Country Matters

Country Matters

Collected Reports from the Fields
and Streams of Iowa and Other Places

by Vance Bourjaily

THE DIAL PRESS   NEW YORK   1973

Grateful acknowledgment is made to the following publishers for permission to reprint
from copyrighted works:
Random House, Inc., for material from *The Immense Journey* copyright © 1957 by Loren
Eiseley.
Grove Press, Inc., for material from *The Palm-wine Drinkard* copyright © 1962 by Amos
Tutuola.

"Eat Awfully Well" originally appeared in *Audience Magazine*; "Eight Months on Full
Feed" originally appeared in *Harper's*; "A Pot of Jacob's Guile" originally appeared in
Woman's Day; "The Mushroom Column," "Charmio's Column," "The Column from
Mexico," "The Dog Column," "Closing Days (The Last Column)," "Memoirs of an
Ace," and "The Catfish Column," originally appeared in *Esquire*; "Famous Writer Says
Hunting Is Humane" originally appeared in *The Saturday Evening Post*; "The Ninth
Upland Game Bird" and "Rainbows Drowned in a Bucket" originally appeared in
Playboy; "The Men Out Hunting," "Heavy, Heavy Hangs Over Mifflin Street" and
"Death in Africa" originally appeared in *The New York Times*; "Something New for the
Old Gun" originally appeared in *The American Sportsman*; "The Corn of Coxcatlán"
originally appeared in *Horizon*; "Seawalking" originally appeared in *Holiday*; "Going
Out Less" originally appeared in *Sports Afield*; and "Peace Prize for a Fighter" originally
appeared in *The Atlantic Monthly*.

Printed in the United States of America
First Printing 1973

Designed by Lynn Braswell

Library of Congress Cataloging in Publication Data

Bourjaily, Vance Nye.
  Country matters.

  1. Hunting. *2.* Outdoor life. *3.* Country life.
I. Title.
SK33.B68   081   72–12660

It is a matter of something deeper than decorum and warmer than justice that this volume of journalism, which has been my family's trade, our way of surviving and gaining some place in this country, be dedicated to my parents.

In it, one was farm-born; to it the other emigrated as a child. Following them, my two brothers and I have all relied a good deal on writing for journals, though not always as primary careers.

My book is dedicated, then, to two journalists whose lifetime professional standards for themselves (and their sons) were set as high as imagination could reach:

> *Barbara Frances Webb (Bourjaily, Larkin).*
> *Born in California, 1905. Died in Ohio, 1965.*

> *Monte Ferris Bourjaily. Born Ka'ab Elias, Lebanon, 1896. His work still appears five times weekly.*

They've met their deadlines, and the work is good.

Contents

Country Matters

for

THE READER

Some of the pieces in this collection are almost ten years old, one even older, and some are quite new. What they have in common is that I was both interested and convinced by what I was saying when I wrote each one. What interests me now, looking at them all together, is how some of my views have changed, and how the situation, too, has changed; and how sometimes both have stayed the same.

Until the final, self-indulgent section, all the pieces are related—though one or two rather distantly—to living in Iowa, which is pretty much a rural state still, and to being active outdoors. Ten years ago, there was a much more restricted collection. It was called *The Unnatural Enemy,* and all the pieces were about hunting. I was newly come to Iowa then, and to a situation in which hunting, particularly wing-shooting, was possible at certain times of the year in a relatively untrammeled way. It became a passion for me in my late thirties, and the first nonfiction book has had some persistence among hunters; and even among readers indifferent to hunting but interested, I guess, in other men's passions.

There was something impure about the passion, as I meant to suggest in the title: in the chain of natural enemies (cat for dog, crow for hawk, deer for snake) a man, I had to acknowledge, has no logical place. Writing of hunters as specimens, as an untrained zoologist, and with myself as the chief object of study, I had to realize that insofar as I was any wild creature's enemy, it was unnatural.

Since then I've been honestly puzzled, at times, trying to decide whether I had any function at all in nature, other than as one of the ambulatory creatures to which burrs cling, thus enabling certain weeds to get their seeds distributed.

If that seems to you to imply that one of the changes mentioned will have to do with the way I hunt, you've read it correctly, and can pursue it in the opening note for Section 2 and the closing piece of Section 5. As the degree of separation indicates, the sequence of the book isn't chronological; however, I've dated each piece with the time of its first publication.

I've also supplied the name of the magazine in which each piece first appeared or, if it hasn't previously been published, noted that.

The lead piece, "For Ophelia," is very recent, and since it seems to govern the rest in a rough way, I've picked my section titles from its text. "For Ophelia" was pretty heavily edited in its magazine form; I've gone back here to my original version, less because I have anything much against the editing than because to let it stand would make this a work of collaboration. I've just learned that *Audience*, for which it was written, is being discontinued, and I'm sorry. It was a genuinely creative try by some first-rate people.

If nothing else, this is a personal book. Since consistency is not one of my strong personal traits, I've let some pieces stand about as written, felt free to rewrite others, and gone hog-wild with the new ones, with no magazine editor to consider. And I've indicated which pieces have had which treatment, though I'm damned if I know why I think you'll care unless you're majoring in bibliography.

I ought to add, about collections like this one, that writing articles is a regular part of most American writers' lives these days. The reason why is simple enough. There aren't many periodicals left that publish such short stories as we might feel like writing; so, aesthetes to the marrow, we don't often feel like writing them. And then there aren't many stories, at the end of five years or ten, to collect. And our publishers, fellow aesthetes every one, don't often feel like publishing story collections when they do come along. People's short stories get incorporated into, or become the seeds for, their novels as often as not.

This is not to say that there isn't some beautiful work being done in the story form, but I have written before in honor of those who do it, and to mourn the passing of a general audience —hence a strong market—for their work. And will likely write of this again.

Meanwhile, the market for nonfiction is a strong one. And most novelists have times between novels, or between drafts, or when the work has slowed down, or when the bank is sending overdraft notices, when it seems like a pretty good idea to write something that will be out of the typewriter in less than three years. And which might sell. This is likely to be an article, either an assigned one, or one the writer thinks ought to interest some editor or other (and his readers), or sometimes just something the writer feels very much like writing. In the last instance, it's not unlike joining in a conversation with a group of people and having something preemptive on your mind, so that you make them change the subject to hear about it. I'd like to think that the best pieces come from that kind of impulse, but I'm not altogether sure. Among the hunting pieces, "Something New for the Old Gun" was one like that—and a long time selling, too.

Inevitably, when any literary form has a commercial vogue, the whole form improves. Pieces of nonfiction in the first person, whether called by a dull old English lit. term like "familiar essay," or a hot swirly mod term like "the new journalism," have been written for centuries, mostly in rather short takes but often enough (by De Quincey, Thoreau, Turgenev, Orwell, Miller, Hemingway, and many others) at book length so that it seems rather curious to have some of the talented hands who presently write it claim innovation among their achievements. I have even seen the odd plea entered that "the new journalism" has replaced the novel; the novel being in pretty lusty shape itself these days, it would seem to me more accurate to say that first-person nonfiction, with the author as a character in the experience he is reporting, has replaced the short story for now—at least commercially. And that it is attracting some first-rate people. And that it has given novelists who have the need and the ability to handle it an opportunity to do a certain kind of short work between books, and a longer form, more used now than formerly, to work with if they choose. And at the same time, developed some good specialists who don't write novels at all. Fine with me.

But this is not an example of that longer form—*The Unnatural Enemy* comes closer to being that. This is only a collection of some pieces I've enjoyed writing, mostly; about a part of my life I've enjoyed living. Mostly.

for

OPHELIA

First published in a considerably edited version in Audience, *under the title "Country Matters," January, 1972.*

HAMLET: *Do you think I meant country matters?*
OPHELIA: *I think nothing, my lord.*

Nothing, Ophelia? Here's a small thought to start with then:

Finally, in this world, I have bred, raised and trained my own dog and my own horse.

I will not spoil the sentence by correcting instantly for truth. Nearly all that follows turns that indifferent blade against me.

Less finally in this world, mortality aside, I wallow three books short, with eighteen months to go, of a sanguine, boy's goal of ten in print at the age of fifty. I suppose the same circumstances which permitted dog and horse give me what chance I have of raising the three books—one is delivered, one half-trained; the third exists as a dark, ambitious cluster, like toad's eggs, in the deep end of the mind.

You are young. Do you wish to turn your own life back towards this bypassed kind of thing? I mean life in the manner of Squire and Mrs. Western, though the bookwright is an old hand-forger too, left over from another age. Let me advise you that it will not be possible to begin until you have some space, land of your own, on which the dog and horse may run. For me it has been seven hundred acres in Iowa. It could be done in a tenth the space, I know, and in some part of the world with a less comic reputation, if you liked.

If it were a young man I was addressing, he would see before I could finish saying it, that to come out with the smaller fraction —one satisfactory hunting dog whose parents he had owned and mated—would mean starting with one of three things: a taste for bachelorhood, enough money and energy to live two quite separate lives, or best (I think) a certain kind of wife.

But you are a girl. I could tell you of a great, stumpy maiden lady hereabouts who owns five farms, on which rib-sprung horses, broken dogs, bald cats and barren goats collect, but it would break your heart to know or be that lady, even if you had her money. So I think that for you to have a woman's share—no, I cannot characterize it as liberated or not; that is some other, abstract area of discussion in which a working partnership is somehow not based on such particular, unremarkable strengths as which can hitch equipment to the tractor, which find the time and patience to keep records. To have the woman's share (I was saying) of the kind of life I am writing of, you would need the spinsterhood I cannot wish you, or your own means to a double life I cannot quite imagine, or best (I hope) a certain kind of husband—one, apparently, in some respects like me.

But which are these respects I cannot say.

I hope for your sake they are not altogether matters of appearance, for I am short, thick now around the waist, thin-haired and

for Ophelia

turning leathery—not nice leathery like white kid or mocha suede, but like the fingers of an old work glove. It is possible, I guess, that appearance could have more to do with whether your husband will commit himself to this quite unmodish style of life than I think, lovely mocha O. Can you tell? It might be kinder not to let me know.

Most likely, after all, my suitability proceeds from points of character—maybe the one indicated by my wincing at the ring of a telephone. Or the one which causes me sometimes to like to drink alone, late at night, after my wife's asleep. Or by my fiercely loving our children—I try not to frighten them with it —and therefore demanding quite a lot of them.

That I relish my own jokes? I can be in a hilarious good humor and irritate you by forgetting to say why, or tell you what's funny. Or the secret sullen streak—sometimes I am cross for a whole afternoon or evening without saying so, or explaining the reason.

Perhaps you can deduce the kind of husband you will need from this: that socially I am as impatient with interruptions in our self-paced, country pottering as I am bitter in complaining that we never see our friends. It is the potential, I suppose, for this, or one of those other kinds of male behavior set forth above, that you should try to locate in your white-kid husband, to be sure of having one who will wear and tear and toughen into one like me.

Quiet, child. Don't tell me of the new, contemporary alternative, all communal and nice. The resonance of that is altogether different from an individual, landed family's pride in its production of horses, children, books and dogs.

The dog in question is a Springer Spaniel. We allowed our son, then in fifth grade, to name him, and the child said, "Pottowatto-mie."

The dog is four years old now and we still call him Pup. We

11

try not to let Pup know that we like his sire, Bix, whom we have
owned for a long time, a little better.

2

Choose your dog, Ophelia, as we chose Bix.

Let me assume though that you won't do anything as dumb as
to pick one of the breeds that have no function—you weren't
going to, were you? In the country animals without function are
neglected, like old farm machines rusting in tall grass. It will be
a sporting, working, watch or guard dog then—they all crave
affection and give amusement, in their plainer way, as much as
any Sealyham or Afghan.

Now, since you know nothing, do not go to a kennel, or a pet
shop, or confuse yourself with books; dog-book writers are the
most simple-minded of advocates. Go to a friend you really like,
who has a dog you really like.

Our friends the Lardners had a Springer bitch, a four-legged
sofa cushion whose hunting instincts were mostly evident in
dreams. But four Lardner children grew up mauling and lolling
on this incredibly good-tempered dog, with never a curled lip
out of her; she just didn't acknowledge abuse. In the field she'd
sniff curiously around, sometimes an ancestral tingle would communicate itself to her at the scent of game, be evident in lazy
movement at the base of her tail, and she'd look up and smile.
If I liked to shoot birds over a dog, I also had small children.

Here is some more general instruction about dogs: breed
means everything to show and field competitors, to trainers,
handlers, kennel clubs—but to you, once you have decided on
a group of breeds (hunting, working, guard, etc.), particular
breed means nothing at all. This is because there are by now,

within every breed, various strains selectively and often disas-
trously bred for certain stupid characteristics.

Among the hunting breeds this has reached a point of absurd-
ity. There is a show strain, bred for appearance; a field trial strain,
bred for speed; a gun dog strain, bred from discards from the first
two, for service. The first category is useless, the second brain-
less, both too high-strung to be borne with unless you feel compelled to artificial competition; in the third there will be some
good individual dogs, and a lot of bad ones. So your only chance
is to find an individual dog you really like, and your only way
of forming that attachment is for a dog belonging to a friend.

Wait the friend out. Eventually he will do what all dog owners
do who cherish their dogs—breed a bitch, put a male to stud.
The drive to promote reproduction in our pets and favored
animals is a human urge Freud could have had some fun with.
Big Sig. (I wonder if he knew this Mexican scene: it takes place
at a *ganaderia,* where fighting cattle are raised. The virgin heifers
are tested, one by one, for courage—will she charge a horse?
Will she charge a man? If she does, she is sent out of the ring
through a door above and beside which the ranch owner stands.
As she goes by, he holds his arm, palm down, an inch or two
above her, so that the whole length of her body passes just under
his hand. If she is thought unworthy of being bred, he signals that
she is to go out a different door. Spanish country matters.)

What you are aiming to get, probably not free, is the pick of
a certain litter, or at least an early choice. Now you are looking
at a basket full of pups that have inherited very specific traits you
like from at least one parent. There is a good chance, by the way,
that an early choice is as good as first pick, because most people
are going to look with misty eyes at the little squealers and pick
for cuteness, color, nostalgic resemblance to a past dog, or,
worst, because that poor little one there is always getting pushed
aside.

You want the pup that does the pushing.

"You did pick the boss of the litter?" my wife asked, when I described my visit to the Lardners to mark the pup we'd like to have.

"First to climb out of the basket and commit a nuisance," I said. "And look around for something to chew up."

You can cut down aggressiveness and adventurousness by training; you can't impart either one.

Men often project wishes in the names of their dogs. My friend Richie Lyons always names dogs Pete, because he wished that had been his nickname as a boy. Bix the Springer pup was named for the legendary trumpeter Bix Beiderbecke, one of my personal heroes; oddly enough there was a real connection, too. The Lardners had bred their sofa cushion to a fine gun dog named Major, who belonged to Lou Black. Lou had been the banjo player in the Original New Orleans Rhythm Kings, was thus one of the men from whom Bix Beiderbecke learned music, listening to them as a boy.

Lou Black, Dek Lardner and I used to hunt together, fish sometimes. Lou was an extraordinary wing shot and tackle handler, a function of the same dexterity and concentration which made him a great banjo player, I suppose. We used to talk endlessly about jazz and sporting dogs, and he approved my choice of Bix:

"That's my favorite of all the pups Major's sired," Lou would say.

Bix was, still is, built like a cinder block. He is one of those nice, genial, somewhat slow-witted creatures, without the brain-size to conceive dishonest or malicious thoughts. I know people like that, and treasure them, too.

Intelligence is an overrated thing, Ophelia. Don't get smart. Bixie never has, and his meals always come on time.

He has never gotten over the cinder-block look. Seeing him,

people think him overweight. Responding to his frank, dopey cheerfulness, they pat him and feel, under the soft hair, a muscularity so hard you can hurt your hand on it. As a gun dog he is diligent and good-humored, rather than slick or fast. His pace suits me. Once I had a splendid pointing dog, and I miss the elegance of that. But the Springer way, which is simply to find and flush game at close range and then retrieve, is good enough for pheasant country like this.

When Bix was a couple of years old, Lou Black found a bitch to buy. He'd been corresponding with kennels and private breeders all over the country, looking at bloodlines and photographs, and talked the matter over so often with us and the Lardners that we all felt we'd participated in the search which brought Meg to Lou from California.

Meg was a charmer.

She was that special dog that turns up in a businesslike kennel which the operating family can't resist and so, against their principles, take into the house. She had the silky, curly hair Lou wanted (Bixie's is straight and coarse), not just on her ears but all over, and she had eyelashes like the flirtatious cartoon thoroughbred to which the alley mongrel foolishly offers his blue-ribbon bone.

Lou was dippy about her.

"I just hope Major's not too old," said old Lou. He had located Meg to keep a line going: he'd owned Major's sire.

And I inherited a jazz banjo player's dream of a dog, for Major was too old. A season or two went by and Lou phoned me; I agreed that Bix should serve as stud in his sire's place.

We are not in a hurry out here. Sometimes I guess we ought to be. Another season passed, and before Meg was ready again to be bred, Lou died. We went to the funeral and came back with Meg. Natalie Black and the children wanted us to complete Lou's scheme.

Whatever it was my wife liked in girlhood when I won her, she now quite distinctly prefers character to charm in animals and humans both. In a situation in which her devotion is divided among her family, thirty Angus cows and a bull, five horses, a pony, forty-two sheep and two rams, a couple of dozen chickens, a pair of peacocks, the dogs, occasional pigs, the steers and lambs being fed for slaughter, and whatever cats happen to be stopping off, she does not take much to individual creatures whose central wish is that she indicate preference. She has preferences; they go uninidicated, being for the independent, the consistent, even the mischievous animal—not the dependent and temperamental, no matter how fine their coats and winning their ways. Winning ways rather put my wife off.

So poor Meg didn't get along too well during her time with us. When she ran around crazy, it wasn't considered cute—it was called neurotic. When she pressed against the human leg she probably got an absentminded pat, but it was found to be as much cloying as it was lovable. And when she walked away winsomely from a pan of dog food, ogling the refrigerator, the dog-food pan just got picked up behind her. Sorry, Meg.

In the field that fall she showed enormous hunting instinct and energy—she was as busy a dog as I've ever tried to shoot over, and I like a dog that keeps buzzing. But she was uncontrollable, and she thought retrieving was nasty, something low-class dogs might do, nice ones never.

In the spring, hoping to combine good qualities, aware we might not discard bad ones, we bred her to Bix. Rather, the vet did. Meg would flirt, but wouldn't stand, and the job finally had to be done by artificial insemination. If you can see, in terms of my invocation of Big Sig not long ago, some grounds for male disaffection on his dog's behalf at this indignity, consider, Ophelia, whether, like my wife, you would have found the business made a lady yet less fond of Meg?

Country matters. What Hamlet meant by his improper remark ("Shall I lie in your lap?" "No, my lord." "I meant my head in your lap." "Yes, my lord." "Do you think I meant country matters?") was just that. Not sex. Sex is a city word for a city hang-up. There is not the time nor the smog nor the density out here for sex—only coupling; romping; ragging; harvest moon sentimentalizing; passion, sometimes leading to violent attempts; not much adulterous opportunity, though a farmer will take him a six-pack of beer and go round to see can he help out a widow woman by ploughing her garden for her . . . what the farm wife and the hired man might do if the farmer were away on a fishing trip, and there weren't so many children around, I can't be sure. But there is much boy-and-girl excitement, pregnancies, mistakes, marriages; hard work making a fellow physically tired at night; boozy weekends to make up for it; driving around in pick-up trucks to country dances; frustration often, release sometimes; dark things sometimes, of course; all the secret things and practices, I suppose, mostly between consenting partners; sometimes the consent a little one-sided, but rarely without provocation thereunto . . . all of it, anyway, light and dark, carrying with it awareness of the obvious: there maybe are lines to be drawn between human and animal behavior, but the reproductive urge, its fulfillment and consequences, is not the place to draw one. No one who lives in the country would buy a book called *How to be the Sensuous Woman,* or man, or pig, or horse, or cow or caterpillar.

Rather, we exchange wisdom: some neighbors came by to talk about buying a couple of Red Angus from us. The conversation turned from the artificial insemination of dogs, as with Bix and Meg, to the more ordinary sort—the artificial insemination of cows with semen from very expensive, faraway, prize-winning, purebred bulls.

My wife asked: "How do you know exactly when?" That is,

in a particular three-week period, at just what hour to catch up
the cow in the head-chute and use the syringe you've been keeping in the refrigerator up to now.

"Some say take her temperature," the neighbor said. "Most
just leave her in the herd and watch for her to start bulling."

"I wouldn't always have the time and help to cut her out and
bring her down without notice," my wife said. "The stuff's expensive and perishable, isn't it?"

"I know. I think the best way's to keep her out of the herd
where she'll be handy. And set a fifteen-year-old girl to watch
her. She'll let you know when the cow's ready."

3

Meg had a big litter, and our son violated all our hardhearted
pup-choosing rules in picking a male: he liked the one with the
darkest markings. We argued briefly, but honored his choice.

Since I'd already trained Bix in a way that satisfied me, I didn't
have much hesitation about working in my eclectic way with
Pup. In training I use bits picked up in various ways: from a
conversation with a professional, that one way to insure against
gun-shyness is to call a pup to supper with a cap pistol. From a
book: never help him over a fence—let him learn to climb or run
around until he finds a way through. As a result all explosions
delight Pottowattomie, and he can climb anything including the
side of an eight-foot, cyclone-fence dog pen. But most of the first
year's training was no more than what you'd do with that Sealyham or Afghan—housebreak him, teach him to come without
hesitation, to stop on command, sit and stay. In the field, and I'm
not sure where I picked this suggestion up but it surely works,
Pup was allowed to spend his first hunting season skylarking. He

ran up a lot of birds out of range for me, admittedly, but he got me a few shots and he had a marvelous time. As a result, hunting is both the purpose and the joy of his life; there's nothing at which he has a better time.

In the second spring and summer, we began working birds, pigeons which I'd catch in the barn at night, climbing up over baled hay with flashlight and gunny sack.

Theoretically, what you do is tuck the bird's head under its wing, rock it back and forth a couple of times, and then plant it in long grass where it should stay until the dog is about to find it, flying up just as he does. I never got very good at pigeon rocking, though; my birds were either still alert enough to fly away the moment I set them down, or so dopey that Pup would catch them before they got started, perhaps bringing them in but not without injury. As often as not when the sequence did work right, I'd spoil it by being so distracted watching that I'd shoot in haste when the bird did fly, and miss it.

I'd thought my wife might help, you see; she's a good natural shot, and has a nice touch with animals—but she found she wanted to give up hunting just about the summer Pup was trained. I settled for getting my boy—he was ten then—to release the birds for me by hand, one by one, at the edge of the farm pond. They'd fly out over the pond, I'd shoot and drop them in the water (most of the time), and then Pup would retrieve on command. The only difficulty with the procedure was that pigeons didn't smell or taste or feel right to him, and though he'd get them in to shore his inclination was then either to spit them out or chew them up, rather than bring them to me.

In the same season, I taught my boy to shoot. We did pistol, rifle and shotgun, and like his mother (unlike his father) he was naturally good—even with the shotgun which, while not as difficult as pistol shooting, is more athletic in that it involves not just

19

pointing but swinging and follow through, in about the same way you'd follow a moving subject with a movie camera.

The boy shot a .410, first at balloons moving along in the wind, then at croquet balls rolled downhill at some speed, finally at clay birds from a hand-trap. He could hit them fine.

The first Monday after Labor Day, with the opening of dove season in Illinois, which is sixty miles from here and to which Dek Lardner had invited me, I took Pup; I would have to say that my training paid off. I was sitting under a medium-sized pine tree, waiting for pass shots, and the dog had been told to sit and stay behind me. I didn't hear him leave, but after a moment, when I looked around, he was gone. It was hard to believe; in fact, I could hear him pant. It was a puzzled minute or two before it occurred to me to look up. There, balanced fairly comfortably on a branch six feet up, was the dog who had learned to climb anything, and at that moment doves appeared out front. I shot quickly and luckily, a dove fell, and I told Pup to fetch—his first real, hunting season retrieve. So out he leapt, rather than climbing down, using my head as a springboard, found the bird without difficulty, sat down and ate it. I guess gunfire still suggested mealtime to him.

We finally did work out that he wasn't to eat doves—though they were apparently too much like pigeons in scent and feathering to be handled seriously, and he never brought one all the way in. With pheasant, quail and ducks, later in the fall, to my great relief, he did and does the proper thing.

He is, in fact, better than Bixie in the field—a smarter dog, inheriting it from his mother, faster, trimmer, prettier to watch, less dependable, and more eager to please. That last, another inheritance perhaps, is, oddly enough, a defect. Unlike Bix, who seems secure in the conviction that no one could possibly be displeased by him, Pup does the equivalent of Meg's nervous cuddling and running around. He makes up to people unnecessarily. He seems to need reassurance that he is liked and approved of.

But it is also possible—there is no way of being sure of this with a dog—that he is often in some degree of pain. He has poor teeth, and a low resistance to infection in places like his ears, so it may be that the reassurance that he needs is something more like being promised things are going to be okay.

4

That is the dog, then; not so much a perfect as an interesting dog. And in a moment, I will write about the horse. But let me digress, Ophelia, as when walking in our woods to hunt for mushrooms I stop off sometimes to see a flower or a nest; let me tell next about three apricot trees, and a lamb.

—What?

A device? Ophelia nothing but a device? Quite wrong, reader. I had a letter from her just the other day.

I have changed her name, to protect her innocence, and alleged a false association with a certain Hamlet.

She lives in New York, not very happily. She does not like the rudeness, dullness and bad air. One winter day she saw, in *The New York Times,* a picture of me standing in the back of my Ford pick-up, throwing out hay to cows and horses. The story which described me as a "dirt-farmer and champion novelist"—a little hyperbole there on both counts—seemed to charm her, and she wrote. If she hoped she might reach and charm Hamlet, she was wrong, of course. Polonius is a tireless interceptor of young girls' letters.

She wondered if she might like life any better if she lived in Iowa.

21

She had some images of that. One in particular which touched me was of herself in a cotton dress, stepping barefoot out a cottage door in the early morning, into dewy grass, with the strong, sweet smell of lilacs in the air.

A man in middle-age, living in the country, I identified her with all the tense, perfect, wistful New York girls I used to see, and had a dew-image to match hers, that I'd carried around in those days: a stoneware crock on a polished walnut table, in a dim, cool dining room with limestone walls, where no air-conditioner need ever whine and blast. There are fresh-cut flowers, the crock is full of buttermilk from this morning's churning, and my dew stands in drops along its sides. Either my mother or her mother, farm girls and schoolteachers from Ohio, taught me to picture that, but I forgot to tell Ophelia in my hasty answer. That is why I'm writing for her now—

There are three apricot trees I planted, two on one side, one on the other, of a white wooden stile we made across the fence, behind the house, into the bluegrass pasture on the way to the woods. I don't suppose either my mother or her mother would be surprised—if they were still on hand, and whatever their feelings about the disappearance of wooden churns and natural, uncultured buttermilk—to know that each of those little trees seems a distinct personality to me. One I think of as sturdy, small, muscular and undemanding. Next to it is my wild, impulsive tree, which sends out all sorts of unnecessary, lighthearted shoots between prunings, a happy, attractive, scatterbrained tree in need of considerable protection and correction. The third, my largest, is now twelve feet tall but grew too fast; it was ambitious, serious, a sincerely misguided tree that did try to please but is now in failing health because the three branches which spread from the main fork are too heavy for the trunk below them. If I'd known, if I'd been the wise friend my third tree needed, I'd have cut off one of those burdensome branches before they all got so fatally heavy.

You see? And did you ever taste an absolutely newborn lamb? Now stop it. Girlish outrage mars your lovely face. I said taste, not eat.

My wife had been explaining to me that each lamb when born smells and tastes, as the ewe licks it clean, so particularly of that mother's womb that she knows, among several born at the same time in the same area, which is hers. There can be no mistake.

All night we have been going to a pen where a lamb struggles to survive, after hemorrhaging from its navel. I have tied off the navel with monofilament fishline, using the same tight knot I use to put a trout fly on a leader, and it seems to work.

A professional sheep man would not have done it, knowing that to save this one, weakened creature would result in his being involved, perhaps for weeks, in individual nursing. This, of course, would have to be done at the expense of time needed for the regular care of the healthy animals in the lamb crop. Sentimental as all amateurs are in every field—the root of "amateur," E. M. Forster once pointed out, is the Latin word for love—we cannot let our lamb go, as a professional would. But the lamb is too weak to stand by itself, and lambs cannot nurse lying down.

Every hour we go out, I hold the big, desperate Corriedale ewe pinned against the side of the pen, my wife picks up the lamb and steadies it on its wobbly legs beneath the udder, guiding a teat into its mouth. Interchangeably, she pins, I guide. When we go back to the house to sleep for fifty minutes, we wash our hands but the taste of newborn lamb is incredibly penetrating and persistent on my fingers: sweet, bitter, woolly, bloodsalty and even a little sour.

I know of no taste like it and believe now without question that this mother, knowing the taste of afterbirth which (as farm animals do) she has eaten, knowing the particular mixture of blood and mucus from her own insides she has cleaned off her lamb, could never imaginably be given in the dark some other ewe's lamb to suckle; the lamb is, in a way human mothers couldn't hope (or fear) to feel, a piece of herself. Or do human mothers, too, have this knowledge in some particular, uncommunicable way of their own?

Country matters.

5

About the horse. He is, like me, half-Arab, and so I gave him half my family name: Abou. There was an *A* sound in front of Bourjaily before it got transliterated out of Lebanese Arabic.

It is likely my paternal ancestors were less fanciers of horseflesh, or even camel, than they were of goat, but I think even vendors on the streets of Damascus, who have never ridden, nor walked on anything but cobblestone, feel some atavistic emotion of proprietorship about the race of Arab horses. They are as different from all other horse tribes—says my wife, whose ancestors came from Denmark and Nebraska—as Siamese are different from all other cats, and in rather the same way: intelligent, inquisitive, fearless and happiest when attached to particular persons. They are a race of horses that sleep lying down, and it is not uncommon in the desert for a rider to sleep with his head on his horse's flank for a pillow.

Quite oddly, if Abou's sire resembled mine in bloodline, so did his dam's line resemble my mother's: part Welsh pony, part saddle-bred, part western, all from lines quite long-established on this continent.

Abou was the first of three colts born here on the farm; he is a strikingly pretty little gray, but too small really for anything but a child. He stands perhaps thirteen hands. Since I am short, I fit him and enjoy his size; my wife, the real rider and horse-trainer here as perhaps you have gathered, loves him very much and is too long-legged for him. She and I are the same height, five-foot-seven, but her legs—to judge by the adjustments I have to make when I use her stirrup leathers—are a good two inches longer than mine. By chance, this is reversed in our children: we have a small daughter and a tall son.

I now deny my own claim to have trained Abou. I did assist, holding the lunge line sometimes when we worked him in circles, Abou wearing a lunging caveson, a special sort of halter which presses against the side of the nose if the horse goes off his path. This is standard enough procedure, but if I am still at the eclectic stage in my dog-training methods, my wife has by now reached the next stage, which is synthesis and personal style. If you were to ask, for example,

"Is that horse broken?"

She would say, "Certainly not. It's trained." She will take an extra year of gentleness, firmness and patience to establish habits quietly, and avoid forever the point of conflict of human with animal will which has to be won by violent strength and punishment to establish mastery, to break (that is) the horse.

I don't much raise my voice or hit at dogs, either. Come to think of it, our quarrels with people and, but rarely, one another, are low-voiced. Neither of us likes scenes, having been raised by parents who seemed to enjoy them as a form of recreation. Each of us can be calmed by a walk through the woods, or a swim in rainwater in the farm pond—and that is something more about living in the country. It is a great dissipater of overintensity, a universal medication, a shock absorber. If life sometimes turns unavoidably dramatic, especially in winter when emergencies take one into fearful cold, out of the home cave of fire, fur and stone, the setting is nevertheless all wrong for inflating those times to melodrama.

So the horse-training was done, a little each day, with caveson and lunge line; then with one of us on Abou's back and the other

25

on the line; finally with riding small circles with no line, the other merely standing at the center until Abou could be ridden with no bit at all.

There is a bit in his mouth when he goes out, but if he's handled properly it seems no more to him than something to play with, because all the signals that he gets to turn, stop, go, speed up or slow down, come from pressure with the legs and feet, shifts in body weight.

Alas, Ophelia, he is a better-trained horse than I a rider. I do not accurately use and understand those exquisite signals which my wife sends a horse as automatically as I brake and accelerate a car.

Here, then, a fantasy begins to come apart. When we bought the farm, there were to be beautiful fall mornings like this: me on my horse, shotgun in a saddle holster, riding out to a bird field to hunt upland game, my boy riding beside me. I'd have taught him all I know about how birds lie in different kinds of weather, how to run the dogs, leave the horse, take the shots. The dogs would be quartering in front of us; there might even be a guest along, on the third colt.

Okay. Already the horse is trained beyond the point where I could use him that way; when I ride it is always with my wife, for I am unwilling to risk letting my faults as a rider become his as a horse. Need her to keep an eye on me.

The dogs, next item here, I cannot hunt together. Identical in breed, closely related in particular family, they are too different in hunting styles to work well as a pair. Bix thorough, a little ponderous, always willing, clumsy enough sometimes to be amusing, wonderfully tenacious once a bird is down so that he seldom fails in a retrieve. Pup fast, dashing, full of bounce and coordination, a fragile, superb little athlete—somewhat forgetful on retrieves, which after all take place after the excitement's over. He doesn't track wounded birds well, sometimes chases

for Ophelia

those I miss or don't shoot at, but is always dazzling to watch work. People who know dogs praise him more often than they do his solid sire.

And the boy: last fall I said, "Come on. You can hit clay birds fine—let's go after some real ones."

He hoped it wouldn't hurt my feelings if he declined. "I don't think I want to kill anything, Dad," he said, his twelve-year-old voice still high. "But you go ahead and have a nice time." I should have known. We fish sometimes, but he always puts his own catch tenderly back, though he's happy to eat mine.

Disappointed? Not at all. Proud as hell of the kid. The pup. The horse. The woman.

If there is not often a guest, I can explain that too as a matter of pride: my wife and I are rootless people, born in towns we never knew, brought up in others that will not know us again. Once I wrote, in an autobiographical sort of book: "I was always a tourist in the worlds of your world, and never found the one in which I could belong until I learned to make my own." This, you see, we have learned to do, on our farm; it was not always painless, but it works. So if there is no red book or blue in which we are socially registered, then no one much registers on us socially either. We have friends—occasionally one hunts with me for that matter—but they are quite diverse, representing no particular group, or stratum, or background, or location, or other system of stability. So be it.

And for our children, be it differently only if they wish (and the world will). I think it can be; as things go now, they are the children of old settlers. We have been here long enough to see several neighboring places change hands; and long enough to find that as reality replaces fantasy, things get more complicated and much more interesting.

6

What more do you need to know? How the crops are planted? On shares, by a neighbor—it is very technical and, unlike the animal work we do ourselves, requires beautiful, very expensive equipment. What else do I do? So many things there is never time enough—build ponds, plant brush and feed for birds, put up nesting boxes, photograph things sometimes—less hunting, more conserving than I used to think I might. Eat awfully well. And my wife? So many things—sees to the gradual remodeling of the house, shops, drives, sells hay, gardens with me, gathers berries. Cooks awfully well, with the meat she raises, and the vegetables we plant and the wild things that we hunt and gather. Do we get away? Sometimes. And are not always straightforwardly pleased to get back. An isolation has been overcome. It has never been bad for us to overcome it, only more than we could afford.

Yes, of course there is something I have put off saying, and it cannot be left out: the deaths.

Dressing of game and chickens, hauling of steers and wethers to the butcher, constant losses by accident and diseases—but mostly through age—of creatures we share the place with. Country people outlive many generations of domestic and farm and wild animals. There is conflict: last week I was away when a coon started getting into the chicken house at dawn each day, and killing hens. My wife, who had loaned her twenty-gauge to a friend, not intending to use it any more, had to shoot the coon with my big twelve-gauge gun. She called me up on the road at five that morning, upset, if not in tears. It hurt. The whole thing.

Generally, you do not let these things touch you—but let me write, here, of one more dog. He was the elegant pointing dog I spoke of, Moon, my old Weimaraner—huge, intelligent, tough

28

and beautiful. I didn't train Moon; he trained me.

When we had had him for eleven years—in Connecticut, Uruguay, Chile, California and finally here—he began to fail. He ate hardly anything, and what little he did eat didn't seem to nourish him. We tried every way we could to help—even (did you know such things exist?) a special formula of dog food for senile dogs, like pabulum for old men and infants.

He became incontinent; being almost catlike about cleanliness, he hated that as much as you would. He went from eighty pounds down to thirty-five, and I knew he'd have to be put down.

I took him to the vet. He'd known Moon for close to eleven years, too, had shot over him with me, sewed Moon up more than once when he'd ripped open his stomach leaping barbed wire, done surgery on him.

"How do you do it, Jim?" I asked. "Is it chloroform, or what?"

"These days just an injection."

"Fast?"

"Instantaneous. No pain. Just goes like that."

"Okay."

"Leave him with me."

"No," I said. I couldn't believe Moon wouldn't know why I was leaving him. He was so damn sensitive to me. He'd have felt and disapproved my cowardice, if I'd left the room.

So I lifted my old dog onto the operating table; he was too weak to climb up by himself. Stroked him. Talked to him. Told him he was a good dog. Moon was looking at me when Doctor Jim Lowe found the vein.

Country matters, girl.

1 "Eat awfully well ..."

There is nothing basic which is difficult to understand, but apparently the human mind is an organ whose function it is to make simple things complicated. Consequently, human life is a form of animal life made willfully—or playfully—complicated by the special development of this soft, infolded organ up between the ears.

In the same way, perhaps a horse's life is made complicated by the horse's contrasting, bred-in and evolved special abilities: to move fast, pull heavy things slowly, bear certain weights, and live, in most cases, curtailed of reproductive opportunities. For each of these there is a resulting physiological and psychological complication—did you know that when a horse has indigestion, his hooves hurt?

Or, to pick an undomesticated creature, an owl's life is

made complicated by its need to hunt, its special eye development, by the fear it lives in and the fear it causes.

But in thinking about man the animal, the basics are the same as for horse the animal, and owl the animal. The same is true for all the other kinds of animate life I am capable of thinking of— I am not capable of thinking of the needs and complications in the lives of amoebae, bacteria and viruses. Maybe their basics, too, are nourishment and rest, and hey, Doc, go easy on the penicillin, willya?

To get rest in many cases requires shelter: protection from the weather and from predators. It becomes more complicated when we extend the idea of predator to that of enemy—something that doesn't want to eat you, it just wants to kill you. It becomes more complicated in another direction when we extend the idea of shelter to include comfort. It becomes magnificently complicated —a really fine example of what the remarkably developed human brain can come up with—when the need for shelter gets involved with aesthetics.

I haven't had much occasion in my life to think or write about shelter, perhaps because at the level of protection it has generally been mine automatically—except now and then, as was true for almost any man my age, during the Second World War. At the level of comfort, for I am a middle-class American, shelter has generally been mine automatically, too, in some degree. Even the big, aesthetic complication has sometimes, not always, been one I was in shape to experiment with—but why was it that every batch of wall paint my wife and I mixed up when we were young, looking for a combination of lightness and warmth, turned out that awful flesh-pink color?

In any case, the only occasions I seem to have had to write about shelter at its interesting, complicated, aesthetic level came a long time ago, when I was a staff writer on the *San Francisco Chronicle* and covered architecture. I don't even need to look through my clippings from that time to know that there is nothing in them worth your present attention. As a matter of fact, I don't think I could find the clippings.

Nourishment for man the animal, unlike shelter, has no simple forms, not even for a stone-age gatherer: he's got to know where to find the good stuff, and how to avoid the bad. When we add hunting and fishing and trapping to those techniques, and then growing and cooking, and live in a culture which permits all of them to some extent, we are into an endlessly complicated, if generally pleasant, subject. It seems to have been one on which I've used a fair amount of typing paper. I've chosen three pieces about food for this section which I thought might be of interest; two of them are even relevant. One, it turns out, deals with raising, one with cooking and one with gathering.

The first is also, as far as I know this morning, the most recent of my articles to appear, having been in *Harper's* for March, 1972, and caused an outcry around here. The newspapers and broadcasters picked it up; it criticizes the American meat supply pretty harshly, and meat's the business a lot of my neighbors are in. Some said ouch, some have stopped waving as they drive by, but there are others, I'm told, who are willing to defend my views up at Orval Yoder's Windham Garage, which is where the local debating society meets. I was tried for heresy in a friendly hearing on the editorial page of the *Des Moines Register*—found innocent, I'm happy to say, but the letters page of the paper is full of dissent from that verdict today. *Harper's* cut the piece quite a bit; I've restored the cuts.

Harper's sent me a bunch of letters they got as a result of the meat article. They were mostly typed, and mostly intelligent, and I had a funny reaction to them. I didn't feel like answering them, or commenting on them, because it seemed to me they were mostly jabber. Jabber is another of those products of the specialized human brain, kind of an idle product really, and I felt there was enough of it in the world already. I felt a little badly that my article had set off more of it for people, and thought that maybe the article itself was jabber, too. There were some other letters, written in pen or even pencil, from elderly people, who'd seen a digest of the article in the *Register*, and who wrote to tell me how good meat tasted when they were young, that they couldn't buy much of it anymore, and how they felt cheated and sad by what little they could buy, and I answered those letters.

The next submission, the one which is admittedly not too relevant in a book called *Country Matters*, goes back for its original publication about twenty years. It was in *Woman's Day*, around 1952. I think it may have been the first magazine piece I ever sold, outside of some poems in *Poetry*, and I may not have much better reason than sentiment for printing it again. The fields from which it reports have probably been out of cultivation for six thousand years. At least there's more than one kind of sentiment involved; it deals with my grandmother, and in it she is doing what she loved best to do, which was cook.

The piece was and is called *A Pot of Jacob's Guile*, and it has interested me to type it through again, just to test how my prose of twenty years ago feels under more calloused fingertips. The process led me to change half a dozen words, mostly in the interest of clarity of directions, for the piece is essentially a recipe. I winced a few times at winsomeness in the language, but on the whole it seemed all right—another sort of sentimental indulgence, if you like. And the recipe is one of the world's basic ones.

Something nice happened: one evening a year or two ago we were invited to dinner by some friends named Ringo—Elbert teaches in the Spanish department at the university I work for, and had helped me with my Spanish; and he and his wife have been gardening, eating organically, baking their own bread, and other newly discovered youth practices, since some time in the

1930s. At the Ringos' that evening we were served 'mjeddrah, the subject of my recipe, and were told the story of it much as I tell the story. They had read about it years ago, they said, in a magazine; they weren't sure which one, or who'd written the piece, but had been cooking and eating the dish with pleasure ever since. Their 'mjeddrah was just right, too.

I think I got up and did a little dance around the table. That sort of thing should happen more often to a writer; but I wish Grandmother Bourjaily had been there to dance with me, because that sort of thing should happen really to a cook.

Listen, you might want to try 'mjeddrah. I don't suppose it's macrobiotic, but it's cheap and its good.

The final piece in this section deals with wild mushrooms. It was the first of half a dozen columns on the outdoors I wrote for *Esquire* in the sixties. Again, I've left it pretty much as it was, though in addition to retyping this time, I've thought it proper to add a note bringing my mushroom experience up to date.

There is probably another piece I should write to complete the account of how we eat—one about gardening, but there really isn't anything very striking or individual about the way we garden and preserve, or fail to get around to preserving. We are still amateurs at it in a farm region where family gardening is a tradition, though one honored, by now, in an odd sort of way: the farmers themselves have largely given it up. Getting a garden made conflicts all too exactly with the big spring push to get the crops in and cultivated. Take a man—this would be a small farmer—with 120 acres of corn and soybeans to plant; he's going to have a seed and fertilizer investment, in addition to his overhead, taxes and interest, of three to four thousand dollars. He is going to be looking for a gross return of ten or twelve thousand dollars. This will pretty much be his income for the year—when you subtract costs and overhead and equipment and gasoline, it won't be much of an income, but that isn't my point. My point

34

is that it's not going to be very persuasive to point out to him that the time and stoop labor spent planting, keeping up, harvesting and processing vegetables from a garden can save him three or four hundred dollars a year on his food bill. Since field-work time and garden-making time come in the same season, he's going to have to be in the field—and so are his kids, after school hours, if they're big enough. And so even is his wife, apart from housekeeping hours, in various supportive ways, and if she doesn't work at something in town.

If the family place is on a larger scale—240 acres, let's say— we are getting into what the tax accountants call a cash-flow situation which calls for pretty careful management; the net income may still not be much, but the flow of money through the bank account is now up around thirty thousand dollars a year, in and out, and perhaps there's a man hired at times to help in the fields. But the kids are still going to be needed out there, on the spare tractor, or working fences or choring, and the wife now has some complicated books to keep. But she's also at a changed economic, hence social, level now—if the farm itself is paid for. She and her husband are capitalists, no less than store owners and other small-business proprietors; bridge clubs and PTA meetings and fashion shows, why not?, are now appropriate to her station. She will garden only if she has a real liking for it; generally speaking, though, having been farm-raised in harder times, or when the wartime food shortage made a child's garden work patriotic, she will have grown up feeling that gardening is drudgery.

I know a number of farm families around here, and hardly any of them raise much of their own food. Either it isn't economic or it isn't fun.

The great repository of gardening and preserving knowledge is in the very small towns, rather than on the farms. In these towns of under a thousand live the jam and pickle makers, the tomato canners, the adherents of special varieties of pole beans and cabbages, the fruit-tree planters, the ones who know how to keep out cutworms without chemicals—all the lore which a good many of today's urban-raised young are so eager to learn. In these towns live the retired farmers and their wives, and here, too, the sons and daughters who were raised on the farm and miss it, but who now work in the larger town nearby as carpenters and nurses, master mechanics and elementary school teachers. (I am not including more highly paid professional and managerial people; they live in the larger town itself and have smaller yards. If they care at all for growing things, it is more apt to be roses or evergreens than cauliflower. They are less likely, perhaps, to be farmers' sons and daughters, but when they are, they have been driven by rather powerful ambition, the origin of which probably included a drive to escape from the farm. And the garden.)

In any case at our farm, and this is true of another sort of professional person and his family who have chosen country living, we do garden and enjoy the stuff we grow. Most of it. My carrots weren't worth a damn last year. But our efforts are neither expert enough nor funny enough nor odd enough for me to describe. So I don't guess I'll write about gardening, but someday I'd like to do a piece about all the different kinds of oysters in the world, and one about applejack, and maybe sometime I will.

*First published in a briefer
version in* Harper's *for
March, 1972, under the
same title—which was one
they suggested.*

Eight Months on Full Feed

My neighbor down the road in Sharon Center, Iowa,
raises 3,600 pigs every year for you to eat, but he
doesn't like his own pork very well.

Whenever he can get me to agree to it, he brings me a
dozen hogs to raise on shares—six for his table, six for mine.

This has nothing to do with skill, luck, intuition, or
knowledge on my part. Quite the other way, in fact—it
recognizes that I am a hopeless amateur who couldn't survive
six months in the pig business, who still feeds pigs the way
some very different country neighbors did, long ago, on
mountain farms in the back country of southwest Virginia.

My pigs get slops, scraps, overgrown stuff from the garden
—especially, this year, a kind of hybrid zucchini which seems
to zoom from thumb to ballbat size overnight. And they get

little enough genuine hog feed so that they have to spend most of the day rooting, grazing, chewing bark and catching beetles.

They inhabit a ten-acre pen, half timbered over, with enough tall grass, weeds, brush, gullies and other opportunities for concealment in it so that most of the time I don't know where they are. They break out of this pen, now and then, and have glorious times raiding cornfields, garden patches, and other parts of the timber for acorns, hickory nuts, carcasses and the roots of rare, endangered wildflower species. They get chased back—coaxed, cajoled, cursed—and when they're in again, glowered at.

When, after seven or eight months of this, they have reached market weight—around 215 pounds—they are long, lean, well-muscled, crafty, and somewhat disgruntled omnivores. The loins and chops, shoulders and fresh hams we get (assuming we can catch and load the pigs) are superbly firm and well-flavored. My neighbor cheers.

At the professional pig operations, up and down the road, the animals are fat and dully contented. They reach their market weight weeks earlier than mine do, eating all they can hold, day after day, generally in outdoor confinement. Their feed formulae and genetic backgrounds have been worked out by computers to enable them to reach the magic weight just as fast as possible.

This is economically imperative. Daily costs are very, very high, and the minimum investment for profitable pig-raising somewhere around $150,000—based on the value of broodstock, land and normal machinery for a 240-acre farm capable of producing part of the feed, which is not a large farm these days. An extra week or so of feeding, obviously, would change profit to loss. (My neighbor reminds me that it often works out that way without the extra weeks, but that's another matter.)

What this means, really, is that commercial pigs don't quite mature. They are grossly overweight, sluggish, late adolescents. The meat is soft, the fat watery and the bones small. But you know about that meat: for as I've said, the pork my neighbor raises, and the other professionals like him all over the country, is the pork you buy.

This situation is repeated in variations with almost every kind of meat available in this country, which eats more of it than any other in history. This is dietary democracy, I guess—that our basic food is not a starch, like wheat, corn, or rice, but animal protein. Whatever the sociology of it, there is no question in my mind about this, after five years of raising all the meat my family eats and comparing it occasionally with what is served in restaurants and other homes: that Americans buy at high prices, cook poorly, and eat in incredible quantities, the lowest quality meat possible.

Having dealt with pork, let me review the rest of the national meat counter for you, item by item, saving the worst, which is beef, for last where it belongs.

But before I start on the project, let me make it clear that my bias is not like Cousin Ralph Nader's. His concern with sanitation and butchering practices is a health officer's, not a trencherman's—its bearing on the pleasure of eating a piece of meat no closer than the relationship between cleanliness and desirability in a person. Having the first may be basic, but it hardly guarantees the second. Thus, if every feeder and butchering plant in the country adhered to every item in the pure-meat code, or whatever it's called, we'd still have lousy meat. In fact, as I'll try to show when I discuss cured meats, there is an uncomfortable undertone of the sumptuary in consumer crusading, and we are already losers in quality from some of the meat-inspection practices imposed.

My bias doesn't have anything much to do with the present clamor, in a part of the population, for organically raised foods, either. My way of raising pork and beef is generally, but only coincidentally, organic—not at all so philosophically. I would not

39

omit the vitamins, minerals and added synthetic proteins which go into what manufactured feed my animals do get, nor take the cattle (for example) off a kind of salt we use in the summertime which includes a chemical that keeps them free of face flies and cattle grubs. One is warned to discontinue the stuff four weeks before butchering (which I do, of course), so I assume the purists would be against it; but I seem to prefer it to grubby steers and blind calves.

It's sad, but not uncharacteristic, that one couple I know who went to considerable lengths to get a quarter of strictly organic meat were, essentially, victimized by means of their own purism. What they got, I'm afraid, was nothing more than a feedlot animal which hadn't been through the feedlot; it was nothing in the world but thin.

On to other particulars: I'd assume that most people by now have heard—and even done—a certain amount of bitching about American chicken. It is factory-raised, indoors and immobile, chemically fed, and while I think the birds reach a kind of forced, physiological maturity, the only flavor they have is what will be absorbed from the cardboard and plastic wrappings they're presented in.

What may not be so generally known is that in France, using its cuisine as the universal gastronomic yardstick, they also have factory chickens—for the poor, penurious and undiscriminating. Stores also offer, but at a premium, what are called *poulets de Bresse.* This can refer to a method of raising as well as a breed, and in the first sense I've got a yardful of *poulets de Bresse* down by the house. They get that way simply by being let out in the sun—as soon as the bird dogs have had their run and gone into the pen for the day—to eat grass, grasshoppers, gravel, and scratch for worms, weeds, and watermelon seeds that the children spat out on the lawn last evening.

These chickens get some grain, of course—whole and cracked

grain, though, not mashes; again, it takes them a week or two longer (in each weight category) to get first to broiler, then to fryer, roasting and eventually stewing size, but by the time they do they are very healthy, active birds. In fact, it's a sight the children quite enjoy, seeing me with an axe in one hand, a piece of wire shaped as a leg-snare in the other, trying to chase down a *poulet de Bresse* with *coq au vin* in mind.

In this situation, I suspect that, except on marginal farms (large ones don't keep family flocks of chickens any longer), and in restaurants of unusual quality, the only flavorful chicken you could buy in this country would be, of all despised things, the ones used in making frozen chicken pies, canned soup, and maybe those served at some of the pressure-cooked-"fried chicken" places. This is because that meat very likely comes from older hens, raised for egg-laying primarily, so that at least they've been allowed to grow up. Furthermore, they've been fed for egg-production, not fast gain; they may not have seen much sunlight, but, because eggs need shells, they've had some grit in their gizzards. Their eggs may not taste like much, but at least the creatures that laid them wind up as birds, not blobs.

In more special poultry, I've had pretty good capons, which I think must have had a version of the *poulets-de-Bresse* treatment, and I find the so-called Rock Cornish Game Hen fairly good. It's a little creature created to take the place of game on the menu; it doesn't do so quite as successfully as guinea hen—something you'll find in even modest restaurants most days in France—but I couldn't tell you where to locate guineas at retail here, except in the most expensive stores in our largest cities. I couldn't advise you very well on where to run in and pick up a goose for roasting, either.

The Rock Cornish doesn't compare badly—except that it suffers in quality from freezing—to game-farm-raised quail and chukkars. These, because they're raised in pens on something pretty much like chicken feed, have little wild flavor though good natural characteristics. Game-farm pheasant, too (and all game sold or served commercially must, by law, come from farms unless imported) is a bird which has domesticated reasonably well from a flavor standpoint; it tastes, more than anything else, like chicken used to. The two have a common ancestor (the Red Jungle Fowl), which would seem to account for it, and if domesticated game is different from wild—to my taste inferior —it is still an interesting, if not a common, item.

There is one pleasant exception to my dismal summary, which is duck. Now it's perfectly true that wild duck, a lean, red-meated, high-flavored marvel, which should always be eaten rare as beef, is nothing like domestic duck. Nevertheless, perhaps because ducks have been raised and fed for many centuries in many cultures, with cuisines as exacting not only as the French but also quite importantly the Chinese, an excellent table bird has evolved which need be nothing like its wild ancestor. Added to this history is the fact, I suppose, that duck is not madly, only steadily, in demand, so that fast gain on a large scale has not attracted its producers. The result is that what is called Long Island Duckling (I'm not sure why) becomes, in my opinion, the one thing worth the money among all the sorts of poultry consistently available in your supermarket. It even freezes well.

The opposite, I'm afraid, is true of turkey. Here, with the consumer as the subconscious national conspiracy's most eager participant, we have been undone by some polltaker's discovery of a small statistical edge in favor of the first-choice answer to the old carver's question: "Which will you have, light or dark?"

This, combined with the census man's report on the dwindling size of families, has resulted in the noble American bird's being bred out of existence—replaced by something half that size with a strange, bulbous breast on it, susceptible to raising methods aimed at a seasonal market. This is what produces all those acres of sliced, dry, grainy but indubitably white meat which appear on our plates at Thanksgiving and Christmas time, to which I would have to say (but here on the farm I generally shoot pheasants or a wild goose for holidays), "Neither light nor dark, thanks. Just a little of the dressing."

Turkey's not bad smoked, I concede, if you can find a real smoked one; by no means do I mean the presliced, pale, packaged stuff, sold with other luncheon meats.

Turning to mammals: our situation with regard to lamb is not yet bad. It may be, shortly, but for now the situation is in one regard like that affecting domestic duck: the demand is steady, but not yet large-scale enough to bring the cost-per-pound-of-gain specialists and genetic tinkerers into massive action.

Otherwise, lamb in this country is uneven in quality. There is excellent hothouse lamb—meat from very young animals which provide tiny legs and racks—a specialty which relies on a special market (certain ethnic restaurants and national-origin groups). As for the animals which produce larger chops and roasts, and which are really young mutton, they can be very good or quite indifferent, seldom bad, depending on what conditioning they've had. When they are bad, as often as not a mistake has been made in the slaughtering; mutton has to be cooled out fast after killing. But no one I've heard of does anything (yet) much different from what we do here on the farm with our sheep: that is, graze them as long as possible, and feed out the wethers on enough grain to fatten them for four to six weeks before slaughtering—unless they've been on a legume pasture, like trefoil, in which case they're quite fat enough already. But lamb or mutton directly off grass can be tough and a little strong; you can run into this from a flock of meat-type or dual-purpose sheep in which the year's young have been kept over, so that the producer can get the wool from an additional shearing. (With wool-type sheep, meat production is so completely secondary that the animals are

43

quite old when culled, and if their meat is used at all I presume it goes into pet food.)

Let's say, then, that you have a fifty-fifty chance of getting reasonable lamb at your local supermarket, but I have to add that these odds could worsen quickly. I look, occasionally, at sheep-grower's trade journals, and have noted that there are fired-up advocates now of shorter production cycles, confinement feeding, and heavy consumer promotion. One article I saw even suggested that, to overcome prejudice, lamb should be bred and fed to taste more like beef.

For God's sake, let's run the polltakers out of the butcher shops.

The same kind of uneveness that affects lamb applies to American veal. There are producers who, like the hothouse-lamb boys, specialize in real, milk-fed veal, and I expect they, too, have a dependable, if not very widespread (though certainly very high-priced), market, from better restaurants and certain national-origin groups. If your neighborhood stores provide this, you're in luck; you might even be able to buy sweetbreads, and real calves' liver.

A good deal of other veal, in less-favored neighborhoods, comes from the unwelcome bull-calves born in dairy herds. These, as with the second sort of lamb I discussed, may provide good or bad veal depending on the care which the dairy farmer has time, or inclination, or understanding—or customers—to give the calves.

Some of the cuts from this haphazardness can be pretty good —I can illustrate from our own, hardly ideal practices with veal. From our beef herd we pick a calf or two which seems weak, or has a defect, and use it off grass and mother's milk for our year's veal supply. I can recommend our stocks and stews, in which the bone and marrow are important; the roasts are quite good for casseroling; but I'd have to admit that the veal chops and cutlets in our freezer are no better than fair to stringy, even though the flavor is right.

I promised a bitter paragraph about cured meats, and may as well produce it now before I come to the big hoax, which is American beef.

Cured meat—from the dry sausages like salami, to the moist ones like hot dogs and bologna, to the pâtés like liverwurst, to fresh pork sausage, to bacon and ending most dismally with American processed ham—are simply not produced well in mass. Like bread and pastry, there's no way of making good cured meats if attention must be paid to irrelevancies like shipping and keeping quality, standardization of batches, appearance on store counters, economy of ingredients, and so on. Just as home kitchens and small bakeries produce what little decent bread and pastry gets eaten in this land, so (Cousin Ralph, sir) did small butcher shops and lockers, along with farm homes, produce that marvelous variety of idiosyncratic and regional sausages, scrapples, pâtés, bacons —and above all country hams—which used to be among the glories of the American larder.

The point probably is that these things were and must be preparations—not just hunks cut off a carcass. They were made. There were recipes for them. There was a man with taste buds and preferences and tradition—family or national—and particular judgment and understanding, who rolled up his sleeves (yes, of course I hope he washed his hands, sir) and made them. Chopped or prepared the stuff, added the spices, mixed and tasted until he got it like he thought it should be.

Now of course, some of this still goes on—I guess, for one thing, the situation with regard to country ham is so glaring that, once again, a specialty market keeps it going in a small way. But the pure-meat laws played right into the hands of Swift, Wilson, Hormel & Cudahy—and I can't help it if that sounds more like an ad agency than a group of firms engaged in preparing good things to eat.

The new laws, mostly directed at meat inspection, promptly closed down the small slaughterhouses and lockers, and sent the master sausage-makers into the aluminum-siding business or used-car selling. A small plant, grossing sixty or seventy thousand a year, with the proprietor and his wife, one assistant and an errand boy, simply couldn't comply with a law which required forty thousand dollars' worth of new boilers, steam hoses, air-conditioning, special sinks and stainless steel counters.

And there went *all* our cured meats of any merit, and they won't be back. Thanks, cousin.

What I had better start with about beef, and I am about to become one of my own villains now, is what *Larousse Gastronomique,* the encyclopedia of cookery, has to say: "The best meat, especially for roasts, comes from five to six year old, grass-fattened oxen." Unlike the British translator, we'd say steers in place of oxen.

But the beef you'll eat tonight, tonight and most nights being your night for it, will come from an animal aged less than two years, who last saw grass so long before his death he's forgotten what color it is.

Nor, to be fair, do I believe there's been much beef around in France since feudal times that reached the age Larousse recommends. Operating, in a way at times ridiculous what with today's shortage of serfs and knights, as much as possible like a feudal lord with regard to my lands and herds, and though I make only a small part of our living from the cattle, I have nevertheless not yet been able to afford to keep a steer going past the age of three and a half.

The land and feed are expensive, the family gets hungry, and the big, well-grown animal uses pasture in proportion to his size. At the same time, the weight gain at that age for an animal on grass is very slow—thirty to forty pounds a season; we can, and do, put on about the same amount again with some winter months of hay and graining, the great quantities of hay assuring that the weight won't go on too quickly. Thus the grain, which is necessary for nicely finished meat, goes in slowly enough so that the fat will be distributed all through the tissues, not simply be a thick, separate layer covering scrawny meat.

Even if I have lacked the character so far to keep one till he's six, our family steers at three to four, raised on grass and properly finished out, give us flavor and length of bone, meat that is at once firm and tender, meat that can take (and needs) a certain amount of aging before it is used or frozen. Every cut is good —the brisket and chuck no less than the sirloin, round and ribs; and the chunks of tenderloin, *filet mignon,* those pieces of meat which in American restaurants cost the most and generally have a flavor somewhat less pleasant than that of average hamburger —regains here its stature as the supreme morsel, not the puzzlingly overrated one.

It makes my villainy, I guess, the blacker to tell you this: when my wife and I were young and lived in New York, we used to walk quite frequently past a celebrated, theater-district steak house, which displays in its windows the cuts you can have for dinner.

We were poor, as young couples are apt to be, and would stand hand in hand, looking at those steaks and roasts and yearning. Twenty years or so later, after we'd got our farm and been raising our own meat for a while, we were asked to that restaurant for an expense-account, business dinner, and you can guess the rest of the story. My wife ordered *filet,* I asked for porterhouse. I recall the first bites, and the unbelieving glance that passed between us. The lean parts of the meat had virtually no flavor at all, and the fat surrounding them an odd, metallic taste —like that of tap water which has stood too long in the pipe.

Neither of us, comparing it silently with our meat at home, was able to finish what we were served, and not because the portions were especially large, either. We filled up on salad and baked potatoes, and enviously watched our eight-year-old son polish off a two-pound lobster.

My villainy is this: each year we keep out what steers we want for ourselves, and sell the rest. Those we sell are seven or eight months old, and have recently been weaned. They are sold at auction to men who operate feedlots. Thus I represent, on a very small scale, the first link—it's called a cow-calf operation—in the bad chain. I forget those calves as fast as I can.

They spend the next four to eight months in pens in the feedlot, fed all they will eat of grain, day after day, until they reach the weight of 900 pounds (good), 1000 pounds (choice), or 1200 (prime).

That's all that silly grading system is any longer, you see; once it reflected whether an animal had matured properly, and therefore meant something in terms of meat quality. Now all it tells is how many days he's been on full feed—that is, not what his true growth is, but how grossly he is overweight. Those who advise you against buying "U.S. Prime" are absolutely correct. Those who advocate a return to a grading system based on culinary quality should give up opium; the best you could do, without changing the national rearing system, would be "U.S. Fat," "U.S. Fatter," and "U.S. Fattest."

You should understand what being on "full feed" means. When my calves come off grass for the winter, they have a limited tolerance for grain, but unlimited appetites for it, rather like the way neurotic children can be with regard to sweets. Only by starting with small amounts and gradually building the animal's tolerance up can his digestive system be so adjusted that he can eat grain all day long without simply getting sick and dying of indigestion.

So this is what is done. The cattle are nursed onto "full feed," a monstrously unnatural diet, by increasing the ratio of grain to roughage each day, and the kind of grain used simply varies with what crops happen to be raised in the feedlot operator's part of the country. In Iowa, where I live, it's corn. In Texas it's grain sorghum. (In Idaho, I've been told, cattle get a lot of potatoes and in Japan, I understand, rice, which is fed to beef animals in the form of beer. Maybe it works out better that way, but if I were going somewhere to eat beef, I'd go back to Argentina. That's where the grass is.)

In almost any part of our country there will be other things mixed in besides straight grain—soybean meal, for example, which is very oily and fattening, but makes a poor-colored fat from the standpoint of the polltaker in the butcher shop. Plastic pellets, which stay permanently in the stomach once eaten and thus curb the appetite for roughage, are used by some really progressive operators. Various chemicals, of course, are used, some to protect health, others to stimulate growth. But the additives and their possible effect on human health, a perfectly proper worry for consumer-protectors, are not my concern here—I am, while my teeth last, more interested in the savor of what I eat and drink than in cholesterol levels and stuff like that. Please pass the butter—if it's margarine, I'll just skip bread tonight.

What comes out of the feedlot to which I supply calves, then, is our vaunted American beef, "corn-fed" or "western" or "genuine Texas," or whatever the advertising agency decides to call it, and it isn't really beef at all. Nor of course is it veal. It is a new kind of meat in the world really: overfed baby beef. As a new kind of meat I would even agree that there are certain good cuts to it, resembling those of real beef—good, that is, if they're cooked properly. Given its properties, that is to say not cooked much at all. I think the sirloin of this animal, for example, and the ribs quite good, if you don't try to roast them—both far better, as I've indicated, than the tenderloin. There are parts of the round which aren't bad. But there is only one agreeable way of cooking even the best of it, and that is grilling over high heat, to melt off the excess fat as quickly as possible. I'd also say our beef livers are much better than most people think, because the animals are, after all, underaged, and the same is often true for hearts and kidneys. But as for the old, glorious roasts—the standing ribs, the pot roasts and the mighty casseroles, forget them. It's all waste—a thousand-pound animal has been raised and slaughtered to provide fifty pounds of fair meat; the rest may as well be ground into hamburger (and when you cook that hamburger in a pan, you'll improve it a good deal if you pour the fat off as it cooks).

And don't try to make sauce with the drippings.

One thing more, about breeds: the Aberdeen Angus is, of course, our dominant beef breed, chosen because it does mature more quickly than the longer-legged, longer-trunked cattle. Some of the latter are being bred in, these days, because the industry worries about consumer resistance to meat with the fat *on* rather than *in* it. However, the cross-breeding experiments are supposed to produce, in addition to what ag-school and Department-of-Agriculture men called "gainability," something they like to refer to as "cutability." Neither of these should be confused with anything like concern on your account for palatability. The goal is simply a dressed carcass with no change in methods which will have a higher (more profitable) proportion of lean to fat in the same foreshortened feeding time—not a return to the beautifully marbled, deeply flavorful prime meats of the past, slow-grown on grass, carefully finished on grain, slaughtered, hung, aged, and cut by an individual who takes pride in knowing what he's doing.

This bleak outline should at least leave seafood untampered with, and it does; except that it reaches most of the country

for Ophelia

frozen, our fish is better than our meat, naturally enough. On the other hand, certain freshwater fish are being found susceptible to production techniques and confinement feeding. Therefore, don't expect much of trout these days, whether in the store or on the menu, for they are a hatchery product—as a matter of fact, don't expect much of the trout you catch, either, unless you know some real, wild streams. Most of the trout caught by sportsmen have been stocked recently enough to retain the mealy flavor and texture of hatchery feed in their flesh. Even the great fish of the southern and middle-American fish fry, the channel cat, are to be raised, so I read recently, in barns, with separate tanks and feeding formulae for each stage of development.

It all adds a certain force to what a customer of mine in the beef business said the other day, darkly: "Twenty years from now, we'll all quit raising and feeding cattle. This stuff they make from soybeans, imitation meat? We can't compete with that. Hell, they can make it taste like anything they want, give it any color and texture they want."

"We've done their spadework for them pretty well," I might have said.

Note, April, 1972: Since this article was published, there has been considerable new controversy, not about the quality but about the price of meat, and of beef in particular. I find myself on the farmers' side of the price argument—and there would go the rest of the votes, if I were running for office. There are two arguments.

First, a farmer, to be at all successful—that is, to survive—must have technical knowledge and professional experience at about the level of an engineer. He must have developed the equipment-handling ability of a heavy-machinery operator. He must have the capital investment—upwards of $200,000—of a solidly established small businessman, say a store-owner or franchise

51

restaurateur. In planting and harvesting seasons he works, as most men do only in emergencies, every daylight hour and often on into the night with his tractor lights running. And he feeds the nation. What should he earn? As much as a lawyer? School teacher? Novelist? Truckdriver? Average net farm income doesn't come close to that of any of those jobs or professions. Do you know how he finally gets a return commensurate with his knowledge, experience, handling ability, investment and dedication to work? He gets it only when he sells out, because land prices do go steadily up; that means, he gets it only by going out of business.

The other argument is this: beef, up to the past few years, has always been a luxury food. In my parents' home, when I was growing up, and even when we were very affluent, we ate beef once or twice a week. We ate it as hamburger, in meatloaf, or as an ingredient in a casserole; sometimes there was a pot roast, or sometimes a half pound of ground beef bought to make a sauce for rice or pasta. Prime roasts and steaks were special occasion foods; they were always expensive; they were served at birthdays, company dinners, other particular occasions. My mother's family dinner menus included other meats used as ingredients, poultry, egg-dishes, seafood, inner organs like heart and liver, various sausages—and, again, cuts like lamb chops and pork tenderloin were special treats.

Perhaps it was the surge of self-indulgent steak buying after the wartime meat shortages in the forties that got this country hooked on meat, beef especially, to the point where consumers in general feel it is part constitutional right, part habit-forming drug.

In any case, they have demanded of farmers, to feed this habit —and enable them to discard all the other good things there are to eat in this world—unnatural quantities of what used to be luxury foods. Farmers have responded with almost miraculous

for Ophelia

production of what, if my *Harper's* article be accepted, is somewhat lower quality meat.

The price is not, in terms of the farmer's livelihood, very high at all, but it is naturally somewhat higher than that of spaghetti with clam sauce, cheese soufflé, crab-meat crêpes, or—to get me out of this and into the next piece—'mjeddrah.

First Published in
Woman's Day *for April,*
1952, under the same title.
A few stylistic revisions
have been made, and a
note added at the end.

A Pot of Jacob's Guile

With two dollars' worth of vegetables and a set of instructions I inherited from my grandmother, you can prove to yourself that the man on the short end of the world's most celebrated bad bargain was smarter than he sounds.

The bargain is the one described in Genesis 25: 29–34— the exchange in which Esau swapped his birthright for what has since been villainously described as a mess of pottage.

One can hardly blame a fellow creature, coming across that phrase *mess of pottage* if he concludes that Esau was an undiscriminating oaf. For *mess* has one current meaning and only one (outside perhaps of Army, Navy and trout-fishing circles, where it can still mean a group of persons who eat together, or a quantity of food). As for *pottage* it has no current meaning at all; but it sounds unappetizingly like *porridge*, and not a bit like "a dish of vegetables, or vegetables and meat," as my dictionary puts it.

Ever since boyhood I have been aware that the shifty English language had done Esau wrong. Casual though he may have been about his inheritance, I have known that the man was no lout in his attitude toward food. In fact, with my grandmother's saucepan to back him, the biblical bargainer becomes a candidate for veneration by food and wine societies—a man who, though he gave up everything, gave it up for a fine meal.

My grandmother was a Lebanese lady whose life, in the slack periods when there were no young children in her care, found its fullest expression in cooking. She told me once that, except when she was staying alone, she never got out of bed in the morning until she had decided what to serve for dinner that night. This decision must have been taken at dawn, for she was always first up in the household—a short, heavy woman with great physical strength, a wide emotional range, and a slow, tireless, fluid kind of energy.

If the meal on which she had decided required a large variety of ingredients, she might spend her whole morning terrorizing greengrocers and outwitting butchers to procure exactly what was needed. Early in the afternoon, the first, leisurely creative steps would begin—washing, peeling, soaking, cutting—during which my grandmother was relaxed and chatty with whoever might be visiting in the kitchen. As mealtime approached, though, things moved faster and the atmosphere became one of concentration. The lavishness of her personality was absorbed in mixing and tasting, browning, basting, thickening—until finally everything was ready at once to be heaped onto platters and carried to the table.

Occasionally, one of these afternoons would be witnessed from beginning to end by a determined daughter- or grand-daughter-in-law, bent on recording the steps which went into producing a particular dish. Only a few of the simpler preparations could be captured by this method, however, and of them the most infallible—and perhaps the most useful—is 'mjeddrah, or Esau's pottage.

The word 'mjeddrah is only an approximation of sounds in a language I never learned, Arabic, the first syllable of which can't be represented in the English alphabet. One authority (Hastings' *Dictionary of the Bible*) transliterates it *mujeddrah,* but I can't conscientiously recall the *oo* sound as being part of the first syllable, as our family spoke it. The *j,* like the one in my name, would be represented by *zh* in dictionary phonetics, and pronounced like the *z* in azure. But if the word seems troublesome, it would by no means be un-Arabic to invent a name for the dish like *Esau's Downfall* or *Jacob's Guile;* there is already at least one commemoratively named dish in the Arab cuisine, an eggplant creation called *The Sheikh Fainted.*

The chief ingredient of 'mjeddrah is, as Genesis reports, the red lentil, a vegetable which, in this country, is sold from the same shelf as split peas, dried limas and kidney beans. I am not relying on the biblical reference however in asserting that my grandmother's 'mjeddrah and Esau's Downfall are the same dish. Scholarly opinion seems to bear me out. For example, *The International Standard Bible Encyclopedia* (1951 edition, vol. II, p. 1122; article on *Food,* subhead *Lentils*): "It was of 'red lentils' that Jacob brewed his fateful pottage . . . a stew, probably, in which the lentils were flavored with onions and other ingredients as we find it done in Syria today."

Hastings' *Dictionary of the Bible,* (1918) cited above for spelling, is even more positive (p. 540, under *Lentils*): "In Palestine a kind of pottage known as mujeddrah is made from [lentils], universally popular. It is of reddish brown color, and is certainly the original of the 'red pottage' of Esau."

Hastings' "universally popular" was, if anything, an understatement. 'Mjeddrah is served daily in many peasant households, or at least was at the time my grandmother emigrated, late in the nineteenth century. Since it uses ingredients which can be stored dry, it may be made the year round and eaten cold as well as hot. Like the beans the Mexicans call "frijoles," it is appropriate to any meal but a feast; unlike frijoles, which accompany other food, there is enough to 'mjeddrah so that it makes a completely satisfying meal by itself.

In Lebanon, my grandmother used to tell us, the fruit and vegetable farmers among whom she grew up customarily took cold 'mjeddrah with them into the fields for lunch. They would wrap a portion up in one of the flat, supple loaves into which bread is baked, to keep moist; and at noon, would slice whatever salad vegetables happened to be growing at hand into the sandwich to complete the meal.

Because 'mjeddrah is thought of by Arabic-speaking people as peasant food, you will not find it on the menus at Middle-Eastern restaurants. My grandmother may have thought it odd that my brothers and I clamored for her to make it, but the quirk has been communicated to the non-Arabic ladies who have married into the family, and, through their cooking, to a good number of guests.

There isn't anything much you need to know in shopping for the lentils to make a pot of *Jacob's Guile,* except that you don't want the French kind, which are green rather than reddish brown. Besides lentils, you'll need a good grade of long-grain white rice, onions, olive oil, butter and things for salad. The following should feed four people:

In the morning put a cup of lentils to soak in cold water. By evening most of the moisture will have been absorbed, but about an hour before serving time, drain off whatever's left. Add three more cups of cold water and half a teaspoon of salt, put in a pot, cover it, and set it on the stove. Heat to boiling, reduce to a simmer, and stir every now and then to prevent sticking.

Next, cut up two cupfuls of onions, not too finely; heat a quarter cup of olive oil in a skillet, add the onions, half a teaspoon of salt, and cook very slowly until soft and yellow. It is my theory that the smell of onions cooking slowly in olive oil was what got to Esau, working in the field, which might give support to a temporary-insanity plea if anyone wants to enter it for him.

Wash three-quarters of a cup of rice, drain it, and parch it in one and a half tablespoons of butter. I'm not sure that *parch* is a proper cooking term; what I mean by it is that you are to stir the rice around in hot butter for a couple of minutes until it loses the translucence it will acquire when the butter first coats it, and starts looking white and opaque again.

Now add rice and onions to the lentils, with enough hot water (perhaps two cups) to finish cooking the rice. The exact amount of water you must judge for yourself, adding a cupful or less at a time, and being careful to put in no more than rice and lentils will absorb by the time they are cooked done but not mushy.

Some hold that the dish, now almost complete, is properly served with crisp-fried (almost burned) onions sprinkled over the top, and salad on the side. My family has less restraint. Omitting the final onions, we ladle the 'mjeddrah onto our plates, and the salad directly onto the 'mjeddrah. The mixture of hot and cold and contrast of textures are wonderful.

The salad should have greens, tomatoes and raw onions in it; from there on you can add whatever you like. Cucumber, peppers, radishes and celery are all good additions. My grandmother's salad dressing was three parts olive oil to one of lemon juice, quite a lot of paprika, pinches of sugar, mustard, and garlic-rubbed salt. Just before adding the dressing, she crumbled a tablespoonful of dried mint leaves over the salad itself. If you can't get Syrian bread, hard rolls go well with the meal, as do strong black olives and *feta,* the white goat's-milk cheese from Greece . . .

February, 1972. My wife and I used to depend pretty steadily on 'mjeddrah in the lean times which other couples filled in with beans or macaroni products—and still might, I guess, though I had to change "a dollar's worth of vegetables" in the first line of the 1952 version to two dollars, and am not sure that's quite enough.

But we don't seem to cook 'mjeddrah much any more, except in the summer when the garden stuff is really fresh, and then having to overcome the fact that the children aren't crazy about it. I try to tell them that it's their loss, but of course it's mine, even more, and they know it. Well. Maybe *their* children, if those future kids' grandparents get to cook for them? Worth a try; I have a photograph of their great-great-grandmother Bourjaily. I'll show it to them, give them each a gold locket with a copy of this recipe inside, before they go out into the world to meet their Cousins Cain and Abel.

First published in Esquire
*for April, 1964, under the
heading "Outdoors." It
appears here with few
changes, but with a note
at the end.*

The Mushroom Column

I don't know about Spring. I am not altogether willing to
take, as my position on the season, the Eliot Switch,
derived from the familiar opening lines of *The Waste Land*
("April is the cruellest month, breeding / Lilacs out of the
dead land. . . ."). This reversed that traditional poet's stance,
of course, which had been to face Spring naked and ecstatic,
with arms open in greeting; you can get a bad chill doing
that, but every year I seem to try some more decorous but
equally foolish version, going out in the false brightness and
the damp wind with nothing much more on for warmth than a
light sweater. There's a physical ache that builds up, a winter
sickness, that can only be cured by the touch of warm weather.
It's as if I were struggling to get out of a womb of heavy
clothing, to be reborn under the sun with the wildflowers.

The Switch requires that one view this perennial rebirth as a kind of tragedy—because, since we have worn out the world, it can only be sad to see old Mother pushing a few bloodroot nubbins and violet stems into the general ruin. And yes, there's something to it: I can never forget, in my excitement at seeing the ducks come back over Iowa, that they are only the remnants of a great population, on their way back to shrunken breeding grounds where there will be room for fewer and fewer of them as the decades pass. And the sign in the woods pointing to "Nature Trail" has so much broken glass around it that I must keep the dogs leashed and the children from running until we are well past it. There are some pretty sad notes in today's Spring song, though I realize that I am transposing Eliot's ruined European gardens of the 1920s into conservation's ruined woods and wetlands of the 1960s in order to make my claim to fellow feeling.

Or fellow thinking, rather. Actually, I am too inconstant a man to remember to feel that way much of the time—particularly since it is in pottering around outdoors with a gun, or a fishing rod, or a pair of binoculars, that I have found my personal counter to that overcivilized sense of general malaise and loss which I learned (in part) from reading Eliot young. Probably, then, an average of my Spring attitudes would put me about halfway between the ecstasy and the Switch, saying to Spring in effect, and even a little crossly, "Oh, here you are at last. I thought you'd never come."

The most precise symbol of my annual discontent with the way Spring takes its time would be an odd-looking little fungus, with a mushroom stem and a head like a scrap of old sea sponge. This is the morel, a mushroom that grows in pretty good quantity in all parts of Iowa except those places in which I happen to be looking. But I would have to admit that one of the best reasons for my having such difficulty in finding it is that I generally start in hunting three or four weeks too early, as if I could wish the things out of the ground. Yet for one afflicted, as I am, with the need to have something to do outdoors, every day if possible, in unhappy contrast with those who are content merely to be outdoors or walk outdoors, there is no alternative to starting to hunt morels when it is obviously still much too early (unless you prefer fishing in muddy spring water, when it's too early to catch fish; sometimes, and unsuccessfully, I do that, too).

Very likely you are already familiar with morels, but if not there are three things to be said which might easily result in making you think of a patch of woods that you could reach this weekend: first, they are generally considered to be among the best of all the world's mushrooms, with even a source like *Larousse Gastronomique* so rating it; Escoffier, less restrained, calls it the connoisseur's choice among all edible fungi. Second, it can only be had through finding it wild, since cultivation has never been achieved, even on a laboratory scale, though it comes up every year in the same spots; I have an awesomely qualified scientific brother named Paul who is among the many who have pondered the matter, thought cultivating it might be possible, tried it, and failed. Third, to quote from Alexander Smith's *Mushroom Hunter's Field Guide,* the most abundant species, *morchella esculenta,* "can be collected every Spring throughout the United States except in arid regions." Mr. Smith's book, published by the University of Michigan Press, is the particular guide on which academic outdoorsmen around here are relying these days—a fine, scary book which is so full of implied skulls and crossbones that it makes the eating of almost any other wild mushroom an act of high courage. But the morel can be excepted —it's an unusual piece of natural benevolence that the most desirable fungus of all should also be a duffer's mushroom, one which all but the blind can recognize securely.

Recognizing it is one thing; finding it another. Says Mr. Smith's book blandly, as if it were good news, "[*m. esculenta*] grows in many types of places, and specimens may be widely scattered or fairly close together." By the time he has described the typical habitats of *esculenta* and four other morel species, we have the following list: old orchards; beech-maple forests; oak forests; lightly burned over old meadows; conifer forests in the mountains; rich moist soil in gardens; shrubby borders of woodland ponds; swampy areas; river valleys of western states; aspen, white birch and balsam forests containing considerable red pine. Now I can add to that list that various morels around here come up in sandy soil, under the fallen bark of trees I believe to be ash, and that I was once shown a dandy stand of *morchella crassipes* (if I am not mistaken) which had come up all along the perimeter of a private dump. I know a successful morel hunter who says he follows the red elms, whatever they are, and another, a man who feeds his family on morels for a couple of weeks each year, who says it's a question of finding yellow birches. If you conclude from this that the way to find morels is to come upon some through sheer luck and then, having memorized the spot, return to it regardless of soil or vegetation the following season, you will have reached in a moment a conclusion which took me three years.

Many of my morel hunting hours during these three years were spent under the instruction of my friend John Ferrell. Now you'd think that a man who can play the Bartok Violin Concerto so that a jaded university audience ("No, really, not more Bartok?") stands up and cheers at the end—a man who can jump horses and outshoot most of us with a handgun—could find morels if he really wanted to. Not John.

He loves morels; he comes from an old, morel-finding family; he says that he has often found a bushel in a morning, at home in Missouri. But having kept close score for three years, I can testify that John's total find in Iowa since he started showing me the ropes has been eight, and that six of these were dried up and useless.

Assuming that John's eye for Missouri morels is as sharp as he claims, we have in him further proof of my thesis that locating the damn things is a combination of accident and recollection, involving very little of tree recognition or other forms of mycological shrewdness. For not one of John's precepts has ever worked out: he recommended, at one time, southern-exposed slopes in the woods. We have found none on them. He recommended watercourses in semi-open places, with adequate leaf compost; we found the compost adequate for disguising soft spots where you could get mud over your shoe tops, but no morels. He thought Mr. Smith's recommendation of old orchards practically surefire, with the result that I know the locations of thirty old orchards around here, and what you find in them is old fruit trees. And finally, he directed me to carry a stick, and to poke with it among the leaves; this I did along with John for all three seasons, until one day he remarked:

"Say, I've never found a morel by poking a stick around in the leaves. Have you?" Pretty much as if the stick had been my idea in the first place.

That was last Spring. About ten days later, I was out showing someone a fall woodcock covert. This was a man named Gene Hlavka, who works for the State Conservation Commission, and was interested in setting up checkpoints for a Spring woodcock census. The place is sometimes wet, quite sandy, and has soft maple seedlings growing very thickly in it—not a beech-maple forest, no red elms, no oaks, not an orchard. Gene and I were pushing our way out through the seedlings, into some tall, wiry grass; I looked down, and there was a large, moist pitted head looking back at me.

"For heaven's sake," I said. "Isn't that a morel?" In so doing,

I showed extremely poor form—not because it wasn't, it clearly was. The bad form came in mentioning it, since the first rule of local mushroom hunting seems to be secrecy. I should have walked right by and come back later, I suppose. However, Gene is a decent fellow and forgave my breach of the code, settling for no more than half of the two or three dozen morels we proceeded to find right there. Well. He lives seventy-five miles away, and may not be able to get back over at precisely the right time this Spring.

Following that, last year, I made two more finds in about a dozen tries, one equally incidental to doing something else (what I was doing was hunting box turtles, which come out of hibernation about morel time, with my five-year-old boy; it was he who saw the morel). A few days later came the really fine moment, the first time I actually found morels while specifically looking for them. But it was rather easy and impure—I still haven't had the true experience of seeking and finding. The morels were growing around the slabs of what I insist was ash-bark, and what led me there was the way the weeds were all tramped down in a twenty-foot radius around the tree. Someone had been there first, and must have gone away with all the morels he could carry because he'd left quite a few for me.

No, not for me. For John Ferrell. I couldn't tell you exactly how he managed to claim them, but he and his daughter were at my house, looking at a white mare we had just bought with my wife and daughter, when I drove up. It takes a certain aggressiveness, as you may realize, to get people who like horses to pay attention to anything else, and I did make the error, in my childish pride, of shouting that I had a whole sackful of morels, here look, aren't they great? Here, see?

The next thing I knew, John had accepted the sack, stowed it in his car, and they were talking about horses again. Though John did take time to say, as he walked towards the blue sedan:

"Look, down along the fence. The apple trees are in bloom. That's when morels come out, when the apple trees blossom." Since it was he who'd got me out a full month earlier, before the apple trees even considered budding, I took it a little hard. But even conceding that John does seem to have a certain Missouri method of getting morels, after all, what continues to bother me as Spring comes this year is something else he said, glancing into the sack, just before he put it carefully down on the car seat:

"These are all big yellow ones, aren't they? Do you ever find the little gray ones? They're much earlier, you know. Two or three weeks."

Grimly, I went to Mr. Smith's book. Yes, there are little gray ones, *verpa bohemica* and *morchella angusticeps.* And yes, they are two or three weeks earlier . . . I don't see why I'll need my heavy jacket; look how bright the sun is.

February, 1972. The temptation to change a few details in that first *Esquire* column has been strong. The man who wrote it didn't know the difference between an ash tree and an elm, and his cavalier inability to identify the red elm in particular would make me grin foolishly if the whole thing hadn't grown too sad for embarrassment. There has been an extraordinary and tragic change: morels have been so common these last three years that we take baskets out, or plastic bags the size of pillowslips.

Far from concealing my morel places any longer, I customarily invite all the students and faculty in the graduate program in which I teach—a hundred people or more—down to the farm on Mother's Day, and show them where to look. It has become more a matter of gathering than of searching for morels, because the elms are dying.

That is not a scientific statement, only a report of observation. All the mushroom gatherers I know around here agree that the more elms fail, the more morels sprout out of the ground around them, having perhaps formed mycorrhizae—begun to feed, that is—on the decay of the dying roots. I have called a mycologist acquaintance, Martin Rosinski, who is willing to confirm the phenomenon but says the cause needs study. It's possible that there is something intermediate, bacteria or something of the sort produced by the decaying roots, on which the mushrooms thrive.

In any case, you may well find a tree one year, generally at the stage of elm disease at which the bark has started to slip off, with half a bushel of morels around it. They may not be there the next, when the tree is altogether finished. The process, whatever it is, ends. So it may not be very long before we are back again to the scarcity and excitement I tried to describe in my mushroom column, ten years ago. This present moment of great florescence may soon be a legend, which my fourteen-year-old (he was five when I wrote the column) will remember with wonder, and my six-year-old not quite believe, and perhaps neither child will really remember elms.

I have, by now, found all the morel species on the local check-list, even the little *Morchella hybrida* which, according to the books, is rare. I make spore prints, now, and have begun trying identifications by microscopic characteristics, so that mushroom gathering goes on for us all year long except in winter.

There is another book by now that I can recommend, in addition to Dr. Smith's. It is called *The Edible and Poisonous Mushrooms of Canada* (sold by the Queen's Printer, in Toronto), and covers a great many northeastern species, along with telling me what to look for with the microscope.

This self-training, considerably helped by Dr. Rosinski and his predecessor, George W. Martin, has made me a little bolder about eating wild mushrooms. There are eight or ten kinds now of which we are certain enough in addition to morels—the field mushrooms and the honey mushrooms, the sulphurs and velutipes, chantarelles, boletes, and the inky-cap family with its great prize, the Shaggy Mane.

But, like a child, I have saved my favorite for last, and I think the reason may be quite as literary as my having opened the mushroom column with familiar lines from Eliot.

Some years ago, in a magazine I edited, I published a story by Chandler Brossard who used, as an epigraph, the following lines from (if I'm not mistaken) the works of Italo Svevo: "This much I know, Mother Nature is a maniac."

I didn't know Mother well enough at the time to have any basis for accepting or rejecting that diagnosis, but the phrase stayed in my mind. Now she and I have got more acquainted, I do not think of her as a maniac. If I were to personify her (but really my mind is not adapted even to this pagan sort of religious thought) it would be as endlessly irresponsible and endlessly inventive, a creative genius so fertile and so neutral she produces in an eternal coma. Consequently, I have no sense of happy or unhappy endings in nature, only places where one may feel like stopping, and I feel like stopping not with dying trees but with my favorite mushroom, and after it, just for the hell of it, another recipe.

The mushroom is *polyphorus frondosis*—*polypilus frondosis* in the newest edition of Alexander Smith's book, but I haven't any idea why the change. Popularly, it's called the goatsbeard mushroom sometimes, and sometimes hen of the woods. Neither popular term describes it very well. What it looks like is a weird, non-chlorophyl-using member of the cabbage family; and it does have pores, rather than gills. Its fruiting body is rather like a large head of cauliflower in shape and size, and from this head it sends out fronds—short, curled-back, feather-edged branchlets, slightly fanned-out—extruding from the head. It is unmistakably fungus-colored—gray, tan, black—and one goatsbeard can weigh seven or eight pounds. On my place they grow, almost without exception, on white-oak stumps which were logged ten or twelve years ago, on a continuously shaded northwest exposure. And they generally appear right around Eleanor Ferrell's birthday, the twenty-sixth of September—and how the Ferrell family does continue to figure in my mushroom recollections.

Here is the recipe. I got it from a carpenter friend named Bob Bowman whose parentage, like that of many people around here, is German-Bohemian. The Bohemians, especially, are among our most devoted mushroom gatherers and eaters, and they clearly know what to do with the other six pounds of a seven-pound goatsbeard, after you've eaten the first pound sautéed. They pickle them. It makes the best mushroom pickle— maybe the best pickle of any kind—I ever ate in my life:

Separate your goatsbeard mushroom into stems and fronds, discarding any parts which seem tough or discolored—perhaps a bit of the stem near the base. Slice the pieces. Slice an equal volume of carrots, celery and onions. Mix them all up, and fill pint jars with the mixture. For each quart, prepare the following in a saucepan: one cup cider vinegar, one tablespoon salt, a half-cup granulated sugar; peppercorns, whole cloves, whole allspice—light on the corns and cloves, heavy on the allspice. Heat this to boiling. Pour it, jar by jar, over the mushroom-vegetable mixture.

Seal the jars.

Paste the recipe on one, and put it in a time capsule for your child. Because this is lore. This is knowledge. Man has learned to do so many simple and important things, but unless the Bowmans pass them on to the Bourjailys, and the Bourjailys find a way to get the word around, and then someone much younger seals a jar and pastes the recipe on it, knowledge like this can die. And I think its death would cost us quite as much, man for man, woman for woman, child for child, in the world, as it would to forget how to split the atom or reach the moon.

2 "Once I had a splendid pointing dog ..."

This would sound asinine to nine, more likely ten, out of ten people polled at random at Grand Central terminal at the end of a day's work, but the fact is that I reread this group of hunting pieces with strong sense of having had a dog as co-author on more than half of them. Moon, the old Weimaraner, seems to have worked on four with me, and my new dog Bix on another. (But Bix, how the years pass, is a new dog no longer and Moon had gone through and was getting past his prime when the first of these was written.)

Nevertheless I mean to report as an insight, make of me what you will, that when I speak of collaboration I do not mean merely that Moon is present, hunting with me, in four of the pieces and Bix, in his puppy year, in a fifth. I mean that I seem to myself, as I puzzle out the evolution of my own attitude, to have shared Moon's for a number of years, and then moved on to (and past) Bix's. Moon was a disciplined fanatic about hunting; Bix is an easy-going hedonist. To Moon, hunting was life's purpose; it was what made life noble. To Bix, it is only one of the agreeable things to be done, others being to lie in a fresh-plowed furrow on a warm day and watch your master try to drive the tractor; to sit under a broccoli leaf watching a spider, while your mistress weeds; to do traditional dog stuff with bones; to play puppy games, even at the age of eight, with gloves and slippers; and to smell the genitals of friendly cats and, if there be a good stout fence between you, unfriendly pigs. Bix enjoys moving his bowels first thing as we enter a bird field; the need to do it always seemed to make Moon impatient.

Moon's intolerance for anything but the matter at hand seems to me to be present in the first, second, sixth and seventh pieces (and even the third and fifth, though he is not mentioned in them); Bix's dreaminess, perhaps, informs the eighth.

Now I don't claim to have gone all the way with either dog; even at my most addicted, I don't think I held hunting to be noble—I think, rather, that the first essay hereafter presents me going as far in that direction as I ever did. Nor do I take any keener sexual interest in cats and pigs than the next man—I mean not when there are still plenty of seals and giraffes in the world —or chew the fingers out of gloves when no one's looking (still, I can understand that there's just something nice and crunchy about a reversed lambskin glove, with the $18 price tag still on it; I mean when a fellow's right canine tooth goes punching through the lanolin-tasting suede to the crackling wool, I'll bet it's okay).

What I do propose is that, as Moon and I worked together in some harmony of dog-intensity/man-intensity, while Bix and I have approached the matter with more diffusion of values, these moods seem to me to have influenced the prose. It may, of course, be no more than accidental that I happened to change breeds when a change was taking place in me, even possible that I have cause and effect reversed, but, subjectively, I don't think either is so. There is also the possibility that I've got birdshot for brains to an even greater extent than that which has been charged against me once or twice in book reviews—the particular deplorable symptom alleged being that I am said to prefer dogs to people.

Which isn't true at all, of course—how could anyone feel he'd rather take Moon or Bix out hunting than seize the opportunity of equipping and guiding those ten random commuters we were talking with at Grand Central, five paragraphs ago?

Gee fellas, I've only got five pairs of boots. Hey, I know. Half of you hop along, with your loaded guns, on your right feet, and the other half on your left feet, and I'll walk barefoot in front of you, catching birds by hand and throwing them up in the air, okay?

The full title of the first piece in this section goes: UNTOLD STORY OF L.B.J.'S FIRST WEEKS / COIN CRAZE / A FAMOUS WRITER SAYS HUNTING IS HUMANE *(Starring Sophia Loren).*

That was the bottom line of the *Saturday Evening Post* cover behind which the piece appeared, and in parentheses the identity of the alluring green-eyed lady whose photograph graced that cover and whose "views on life, love and marriage" were said to be part of the magazine's contents. I don't recall that the views were striking enough to justify the use of the preceding phrase "an intimate look at . . ." nor that the story of L.B.J.'s first weeks had much in it that I hadn't read before, or even that the coin thing was a real "craze," rather than just a fad. However, editorial license is nothing I object to very strongly, being more a convention than a misrepresentation—but I was surprised equally by my promotion to the ranks of the famous and by the promotion of hunting to the status of a sport "marked [quoting from Webster] by compassion, sympathy or consideration for

72

other human beings or animals." Nope. I don't think I say that. What appears here is the piece as I sent it in, and, I'm fairly certain, as it appeared in the magazine. It was under a standing head they used, "Speaking Out," meant to present controversial opinion, and on the whole I wasn't unsympathetic to the editors. They had a problem.

Nobody ever answered the defense of hunting in a way that seemed persuasive to me, so, in the last piece in the book, I have finally answered it myself.

The second thing here is another of the six "Outdoors" columns I did for *Esquire.* I liked doing those columns, and was sorry when the freedom to use the space as I wished was withdrawn; maybe they never really meant to offer it to me. Anyway, we agreed, not without anger, to terminate the arrangement, and I should add that Arnold Gingrich's *Esquire* honorably paid for the seventh, unused column, over which the disagreement started. Arnold himself, whom I know and like and who is one of this century's first-rate sportsmen, wasn't party to the hassle. This, and the other columns, are still in the form in which I sent them in; in fact all the pieces in this section are, and I'd say on rereading them that I like myself best in the *Esquire* columns, when I wasn't writing to anyone's requirements. "Charmio's Column," the second piece, is one of the few in which I felt sure enough of my experience (and Moon's) to write what became a set of directions, in this case for late winter pheasant hunting.

"The Ninth Upland Game Bird" was written for a magazine which turned it down as not being zippy enough, and then was sold—one of those rare small triumphs in a writer's life—to another magazine for quite a bit more money. It appeared in *Playboy,* which is a pleasant place to publish, not just because of the good paycheck but also because you have a sense of reaching some readers who are different from the ones you usually imagine yourself writing for.

"The Column from Mexico," though it ends with thoughts

about duck hunting, introduces me engaged in quite a different outdoor activity. Archaeological field work is an interest which also produced the piece about prehistoric corn in the following section. As you might gather from the footnote to the mushroom column, I keep finding new things to do outdoors. I don't, by the way, know what to make of the way Mexico becomes the chief locale, second after Iowa, for pieces in this book—a combination of coincidence, I guess, and the fact that I've spent a good bit of time there. Still, it seems odd that in order to get well enough acquainted with a couple of nationally prominent Iowa men— Harold Hughes, now U.S. Senator, from Ida Grove; and Norman Borlaug, Nobel Peace Prize winner, from Cresco—I should have had to go to Mexico. Anyway, that's next section, and the preoccupation with ducks in the column at hand is a true lead into the piece that follows it. In the one that follows I am classifying hunters in a way suitable to the impersonal style of the *New York Times Magazine;* if I don't seem to put myself into one of the classifications there, you can guess easily enough which it would have been.

The thing, however, that I notice especially in the *Times* article is that, even though it continues to have some of the tone of my defense of hunting, it's also the first place—coming less than a year after the *Saturday Evening Post* entry—where I acknowledge the existence of ex-hunters, and speculate about them. Just a little.

Then back we go to dogs, again, obviously, in "The Dog Column" and then "Closing Days," which should be Moon's last appearance. But it isn't. He'll appear as a comic nuisance, I'm afraid, later when I write about trout fishing, but obviously he stays in my mind today as part of the sunset composition in the last paragraph of the last column.

As for "Something New for the Old Gun," I guess there was more that was new going on in my head when I wrote it than I realized at the time. It isn't there overtly, only in tone and by implication: when you find yourself able to sum up your fantasies —and even what you take to be your dog's fantasy—look out. You are becoming too involved intellectually. You're only a step away, now, from having to think things through. Analyze. Conceptualize. For a man with birdshot for brains, the head is a shell-case, he puts in a primer, and some powder, and a wad, and crimps the shell . . .

First published in the
Saturday Evening Post,
*February 15, 1964, under
the heading "Speaking
Out."*

Famous Writer Says Hunting Is Humane

I think a reasoned defense of hunting, an activity I enjoy very much, would be as difficult to compose as a reasoned defense of drinking whiskey or going to the theater. All three are things men do for pleasure. All three come under attack, at times, from the various kinds of puritan with whom the culture of this country is traditionally afflicted. The puritans brought us Prohibition not long ago. They kept theater out when we were colonies (and their influence is still felt in the mindless censoring of today's forms of popular theater, television and the movies). They are pressing now, and sometimes achieving, various laws designed to restrict hunting which have nothing to do with game protection or safety; such laws are in the bleak category of moral legislation.

Now there is no honest defense of any pleasure except to

for Ophelia

say: I do it because I enjoy it. When criticized we are likely to take peripheral benefits (exercise, identification with tradition, relaxing of tensions) and try to make them stand up as central justification. This seems to me a mistake. All we ought really to say to those spoilers who would suppress pleasures they do not share is this: disapprove of me as you will, but to try to give your disapproval the force of law is a crime against freedom.

Beyond this, in the particular matter of hunting, I can distinguish three kinds of attacker, and each deserves a different answer. There are the moralists, who must be answered with an invitation to examine themselves. There are the sentimentalists, who must be answered with straightforward information. The third are simply politicians, who may be answered with contempt. Let us take them in reverse order.

The politicians. I do not mean to restrict the term to those who seek office; any man whose goal is influence, and whose means of seeking it are cynical, is a politician in the bad, broad sense. Often they are men of some intelligence and energy. There were many of them working for Prohibition; the ladies with hatchets could never have put it over without them. They provide the officer corps for crusades, whether to burn books or witches. They are tough men, their inability to see the other sides of issues is self-willed rather than actual; they attempt to lead by organizing the sentimentality of the uninformed, and I shall be done with them very quickly. For if their abilities make them the most effective opponents, to answer them is no more than a matter of exposure.

The example which comes most readily to mind does happen to be a politician in the narrow sense, a member of a state legislature who announced that his opposition to a dove-hunting bill was based on the determination to forestall extinction (if I am not mistaken, he brought up the passenger pigeon). I had met the man, and knew him to be familiar with the methods of modern game management. As will, I believe, become clear, depletion—let alone extinction—of any species by hunting is quite impossible under the controls practiced today in all fifty of our states (and, as regards migratory birds, under federal supervision as well). In fact, and very strict fact, the result of legalizing hunting for a species is to build it up, and many nongame species along with it. The prohibition of dove hunting in certain states is an abolutely clear example of legislation which has no other purpose than to tell a hunter what his conscience should permit. This legislator was choosing to talk nonsense for its supposed political appeal; there are a good many like him. Their crime against freedom is the worst because it does not even spring from genuine moral conviction.

The sentimentalists. These are people whose tenderness of heart and failure of comprehension makes the decent hunter feel that the best he can do is keep his views to himself as, were legislation of morals not involved, I would. To let them go their way, deploring me, while I go mine, avoiding them, seems the most comfortable thing for all parties. But if they are to be used as foot soldiers in a crusade against hunting, then I had better at least make a try at presenting the more open-minded with a summary of the facts.

Hunters, like nature, are indifferent to the lives of individual creatures, but infinitely solicitous of the survival and multiplication of species (there has been some evolution here, of course, from the market hunters and blood sports of the nineteenth century). Modern hunters spend, annually, millions of dollars in state license fees, special federal taxes, and contributions to private organizations, to preserve and increase game. Obviously and admittedly, our motives are selfish. We want those creatures to be there to hunt during the short seasons when hunting is permitted. But what must be understood is the nature of the permission sought and granted; it is not permission to deplete a game species, only to harvest its surplus. Further, the surplus we harvest is always set well under the vast numbers of individuals which—even were hunting not permitted—would perish annually anyway as a result of predation, attrition and disease. To return to mourning doves for a moment, as a good example: this species is classified as game by international treaty, by tradition, and by law which permits hunting them in thirty-one of the fifty states. (And, I ought to add, so classified by its nature—what distinguishes a game species beyond palatability and commonness is a superb natural ability to survive through evasiveness, wariness, speed and protective coloration.) Doves are extremely common, far more so in the United States than any other upland game bird, and extremely prolific; in Iowa, for example—a non-dove-hunting state—a 1963 spring census by the Des Moines Audubon Society showed them to be among the ten most common of all our birds, more numerous than robins or meadowlarks. Now, studies show that of all the doves hatched in a given year, 70 per cent will not reach the age of one. They will starve, die accidentally, get sick, or fall to owls, hawks, and foxes. Nevertheless, in such a state as Iowa the total population will remain stable.

In states where doves are hunted, on the other hand, the birds actually shot by hunters will simply be part of the 70 per cent fatality (a small part—4 per cent, for example, in California). This is to say, hunters will be permitted to harvest part of a surplus which would be taken otherwise by other means. Moreover, the total dove population in the hunting states, from year to year, will increase. This is due to a number of factors, the most important being that hunters' license fees are spent, in part, to expand and create the kind of habitat in which doves can nest, hatch and flourish. In addition, the time when hunting is permitted coincides with the population peak; flocks are huge, primary ranges crowded. The competition for food and cover among the

birds is intense and damaging, and the crowding promotes disease. At the moment the first gun sounds on opening day, these
big flocks begin to scatter, to thin out into secondary ranges for
better protection. A few individuals fall; species prosper.

Through their support of federal, state and private conservation agencies, hunters have paid the bills for establishing pheasants, for preserving waterfowl breeding grounds and refuges,
and for the salaries of the men who protect the game from the
excesses of the greedy. Even more dramatically, the hunter's
self-interest has, in our lifetime, brought back species from the
edge of extinction. The prong-horn antelope was, not long ago,
a vanishing species. This had nothing to do with hunting. The
prong-horns were the victims (as is true of almost any species
which has gotten into survival trouble in recent years) of so-
called progress: clearing, plowing, building, overgrazing, drain-
age. Hunters' money—blood money if you like—bought the
preserves, paid the specialists, financed the experiments, which
have restored the prong-horn to the point where nature lovers
(which includes most hunters) may see these animals from their
cars on the way to our western parks. And each year a small
surplus of them may be shot for sport. The wild turkey, re-
established now in many states, has benefited from hunters' interest in much the same way.

Thus, and with dozens more such examples, it may be shown
that an attack on hunting cannot be realistically based on the wish
to protect game species. Insofar as it is based on a desire to
protect the individual game creature from cruelty and death, the
hunter's immemorial reply is simply that he is no more cruel than
nature, and far less wasteful.

The moralists. If politicians are the generals in crusades, and
sentimentalists the foot soldiers, then moralists are the grand
strategists and ideologists, the men who provide ideas and define
goals. Their sincerity cannot be placed in question, nor can we

say that they are not entitled to argue their opinions so persuasively, if they can, as to make us forswear the pleasures of hunting out of sheer guilt.

The best of them are those whose opposition to killing for sport is based on a moral code of total reverence for life in all its forms, who eat no meat, swat no mosquitos, and will not poison other bugs to improve the quality of the fruits and vegetables on which they subsist. For such men I have a good deal of respect, a certain reverence even, but I do not share their code. And I do not wish it imposed on me (or you) by law.

There are very few such men, of course. The great majority of those who urge that I feel guilt for the game I kill live in somewhat more transparent houses. They see a moral difference of some kind between the unnatural rearing and drab, bloody slaughter of meat and fowl commercially, and the system of game management which raises crops of wild birds and animals to be harvested by men who find challenge and excitement, health and pleasure in trying it. With gentle smiles, these part-way moralists pull on their gardening gloves and dust the roses to kill the merry, high-hopping flea beetle. Gaily they cast the lure which will attract and hook the exuberantly innocent bass. Craftily they place the trap which will drive sharp prongs through the furry back of the comically shortsighted mole. And for lunch, it's cutlets or chops, from brown-eyed calves or woolly lambs.

No, if you are not a sage who can see that the housefly, with its transparent wings and iridescent body is too beautiful to kill, I cannot take seriously the presumption that my morals as a hunter are in worse shape than yours as a gardener, or fisherman, or sanitary housekeeper who cooks good chicken. Growing, catching—even cleaning and cooking—are instinctive things; so, for men of a certain temperament, is hunting.

There is enough in us, I suppose, of the primitive so that to hunt and kill a creature under difficult conditions is profoundly satisfying. The two parts of the sequence must occur together, or there is no satisfaction. Killing, and this is generally misunderstood, is no pleasure at all if the challenge of hunting does not accompany it. I do not relish, for example, cutting the heads off chickens, as I must from time to time, nor do I like trapping mice. Against such simple, necessary and quite dreary killing, let me describe a brief hunt I made yesterday:

It was a windy afternoon, two degrees above zero and with eight inches of snow covering the ground. It seems almost unimaginable, in a way, that I wanted to go out, and perhaps that I did, very much, want to, is demonstration enough of the power hunting has to excite me. As I warmed the car, I thought of the base of a certain steep hill nearby, which has been contour-plowed to permit planting and harvesting a small cornfield. Along the bottom of the hill runs a thick growth of giant ragweed, wild plum, blackberry bushes and small trees—good winter cover. I thought pheasants ought to be in there.

With my big old bird dog, who is called Moon, and a springer puppy I was running for the first time this past season, I hunted the long thicket; there were pheasant tracks all through it, but no birds. A few tracks led, illogically, up the steepest part of the hill, into the wind, and Moon indicated that they were fresh. Up the hill, sliding and scrambling, the pup and I went after him; out of breath, feeling the cold, I was finally running to keep up, as Moon went across the top and into a wooded draw on the far side (for pheasants do not often stay for a dog, as quail will). And suddenly birds went up, near the dog and out of range for me: four hens, then a cock, then another cock. The second cock flew towards me, saw me, turned and swept away down the draw. I might have shot if I'd been quick enough, but wasn't.

Old Moon came bounding back on a fresh scent, and I went after him up another steep bank, towards a second and smaller draw. Just at the edge, Moon pointed. I tried to be both quick and careful, and was almost to the dog when the bird flew, straight into the sun. At first, starting to lower the gun, I took it for a hen. Then it turned slightly, I saw a glint of color on its neck, it gave a confirming cackle and I swung and shot, all in one movement. And the cock fell. It was the kind of snap shot I've been missing recently, and I was delighted.

The bird hit the ground dead, slid along the snow down the steep side of the draw; old Moon plunged down that way and got him, and started to climb back to me, the little springer following both ways, wagging his tail. And just at this moment, from close to where they had retrieved the bird (and where I might easily have been if I'd been alert), another cock flew up. I fired. I missed. But I had my bird, I was warm with pleasure, and the dogs were ecstatically proud of themselves.

Today we hunted another hour—the season will be over so very soon—and raised no birds at all, but I am as pleased, as cleansed, as brightened by my time outdoors in the cold weather as I was yesterday when I saw several and got one. The dogs feel pretty good, too. And I find myself willing to acknowledge that my pleasure in hunting differs very little from theirs: it is an exercise of instinct, training and, to some extent, physical endowment, and we like it.

Not all dogs are fit to hunt nor, in the same way, are all men gratified by it. Nor, for those of us who share this dog's pleasure of hunting (if you will), do I ask special tolerance or understanding. We are as we are, and if we seem to you to act immorally, it is certainly your right to feel so. But I say most seriously that you exceed your rights when you urge that laws be made in the shape of your conscience to block pleasures permitted by mine. When you prevail you commit a crime against freedom, and that is the greatest immorality I know.

First published in
Esquire, *under the*
heading "Outdoors,"
December, 1964.

Charmio's Column

Shall we sit by the fire now, sucking on pipes and
murmuring of hunts long past, watching the old dog's leg
twitch and his teeth bare as he dreams of hunting too?
Gentlemen, I have no fireplace.

Further, our State Conservation Commission, following a
trend in the midwest, has extended the pheasant season this
year into January. Insulated underwear. Down-filled jacket.
Boots. Muffler. Gloves. Just where in hell did I put my
gloves? They aren't gloves really but those big, yellow
deerskin mittens, with the right-hand palm split. I always
seem to find my wife's pair first, and try to pull them on even
though I can see that they're the smaller ones; then mine
were in the pocket of the down jacket all along. I do a little
cheerful roaring about all this: the first problem in winter

pheasant hunting is to get one's spirits up artificially high, to counteract the temperature's natural low. I don't really like cold weather, but once I get out in it will be glad I did.

The next problem in winter pheasant hunting is less personal: where have the birds gone? Many, of course, are gone for good —most of this year's cockerels who didn't know about men and guns, and failed their one chance to pick up useful information. They were the easy birds, and have been gone since the first week in the season. In the following weeks the survivors were around, during the pleasant weather, in conventional places: hayfields at roosting time, fencerows at loafing time, grainfields if you caught them feeding.

They won't roost in hayfields any more this year. There is an annual movement from high, well-drained ground to low, out of the wind. Frozen marshes are a good bet now. Timber bottoms, with plenty of undergrowth. Pheasants are along streams in high grass and willow clumps; sometimes in east-west ditches. They are in horseweed patches, that tall, brittle, gray-stemmed weed. They are in deep draws, sometimes without much cover but with good wind protection on all sides, back in the woods.

For loafing, they go back to these same dense or isolated places, not by ones and twos as they did earlier, but in segregated groups: half a dozen cocks together here, fifteen or twenty hens bunched in somewhere else. They feed less frequently, except on sunny, windless days—or so it seems to me. And they make a quicker job of it. They don't have to get to cornfields either, though of course they still like to. But in the crop of a winter pheasant there is often nothing but weed seeds—black, gray and brown and to me unidentifiable. The pheasant has done just what I might: he has gotten cosy for the winter, and instead of roaming around he will, if he can, and especially on a stormy day, feed in the same protected place in which he roosts.

If I seem to be putting forth information in a somewhat more authoritative tone than I usually feel comfortable in taking, it is easy to explain. For years, before these extensions of the season into winter began, I continued to run my dog through pheasant coverts in the cold weather, day after day right up to nesting time. One of the finest hunts I ever made took place on a New Year's Day, several years ago. I used to use cold beer as a hangover cure, but as I age cold air does it better.

I carried a shotgun, thinking I would shoot a rabbit if I felt like it, though generally I let them go. We were skirting the edge of a big, low-lying weed field when Moon got birdy. He is, as I must have said in this space a number of times before, a Weimaraner, a big dog with a tiny stub for a tail. When the stub begins to vibrate so quickly that Moon's rear end is a blur, we are close to a bird. And so it vibrated.

Moon began to go through the thick, waist-high stuff at a quick trot, and I went after him at somewhat the same gait. Clearly the pheasant wasn't going to hold; soon I started seeing tracks, and learned it was a cock. This, by the way, is the only use for snow in pheasant hunting of which I am persuaded—being able to tell the sex of the bird by the mark (or lack of it) which the spur makes. Following tracks to find a pheasant is something I have tried or seen tried any number of times and, in my opinion, it simply doesn't work. The attention given to tracking gives the bird all the chance he needs to get away and flush out of range, if he's really out there; but generally the tracks I've followed didn't end with a flushed bird at all. They just ended. The flushing took place, I conclude, some moments before I came in sight, along about the time, perhaps, that I came in sound.

On the New Year's Day that I'm recalling, I paused, in trotting after Moon, to unload the gun, and hurried on. It was a marvelous, breathless chase, as the bird went twisting and turning through the weeds, never seen, with the dog now hot, now cold, but seldom checking and me after the dog chuckling and gasping and slipping, now and then, in the snow. Finally the bird went up, a huge one, four or five years old from his size, about forty yards out. I skidded to a stop, raised my empty gun and tracked him beautifully; he was sailing over trees, fifty yards away when I slapped the trigger, and I knew my lead was right, even for the acute angle at which he went away, and ah, how he would have fallen. . . . There was, I knew, a small swamp on the other side. When Moon and I got to it I'd have had a chance to dry-fire on the old bird again, except that three younger cocks got up before he did. As long as I was shooting so well, I saw no reason to settle for a double. I swung my two-barreled gun smoothly after each in turn, and shot a triple.

Thus last year, when the season was extended through December for the first time, Moon and I knew how to change our technique to fit the weather, and were still getting birds when better hunters had given up.

We got, too, so that we knew several individual birds: as fishermen who fish a habitual stream have a named fish or two which they have hooked and lost numbers of times, so I found that in winter pheasant hunting I had some named pheasants— wary escape artists within whose individual precincts I tried to move with particular thought and care. The hardest for me was a pheasant I called "Charmio," because it seemed to me he had a charmed life.

He was—and probably still is, for that matter—a relatively small bird, even scrawny, and one who never cackled when he rose. His method was deception in rising, rather than running, to keep from being shot. In fact, the first time I missed Charmio, Moon was hunting in a little bunch of saplings, tail going maniacally, and I was standing by relaxed and confident. From Moon's behavior the bird was close at hand, and it was the kind of blustery day when pheasants hold well to a dog; I already had one fine bird hanging from my belt. It puzzled me only that

Moon wasn't pointing; he kept working into the same little spot busily and out of it again. Once he stopped and looked directly at me, as if for advice. At this I felt, rather than saw, Charmio rise. He came up from within two feet of my right heel, a position he'd apparently crept into as I waited.

By the time I recovered, wheeled around and saw him, he was far enough out in the dull light to make me hesitate over whether —there being no cackle—Charmio might be a hen. Then, as he got enough into profile for me to see the long tail, Charmio, staying low, got just enough saplings between himself and me so that there was no sense shooting. Unlike you, gentlemen, I sometimes shoot when there's no sense to it and I gave those saplings a fine spraying.

The next time we encountered Charmio, I gave him what may have been a helpful injury: I shot off part of the long, unmistakable tail. There was a horseweed patch near the saplings; Moon was in it and I was at the edge, this time expecting and wanting rabbits. Just as two came out, distracting me, Charmio did too, bolting right at my head. As he rose to clear my hunting cap, I tried to bend double backwards and shoot up at him—perhaps I'd have gotten him if I'd thought to turn; I saw my pellets pattern through the tail feathers as I shot behind him, and the two longest feathers broke upwards, so that he carried them away at a right angle to the rest of the tail.

After that, when we saw him, he was short-tailed and unmistakably himself except when I took him for a hen. The last time I saw him, Moon got him up from the saplings again, and he went straight out, hardly even waist-high, in front of the dog. Then Charmio swerved downwind, climbed a little, and by the time things were clear enough for a shot was sailing away with the wind behind him, fast as a dove or pigeon. I held the shot, trying to outthink him, and marked him down in a ploughed field, of all places and, of all things, into a furrow. I actually saw him land

and run along for a moment in that fast, hunkered-down, cock-pheasant walk which is like the gait Groucho Marx used to use for making surreptitious exits.

I made a big circle, to the other side of the ploughed field, going through some woods for concealment. I felt certain he'd have gone on to the edge of the bare ground, to where grass was growing, but he fooled me again. He crouched out there in the middle, with only clods for cover, watching to see if he was followed. Then he rose, at fifty yards or more, going away at an angle I couldn't solve, and rode the winter wind the farthest I have ever seen a pheasant fly, over the hill a mile away and out of sight.

It is my belief that Charmio will be back, with new tail feathers, in pretty much the same place this year, to make me forget I don't have a fireplace and make me glad I've come out in the cold.

*First published under the
same title in* Playboy,
November, 1966.

The Ninth Upland Game Bird

In 1914, just fifty years ago, in Cincinnati, the last passenger
pigeon died. She was a female, and her single life in the zoo
kept extant the most numerous game bird species ever known
for fourteen years after the final sighting sighting of free
birds.

Long before that—I don't suppose anybody knows or cares
just when—settlers from Europe had begun to import rock
doves, distantly related birds of about the same size, which
we now call domestic pigeons. They were brought in for
various uses: for farm flocks, in the interest of fanciers of the
ornamental strains, for shooting and racing and even message
carrying. And perhaps these pigeons were sometimes brought
over in much the same spirit as were English sparrows and
European starlings—the human urge, an adult form of

homesickness, to introduce an old, familiar species in a new land.

Though we still have farm flocks and fanciers around, as well as men who keep pigeons to race and to use in training dogs and falcons, most domestic pigeons are no longer domestic. They are in the stage between domestic and wild called feral, and many have gone beyond that into true wildness—that is, a state in which their existence no longer depends on man, his structures, or the products of his cultivation in any way; these live in cliffs, and feed on open ground. The majority of pigeons, of course, live the feral life of raiders, nesting in barns or on building ledges, feeding on waste or sharing handouts with regular farm creatures when the farmer's back is turned. They are wary, sharp eyed, bold and furtive by turn—necessary qualities for adapting to the bandit's life. As a consequence, having wiped out our native wild pigeon, we find ourselves with what is essentially a new wild pigeon of very different characteristics. It is one of those ironies of nature which, because it took a century to de-velop, nobody much noticed.

Now usually we count ourselves as having eight chief upland game birds: the pheasants, the various quail, the grouse, par-tridges, wild turkey, doves, woodcock, quail and snipe. (These are gunner's categories, of course, a separation into target styles, rather than a naturalist's grouping in familes.) The feral pigeon is, it seems to me, really our ninth. As are the pheasants and partridges, he is an exotic; as is true of carp, another exotic introduced with great enthusiasm at one time—and, of course, true of English sparrows and starlings, too—this transplanted pigeon is not an unmitigated success. But wisely or not, we seem to have him irrevocably established, and most men I know, whether they think him game bird or nuisance, will shoot one when they have a chance to.

So, for that matter, will I, though it took me a while to get used to the idea. First, I suppose, this was because, in the city passages of my boyhood, pigeons were the birds we fed, watched, admired and, when a mishap came, wept for. Even now I wonder at the insistence of city managers that a town without birds would be preferable to accepting the deposits of dung on roofs and sills which are the price of having life in the air above the streets, squadrons of wings in flight, iridescent feathered bodies picking through parks and gutters. That feeling was part of my initial reluctance to shoot pigeons. Another part must have been my share of the guilt that all Americans carry towards this family of birds, and yet another my feeling that pigeons in the countryside weren't quite wild—that they must belong to someone who valued them.

The country part of my boyhood was spent in the woods rather than on the farm, and consequently I had seldom seen the feral rock dove as other than a city creature until I moved to Iowa. One morning here I was walking back along a country road from duck hunting, with a friend I have written about before and called Henry Akers. We weren't talking; we were rather disgruntled, first from having seen no ducks, then from having walked unexpectedly into a covey of quail. The quail season had opened the day before—in fact, having been skunked locally, we were planning a more distant quail hunt. It's quite possible that, just as we came out of the woods, Henry had said something like: "If we drive south about an hour from here, we'll be down more where the birds are," when twenty quail burst up out of the grass around his feet and went buzzing off. Henry is quicker than I, and had time to send one, unavailing duck load after them; I never even got my gun to my shoulder. The covey scattered into woods across the road.

We were without a dog that morning, and failed at trying to walk up singles. Then, as we resumed our stroll down the road, a quail flew right across in easy range, and Henry and I missed the crossing shot in turn, bang, bang, bang, properly loaded this time. So we were feeling uncharitable when the pigeon flew over. We saw him coming from a long way off, leaving a barn and winging steadily towards us, rather high, straight over the road.

"Damn it, here comes a shot I'm going to make," Henry said, rather grimly, stopped, and set his feet. He's the kind of man who occasionally issues a challenge to himself in that tone, and so I kept my own gun down; besides, I had that panicky thought about the bird's belonging to someone, and was about to ask if this weren't probable when Henry's gun went smoothly up, swung in a fast arc, fired, followed through, and the high pigeon came tumbling down.

Is it true that different birds fall differently? It seems to me that a duck, well-hit, folds its wings and dives. A pheasant, even though it's dead on impact, fights air reflexively all the way down. A quail drops. But a pigeon tumbles, wing over wing, as Henry's did.

"Great shot," I said. Then I asked my question. And Henry, picking up his bird, explained:

"The farmers don't want them," he said. "Oh, I guess there are a few pouters and homers and fancy breeds around, and you could get someone pretty sore if you shot his prize Blue Fantail. But mostly they're living in those barns like sparrows. They feed from one barnyard to another, and if there's any kind of poultry disease on one place, the pigeons spread it to the next. Most of these farmers will ask you in to shoot them, if they know you like to."

"Any good to eat?"

"Take him home and try him," Henry said.

The feeling about pigeons as food around here is, again, the same general feeling that prevails towards carp—that, being scavengers, they shouldn't be eaten. This ignores a European tradition for use of the rock dove, which fills a couple of pages in Escoffier. Of course the bird, while edible enough in stews and casseroles in maturity, has been a delicacy—a broiling and roasting bird—when it was young, full-sized and flightless. This desirability of the squab form acutally was a heavy factor in the tragedy of the passenger pigeon—netters took the young by wagonloads in the spring for sale to city markets, breaking up the huge nesting flocks and aborting the year's hatch. This is still a practice, I learned when I was in Uruguay, in the pampas countries of South America, where there are other New World wild pigeons still thriving.

It was a couple of months after I took Henry Aker's bird home to cook (it turned out tough, but not unflavorful) that I actually saw something of the disregard in which country people hold pigeons and, at the same time, something of what it is like to hunt them in a less than casual way. I know a mechanic, a sort of mad genius with all metallic things. He collects and repairs guns, his thirst for restoring machinery to operation apparently unsatisfied by long hours under the cars at the shop where he works. Call him Martin. He probably handles more guns and shoots them less than anyone I know.

But now and then Martin will get some piece of iron back into shooting condition and want to try it, and when those weekend days come he has no patience for the chances and vagaries of searching fields for game. He knows dozens of farmers whose tractors and other farm machinery he has fixed, and most of them are men with barns—and pigeons.

On this particular Saturday afternoon Martin had just finished adjusting the trigger pull on a Parker I owned.

"It's no duck gun," he said. "But keep it dry and it won't rust up in there and double on you." Somewhere in behind the firing pins, where my cleaning brush didn't reach, it had become rusty enough so that when one pin was released the one beside it was sometimes jarred sufficiently so that both barrels of the gun went

94

off at once. The gun had nearly knocked me down a couple of times—done it quite literally, as a matter of fact, just at the end of duck season. I was standing in some rather slippery mud, fired at a pintail and caused a double blast. I'd done a heels-up pratfall in shallow water, very surprised. Whether it was a hunting joke or a painful matter—the water was intensely cold—depended, I remember, on whether the pintail was hit or missed; he was lying out there good and dead, and I laughed instead of cursing. But now all the seasons were closed for the year, I'd gone along with a gun which had me a little spooked, shooting worse and worse because of it and Martin scolded me for delaying so long in having it fixed:

"Why didn't you bring it to me when you still wanted to shoot? You're going to spend a whole year now remembering how bad it treated you, before you can hunt again."

"I guess I can shoot clay," I said.

Suddenly he grinned his grimy, mechanic's grin. "Aw, let's try on some birds," he said.

"But the season . . ."

"You too fine to shoot pigeons?"

I called home to say I'd be delayed, got in Martin's car with him, and we drove out west of town. He had four or five guns he was going to try, but the only one I remember specifically was a monstrous French thing, made, he told me, for the tropics. It was a double-12 with a curious breech arrangement designed to put enough push behind shells while loading to force them into the chamber, in a place where cases are swollen by perpetual dampness. I rather imagine that gun had shot wild pigeons before, at the edge of some equatorial rain forest, for there are a number of tropical varieties.

The farm we stopped at was a big one, with two barns about a quarter mile apart, and the farmer, when we got there, was feeding buttermilk to hogs. He had the place posted against hunting, too, but when he recognized Martin and heard it was pigeons we were after, the farmer set down his pail and rubbed his hands briskly.

"Let me run 'em out for you," he said.

Martin and I placed ourselves at one end of the barn. Way up near the peak was a small, slatted window, but several slats were broken out.

"That's where they'll come from," Martin said, laying his assorted shotguns around him on the ground, except for the French one which he loaded. It was about four thirty in the afternoon.

"You take the first," he said.

Inside the barn I could hear the farmer, chucking ears of corn and shouting, and suddenly there was a blue and white pigeon perched at the edge of the opening, fifty feet up. It looked down at us, launched itself in a downward arc, and, with an audible snap of its wings, was away and flying. I swung up my gun and shot. It felt rather late but I was quite confident, even on the overhead-going-away shot, since the range was short; I missed.

"Way behind him," Martin said. "They don't take any time at all to get started." He mounted the French gun like a trap-shooter, was ready when the next bird came out, and dropped it.

Imitating him, I mounted the Parker and waited, but what came out was the farmer, from a ground floor opening behind me.

"Doesn't seem to be any more in there," he said, and I was about to lower my gun to turn and look at him when two pigeons came out together. It was beautiful, if I do say so myself. I got the high bird, who was rising straight away from my barrel, and swung to hit the low one in a repetition of the shot I'd missed at first. As a man who seldom makes doubles, and shoots worst when watched, I was very pleased.

"There you go," Martin said.

I smiled at the farmer to receive his congratulations as well.

"What'd you do, miss that first one that come out?" The farmer said, disgusted with me. "I want these pigeons shot, not educated."

He went back to his buttermilk, and Martin picked up a different shotgun, but no more birds came out of the barn. For a moment there, though, looking up at the little window, I'd been as close as I may ever be to living in a past when live pigeons came out of a trap, in pairs or singles, to bewitch a target gunner.

There must be a time of day, which one could determine by local observation, when pigeons could be predicted to be present in a given barn and to come out in this way. This would, I think, vary with time of year, for barn pigeons, though not migratory, seem to change their feeding and roosting habits seasonally— around here they leave town and congregate in large farm flocks in the winter, dispersing after nesting is over.

But my own interest would be less in figuring out how they might set themselves up as inadvertent trap birds than in trying to work out something more like pass shooting. I remember that Martin and I turned our eyes away from the barn and saw a flock between us and the second barn, circling, lowering over picked corn, almost settling and then dashing away into high air again for some pigeon's reason. Even at that distance, a couple of hundred yards away, they had the look of pass birds to me—a style of flight singly and in formation which I associate not only with doves, which are related, but with ducks which are not. It's a style which gives an impression of great speed, orderliness of shifting mass, both in straight flight and in circling, as if such birds were made to outfly the gun rather than depending, as do other gound feeders, on surprising the hunter.

It was five by then, forty-five minutes till sunset.

"Tell you what," Martin said. "They're going to be coming

97

in to roost, here or at the other barn. Maybe both. Why don't I go down there, and I'll bet we send them back and forth?"

That was a fine idea, for all I knew. I unloaded and laid my gun down, picked up his spare shotguns and started walking him to his car in the barnyard; on the way he stopped.

"Will you look over there?"

He pointed to a grazed field, just over the fence from us, where a couple of sows were tending their litters. Out beyond them, fifty yards or more, two pigeons were hopping around, pecking at something or other.

"Good test of pattern at extreme range?" I said, thinking he meant to fire the Winchester pump he'd had ready but hadn't used.

"Here, hold this," Martin said, shucked shells out of the pump, and piled it into my arms with the other four. Then he opened his mackinaw, and I saw more guns, pistols, strapped to his body and sticking out of his inner pockets. The man was an arsenal.

I think the one he selected was a thirty-two, and damned if he didn't set that overweighted body, holding a box of twelve-gauge shotgun shells in his left hand for balance, and shoot the head off a pigeon at fifty yards.

"Huh," Martin grumbled. "Fella brought this back, tried to tell me I hadn't got it sighted in right for him."

We got Martin and his weapons loaded, and he drove off for the other barn in his sagging mechanic's car.

I returned to the first barn and found a place about thirty yards out from it by a high, weedy fence. It was fifteen or twenty minutes before I heard something for which Thoreau's phrase is the most accurate I know—"the slight, wiry, winnowing sound of their wings." Thoreau was writing about passenger pigeons, and it has seemed curiously suggestive to me, ever since I read it, to think that our great naturalist and sometime vegetarian should describe so casually, in *A Week on the Concord and Merrimack Rivers,* how he and his brother "obtained one of these handsome birds . . . and plucked and broiled it." They even potshot it, as a matter of fact, for Thoreau observes that it was one that "had lingered too long on its roost." It has modified a little my feelings about the passenger pigeon, from one of inherited guilt towards one of accepting the unforseeable dooms and reprieves of history, to think of Thoreau at his campfire, a hundred years ago, eating the legendary bird, licking its juices from his fingers, in perfect unawareness of what might happen to its innumerable kind.

I heard the winnowing sound, looked up, and saw twenty pigeons, high and loafing over me. Mindful of the farmer, I tried to shoot very carefully, and realized, chagrined, missing both my shots, that the apparent loafing was ten times faster than it seemed. The birds scattered; one came wheeling back over me just as I reloaded, and I led like a mathematician, not shooting till my barrel was a good five lengths in front. Even so I hit rather poorly, one of those shots where feathers come streaming down and the bird flies on, which meant that I was still a little bit behind. I shot again and finally dropped him.

The rest of the flock were halfway to the other barn by now; I watched, heard the double report of one of Martin's guns, and saw that at least one pigeon fell.

Fairly sure that they'd be back, and thinking that my position away from the barn put me at too much range, I trotted over to stand by the building again, under the eaves. One doesn't precisely have to hide to shoot pigeons, I'd been told, but it's just as well to have something overhead that partially obstructs their line of vision.

There were forty birds when the pigeons came back to me, and they were determined to make it to the barn this time. I picked one just before he could get over the roof, fired, and he dropped onto the roof and slid off over to one side of where I was standing. In a moment the others, who had gone out of sight overhead, came low into the barnyard in front of me and I shot another as they swept by—though I'd be unwilling to swear it was the same bird I aimed at.

I reloaded, thinking it was over for the moment, but the pigeons wouldn't go back to Martin. They kept wheeling; new birds joined them. I moved back to where we'd stood at first, in sight of the small window, realizing they would try to get into the loft that way; the whole flock took to flying off, turning and swooping towards the barn, and each time they returned I had two more shots, though I don't suppose I hit with as many as half of them.

It was, without question, the fastest shooting I've ever had, and I was regretting that Martin, with all those different guns to try, wasn't with me when I heard tires squeal, looked around, and saw his lopsided car pull up.

Even a car coming wasn't enough to discourage the pigeons by now, nor was the sight of me running over to help Martin out with his guns. I glanced back, and there were the birds, suddenly still, settling all along the roof peak in the sunset. And just as suddenly, as we were running back towards them, clanking and awkward, dusk fell and they were gone.

"Inside the barn," Martin said, stopping. "Hell, I'll get us a coon-hunting light out of the trunk; they'll sit in there now, but you can shoot 'em off the rafters with a twenty-two pistol . . ."

"Wouldn't that make, uh, holes in the roof?" I asked. The matter of pigeon shooting was taking on such a wonderland quality that I said it quite tentatively.

But this time the obvious was correct, and Martin calmed down.

The final thing I saw was the farmer with a gunny sack. I'd suggested, after we got our several shotguns cased, that we take the coon light and pick up the birds we'd shot—but the farmer was there before us.

"Let him have them," Martin said.

"Oh, sure. I didn't know he'd want them."

"He'll use them for garden fertilizer," Martin said. "Or else throw them to the hogs."

"Sorry you didn't get more chances," I said, as we drove off.

"Aw, I don't care much for shooting," Martin said. "But sometime when I do feel like it, we'll find us a big flock, and really have a go."

Not all the pigeons I have seen harvested are so disprized. In Costa Rica, on my only Central American hunt, we shot—or shot at—huge gray birds in the dawn, coming out of the fog like shadows, visible as pigeons only for an instant and impossible for me to hit. Dr. Cubero, the man who took me there, to the orchard in the mountain pass just off the Pan-American highway, got five with his box of shells, and didn't seem dissatisfied.

"When I was younger," he told me. "I could hit perhaps fifty percent."

These were true wild pigeons, red bills I'd guess, though I had no field guide with me to identify them and have to rely on memory (and on a description which fits my recollection in Dan Holland's book, *The Upland Game Hunter's Bible*). Since I didn't ever hit one, I can't even guess what lead is necessary. But I can say that for a feral domestic pigeon, rock dove, in full flight, thirty yards up—for I have shot quite a few more since I hunted them with Martin the mechanic—six lengths may be about right if your gunswing is reasonably fast.

The more I've hunted feral pigeons, the more I value them. They are, for the present, still classed as a domestic bird under the game laws of most states, so that the matter of how and when to hunt them is up to landowners and to gunners themselves (except that they may not be used in organized trap shoots in this country, so far as I know). This is, of course, a great convenience, as we train our dogs and test our shooting, but convenience carries responsibility: I wonder, for example, whether they shouldn't be given the spring off, whether as a matter of law or simple gunner's practicality, for nesting? Further: Holland says, in his upland game book, that there are colonies now, especially in the west, of the really wild sort "wherever the ground remains open all year round for feeding purposes." And I wonder if there isn't some way of encouraging this kind of colony?

I don't know how we square it with farmers and city managers, but I wonder, too, if we shouldn't start, quietly, asking our game-management men to make some studies of them—to determine, for example, whether they really are carriers of poultry disease to any important extent, now that most commercial poultry is raised indoors. Whether they actually present any particular sanitation hazard in city streets, now that horse-drawn vehicles have left the traffic pattern. And as hunters, I wonder if we shouldn't begin thinking in terms of learning, even for the barn-dwellers, where they pass and at what times—instead of shooting them at the roost as is most often done, and as I have most often done myself.

I'm suggesting, heretically, I guess, that our feral pigeons are in fact game birds, what game board men call a resource, and must consequently come to be managed as one.

They have even, at least once for me, achieved the most esoteric of what I think of as game bird qualifications: it is a personal peculiarity that I must, in order so to regard a bird, have had the experience at some time or other of finding it so beautiful that I choose not to shoot.

Pigeons? It was, once again, at a barn at sunset, and I was by myself. I had been having desultory shooting, hitting some and missing others, from a flock of thirty or forty which gradually ceased to work the area.

My attention had died away, and I was pondering some unconnected thought or other, when I heard, not a winnowing or wiry sound, but low thunder, and looked west. Two or three hundred birds were dropping towards me and the barn, out of the sun, with orange light streaming all around behind them. They were left and right, high and low, the great flock made up of fifty little flocks, each flying its own complicated figure, and shining with that crazy light that changed them into colors impossible to believe. They took my breath away, and my will to shoot into them with it. It was one of those strokes a man's eyes can sustain but not recover from, which leaves him ever after unable to see, except as a blessing, what the whole world knows to be a nuisance.

First published in Esquire
under the heading
"Outdoors," September,
1964.

The Column from Mexico

The other evening I called home, which is a very small
town in eastern Iowa, from Tlacolula, a slightly larger
town in southern Mexico, and learned from my wife that the
children were well, the bills accumulating, and that I was
about to miss a chance to meet Secretary of the Interior
Stewart Udall.

There had been a call, my wife said, from the office of our
rather amazing governor, Harold Hughes (Democrat, wing
shot, and remarkable to me for the consistency with which he
addresses political matters with an apparently spontaneous
common sense which seems better than merely courageous
for its lucidity and lack of calculation). Secretary Udall was to
be in Des Moines, and some thirty of us were invited to
lunch to meet him. Five of these Iowans are members of the

for Ophelia

State Conservation Commission; the rest of us are members of a large, Governor's Advisory Committee on Preservation of Natural Resources, and I don't mind admitting that I hated to miss the lunch.

At noon, on the date it was held, I was sitting on top of a mound of dirt and stone at an archaeological site in the Oaxaca Valley, holding an ice pick and a paint brush. I was loosening potsherds and grass roots with the pick, sweeping away the debris a little at a time with the brush, hoping to come onto a nicely articulated two-thousand-year-old skeleton of which I had so far found only a couple of disconnected finger bones.

As I write this I still haven't found any more bones and know that even if there is a skeleton, it will be in a pit burial—not a tomb—and that therefore there isn't likely to be so much as a nice, unbroken pot with it, let alone the Jeweled Sacrificial Knife of the High Priest. The others on the dig, a group associated with the University of the Americas in Mexico City, alternate between chuckles and commiseration: none of us really wanted to find a pit burial, and the man who did may be stuck with it for days, rationing himself a little water from a canteen as the sun shines on—and in Des Moines they were eating steak in an air-conditioned room.

But if I had met Secretary Udall, and if the occasion had permitted me to speak a piece (as such occasions rarely do), I'd have liked to talk to him about duck-hunting regulations.

I'm far away from my sources of statistics, so I'll invent one: if there are a million duck hunters in the United States, then there are at least a million experts on what each year's regulations ought to be. As a matter of fact, there are over a million because all the men who don't hunt them any more, for one reason or another, are experts, too.

I'm no exception, of course, though I'm a fairly specialized expert, willing to leave larger matters—season dates and bag

105

limits—to the professionals of the Fish and Wildlife Service and to defend their decisions quite blindly. My special fields of expertise are the Duck Stamp and the matter of shooting hours, and it's in these areas that Secretary Udall's men need defending from me.

The Duck Stamp, as it's commonly called, has a formal name: Migratory Bird Hunting Stamp, and it is my crotchety view that we make a serious error in letting it fulfill its nickname only. It is at present required, at a cost of three dollars a year, just for the hunting of ducks, geese and brant. Its sales, therefore, are subject to great annual fluctuation, usually downward, as individual hunters decide, on the basis of last season's luck and this season's predictions, whether they are going to hunt waterfowl this year or stick to the State-controlled, nonmigratory upland birds like pheasants, quail and grouse.

Meanwhile, sales of the stamp are an urgently important source of money for the refuge and other programs that keep our migratory bird flocks in good shape. But dove hunters, woodcock hunters, snipe hunters, rail hunters—all those who hunt federally controlled migratory birds other than ducks, geese and brant—are not required to buy the stamp. Dove hunters, in particular, are the most numerous bird-hunting group we have —not only numerous, but avid—and I see no reason why they (or we, rather, for I hunt them though I must go out of state to do it) shouldn't contribute to the refuge system, too.

It's true that the program is not directly designed to benefit doves, but this hardly prevents a dove from drinking out of a pothole, breeding on the edge of a marsh, finding rest in a "No Hunting" area, feeding on wheat crops planted for geese, and in general getting protection and sustenance from all kinds of management measures from predator control to tree plantings.

But I'm weaseling. The real argument for requiring more kinds of hunters to possess the Migratory Bird Hunting Stamp is more imaginative than simply saying, "Hey, your dove's eating my goose's wheat. You gotta help pay." The real and imaginative argument was put to me—though not in support of my stamp proposal—in a letter from Roland O. Clement, who is Staff Biologist for the National Audubon Society: ". . . we must come to look on our wildlife resources as a unit, indeed we must see them as part of a landscape, and it is the landscape . . . that must be conserved." To go beyond what I could responsibly ascribe to Mr. Clement, it seems to me too late and too small-minded to try to manage and tax on a species-by-species basis; all of us who find our pleasure, whatever its kind, in joining the landscape should be required to contribute to its conservation.

As to means, I am in some disagreement—gentle, I hope—with the Audubon Society. It has for some time been advocating a second Federal Stamp, a $2 Migratory Wildlife Conservation Stamp, to be sold to those who wish to use the refuges out of hunting season for bird-watching, fishing, photography and so on.

I don't know that I'm fit to judge, psychologically, whether these quieter and less aggressive sportsmen should have a stamp distinct from that required of hunters. But practically, it seems to me that to get this would probably involve the delay of going to Congress and the expense of printing, distributing and administering what are essentially two Federal licenses where one would do.

Sir, I should like to have asked Secretary Udall, couldn't you, by a simple executive order, in order to stabilize and vastly increase the sales of the present Migratory Bird stamp, just require a hell of a lot more people to buy it? If we're going to soak people for the good of the landscape, shouldn't we cheerfully soak as many of them, as simply, and as much as possible? I'm sure we ought to have all those dove and woodcock hunters in—if you want to let the bird-watchers and fishermen off for now, it may not make too much difference.

Well, having alienated myself from a lot of fellow hunters by proposing that they be subject to a nice new tax they haven't had to pay before, let me next propose something which may win a few of them back.

In the last two or three seasons, regulations of waterfowl shooting hours have provided that one may open fire at sunrise and must cease at sunset. Before that, the hunting day extended from half an hour before sunrise to half an hour after sunset—and it was in those two, lost half hours that one saw ducks. They are not, I hope, lost forever, for they are not only the most productive times; they are the most beautiful, too.

Duck shadows going by out of range against a gray dawn sky, faint rose at the horizon beginning to color leaden water, and the wind blowing—that's how duck hunting looked. It was a silent, even mysterious time we had invaded, a time that belonged to the birds in which we were present as hostile and often inept strangers. Ducks in that first half hour would appear in range quite suddenly and be gone, often as not, before the gun was raised. To coordinate it all—attention, concealment, vision, shot, retrieve—was something that didn't happen every morning, though the opportunity for it might. It was excitement, all the way, and at sunrise, often enough, we began picking up the decoys if the day was clear. A duck knocked down might require some searching, by dog and hunter, as the sky lightened, but we seldom quit before we found it. To say *duck hunting begins at sunrise* is to say, *it begins when it's all over till evening.*

I think when a duck is shot, and crippled and flies away, it happens most generally in full light, for then it is clear enough to give one the illusion that the long shot can be made effectively.

The evening half hour, the one after sunset, we need for consolation. One goes out, in the evening, because he has missed so badly in the morning—or perhaps, couldn't get away. The

evening ducks begin to fly just at sunset, and they are almost
always high. Only occasionally is there a shot to be tried, but
there is something reassuring about seeing them then, as the light
fades; one knows that they will be there in the morning. If there
has been a chance to shoot one, fine, but even if there hasn't one
leaves the blind more tranquil, to follow the path in the dark to
where the car is parked.

Now here is where my 999,999 fellow experts are going to
disagree, perhaps, and if they do, let them. I would rather have
those two half hours back than larger limits or a longer season.
I would say: calculate the permissible limit this year and then cut
it in half, if necessary—but give us back those two half hours. If
the limit were to be only one duck that way, it would be better
to have a chance to get him than to have a theoretical two-bird
limit and the best times for getting any at all eliminated.

There's another, even more powerful argument, it seems to
me, though it's possible that it's going to sound a little self-
righteous. Nevertheless, it's true that these cut-back shooting
hours favor the unscrupulous. For every guy in a blind, eyes on
his watch, waiting for the official sunrise minute to come (and the
ducks to go), there's another down the marsh who starts shooting
early. One's tolerance for the ethical character of the man down
the marsh is tenuous enough without his being given so unequivocal a way of proving himself contemptible. Besides, he's
probably getting ducks; and any chance the man with the watch
might have for a post-sunrise stray is gone indeed with the time-
buster working away. He wasn't much of a problem five years
ago—earlier than half an hour before sunrise, he couldn't see to
shoot.

I think wardens would bear me out in saying that the current
time rule is unenforceable; the warden would have to be virtually
in the blind with the time-buster and see him shoot to make an
arrest. A duck too many, or a newly killed one on the wrong day,

are evidence; the sound of a gun going off, too early or too late, down there somewhere, won't stand up in court. It's the man with the watch who gets punished, for by the time he allows himself to start shooting the birds are spooked.

But I become too practical: give us back our lost half hours, sir, not for reasons of justice or efficiency, but because it's in the hushed times, the rose-gray times, when the day hasn't quite declared itself or is dying towards tomorrow's mysteries, that hunting waterfowl is so exciting and so lovely.

First published in The
New York Times
Magazine, November 29,
1964, under the title
"You Can Tell a Hunter
By What He Hunts."

The Men Out Hunting

The man in the duck blind is cold. He snagged his hip
boot on barbed wire, walking here in the dark of 5 A.M.
It is not much of a snag, but enough to let some water in as
he waded around, setting out his decoys. His hands are
mittened, his ears muffed, and his body cased with thermal
underwear, but the damp sock chilling his right foot is really
uncomfortable: armor needs only one chink to fail.

The man out pheasant hunting is footsore. There has been
a lot of walking already today, and he is not in shape for it.
Four miles of fields and borders, carrying a gun which no
longer seems light and with heavy boots to which he is
unaccustomed, are too much. When he gets in the car to go to
the next field, the next border, he fights down the impulse to
say to his companions: "Let's quit. I've had enough for today."

The man with the quail dog is hot and itchy. He wore only a shell vest over his short-sleeved shirt, but the vest makes him sweat. The sweat irritates a long briar scratch on his bare right arm, on this warm Southern morning, and mosquitos have started to find him.

The man with the beagles has four rabbits, and is missing a dog; it is almost intolerable to think of carrying the rabbits— seven or eight pounds hanging from his shoulder in a hip-level game pocket—all the way back to the car, let alone haul them around in the woods, whistling and shouting for the errant pup. The man with the magnum goose gun is cross, because people in neighboring pits have been shooting at high birds, spoiling his chances. The man hunting deer is frustrated and half-lost; he has not seen a deer yet, in two days' hunting, and this ridge seems much steeper than the one he climbed yesterday and planned to be on again. The dove hunter's fingertips are full of sandbur spines. The grouse hunter's eye still stings from having an alder branch poked into it, and on a log in the hardwood timber sits a bored man with a squirrel rifle and a crick in his neck from looking up so long and so unavailingly . . .

Hunting, while seldom a dangerous sport in this country, is often an uncomfortable one. It is also often a tedious one, with game quite scarce in most localities—a long time between shots. It is quite frequently an irritating sport, with the commercializers making a pitch to lure more and more of the inexperienced into it, men who innocently or sometimes deliberately so conduct themselves as to spoil things for others. And success, in our democratic hunting, is always crowned with unregal exertions: it is not really much fun to pluck four ducks properly, or drag a hundred-odd pounds of deer carcass through the brush. Constantly one meets men who, having hunted all their lives, up to a couple of years ago, now have second-hand guns for sale and, instead of knowing this year's canvasback limit, can name you all the middle linebackers in professional football. Nevertheless there are many more, several million, who are still hunters, and the question becomes, *why?* What do they get out of it?

Though anti-hunters will, as they always do, pick up their jolly pens to reply that the enjoyment of hunting lies in the expression by brutal men of their most hideous traits of character, I am not, this time, going to formulate the general defense against this kind of attack. To do so would be to lose the opportunity for making some tentative distinctions among hunters in which there may be more illumination.

Hunters are various sorts of men, and from the sport they take various sorts of pleasure; in a rough way, to which there will be infinite exceptions, they can be divided and understood according to the particular game pursued.

That duck hunter with the cold right foot, for example, is a romantic aesthete, though he might knock you down for saying so. He likes the hush of the world at dawn, the whisper of wings, the gray water lightening and the shadows of birds plunging through mist. He will drive miles, out of season, to watch ducks fly their marvelous patterns. He will take great pleasure in a well-tuned call, a well-made decoy, and perhaps in winter he will himself carve duck figures from walnut or wild cherry. It is no accident that most of the sporting prints and paintings we see are of waterfowl; there is enormous beauty in these birds and in their setting, and in this the duck hunter participates. There is even a moment of painful beauty when a duck falls through the air, displaced from its element by an accurate shot—the hunter catches his breath not in triumph but in wonder at what he has done.

The pheasant hunter is apt to be more gregarious. Pheasant hunting, for most men, is a sociable sort of sport, often involving groups of five or more, walking and hunting together. There are trips from one place to the next, with joshing about shots made or missed and perhaps the passing of a jug. The general heartiness takes the form of quasi-military organization when a new field is reached, with some of the party stationed as blockers at one end, others assigned to walk through driving up birds from the other. The pheasant is not the world's most difficult bird to hit, and a feeling of mutual competitiveness often prevails as to who will get off his shot first, or account for the most birds. Curiously enough, this down-the-middle, regular-fellow aspect of pheasant hunting has an analogy in the quality of the pheasant as a table bird: unlike the exotic wild duck, the pheasant is a perfectly familiar bird to eat. It is a chicken, especially if it has been feeding in cornfields, and while it can be cooked elegantly if one likes, one generally sees it fried or roasted quite straightforwardly.

Quail hunting is a sport involving decorum. While I would not insist that all quail hunters are fastidious men who enjoy rules and procedures, it seems to me that the best of them are (and I should explain that I am trying to categorize each of these sorts of hunter at his best; there are boors, louts and brutes hunting each kind of game, too, but let us avoid them on the page as we try to in the field, searching for the coverts they do not use). The quail-hunting ritual begins with the training of highly specialized dogs, and a great deal of the pleasure comes in watching the dogs perform correctly. There are other refinements attached to quail shooting, as for example what percentage of a covey may properly be taken (never more than half); and who shall walk in on a point, once the covey is boken up and the singles are being hunted (it is done in turn). The double-barreled shotgun and the unhurried pace are correct in quail shooting—one may proceed differently, of course, just as one may catch trout with worms or lose one's temper publicly in a racket game.

Coming to rabbits, we are again concerned with eating, for the rabbit hunter, more than any other, deserves (and even finds unobjectionable) the epithet of meat hunter. He is a man troubled by empty spaces in his freezer. He would probably not be hunting rabbits for the sport alone, with perhaps an exception to be made for jackrabbit hunters in the West—the jacks are much faster and more difficult to hit than cottontails. The proof that rabbit hunters work for meat might lie, for you, in the matter of donations: in a good year you may occasionally, if you are highly deserving, be offered a duck, or a pheasant or even a brace of quail. But you will not be offered a rabbit. It is not a princely gift, to begin with, and the man who shot it intended to get it home for supper. I don't mean that he is necessarily gluttonous, or that there is no fun in shooting rabbits: but it is essentially a harvester's fun, the pleasure of providing.

Squirrels are quite a different thing. The squirrel hunter, at his best, is an American traditionalist. Unlike the quail man, whose hunting manners come, like his shotgun design, from Europe, the squirrel hunter is a rifleman. His exemplars are Boone and Crockett; he moves well and quietly through the woods, or waits with great patience for the chance to place a difficult, well-calculated shot. Ideally, though the practice could hardly be called widespread, the squirrel hunter will use a muzzle-loading rifle—there is considerable trade in them among enthusiasts. And with it he will shoot as the frontiersman did, not to hit the squirrel directly but to bark him—that is, to strike the limb just under the squirrel's head, so that the animal is killed instantly, by concussion, from the impact of the heavy lead ball against wood, with no visible wound. There is another sort of dedicated rifleman around, it should be added, whose weapon is the most technologically advanced—scoped and custom-fitted, embodying esoteric ballistic principles in the way its ammunition is loaded. But these riflemen are not generally after squirrels; their engineering natures require open shots at long ranges for fulfillment, and it is the groundhog by a distant burrow, the crow on a far limb, which most engages them.

Goose hunting, as it is done in many of the major centers like Cairo, Illinois, or Swan Lake, Missouri, seems to me so poor and distasteful a sport that I must exclude the customers of these highly organized places from my discussion of hunting pleasures. Geese are entirely too susceptible of being managed, with the result that great concentrations can be held at a given place, and men shuttled in and out to shoot at them in a way which has nothing to do with hunting. If there is pleasure in it, it is a pleasure I do not understand. But there are states which geese cross in their fall migration whose game managers have held out, so far, against the pressure to develop such areas. Through these states the geese still pass in smaller bunches, spending a day or two at isolated sandbars or potholes spread over a whole region. With luck, the waterfowler will take a goose every second or third season. Where hunting conditions have been left natural, the pleasure of taking a goose is a gambler's pleasure, the pleasure of being by chance at the right place to win a magnificent prize.

Deer hunting is subject to a great deal of sectional variation, and I am no authority even locally. But the deer hunter is, of course, a big-game man, finding pleasure in matching himself against the size and wariness of the creature, and not indifferent to the trophy he may acquire. This must of course be true of hunting other American big game as well—bear and moose, elk, buffalo, antelope and big horn sheep. The deer hunter must be a good woodsman, in the East at any rate, and must learn a good deal of lore and technique. A good deer hunter—I know a few, though they are in smaller proportion to the clowns than in other sorts of hunting—is a good man physically, needing more strength and endurance than do those who hunt birds and small game. Men with this sort of strength, men who have learned hunting skills and woodsmanship to a high degree, quite naturally enjoy entering situations which require their use. It is the pleasure of exercising training and endowment, of learning that one measures up. (In my own region, which is Iowa, where deer are more often found in fields than in deep woods, it is the fox and coon hunters who employ this complex of virtues and aspirations.)

The dove hunter (and in a less widespread way, the snipe hunter) is a man who enjoys shooting. Doves and snipe are small, fast birds, with extraordinarily tricky flight patterns. Even the finest shot may have difficulty in shooting a limit of doves (ten) with a single box of shells (twenty five), and many of the dove hunters I know are trap and skeet enthusiasts as well. It is a somewhat lazy sport, as far as walking and general exertion go, but pleasantly so—one sits under a tree, or by a fence, perhaps, on a warm day, making or trying pass shots of extreme difficulty. As in deer hunting, the pleasure lies in the exercise of skill, though of quite a different kind.

Though I am newly come to grouse and woodcock shooting, a few days' experience convinces me that here again we have an appeal to a particular sort of hunter personality. Success here is in the excitement, sometimes almost continuous, of contending with innumerable unexpected obstacles. It is a kind of hunting which moves in and out of thick brush and deep woods, with every branch a barrier. Birds are flushing quite constantly, but there are chances to shoot at no more than perhaps 25 per cent of them. Even these are opportunities which exist only for an instant—the bird is there (where?), in the clear for just an instant, and then gone, perhaps before the gun is raised. One needs to love the woods, and the birds themselves, to take a kind of wild pleasure in being eluded. Yet when the woodcock are around in good number, to supplement the resident but scarcer grouse, there is, it seems to me, more continuous adventure in this kind of hunting than in any other. Though it may be less productive, it will satisfy certain natures abundantly.

There are, of course, other sorts of game, some of them outside my experience, but my purpose is not to detail them all.
Rather, I am interested in making the point that the term *hunter*
covers a considerable variety of men, seeking a considerable
variety of values. Often one meets a man who, having begun by
hunting everything more or less at random, comes gradually to
specialize on the particular sort of game and hunting situation
which best suits his nature. And while my suggestions as to what
traits of character are reflected in the choice are, as I have said,
tentative, it is possible that something could be added to our
understanding of ourselves if these beginning notions could be
refined and studied further.

First published in Esquire
under the heading
"Outdoors," October,
1964.

The Dog Column

One of the strongest of the several minority hunting opinions I hold is that a bird dog's place is in the home.

Perhaps the most depressing thing related to this opinion is precisely that it should be a minority one, nor will I pretend to be anything but self-righteous about the matter: since I admit no possibility that I am wrong, it must follow that in my view the majority of American sporting men are about as sorry a collection of dog handlers as could readily be imagined.

The basic tenet of this majority, and it is always advanced as if it were a fact, is that hunting dogs are ruined if they are allowed to become pets. Advocates of this fact are apt to know for sure such other facts as that dogs must be penned or tied outdoors, regardless of how hot or cold it is; that dogs benefit from being hauled to and from the hunting field in airless car trunks; that the more harshly they are spoken to or punished, the more eagerly they respond; and that, in a general way, any impulse of consideration, let alone affection, for the animal must be stoutly fought down. This indicator of the handler's infinite virility is for the dog's own good.

The basic tenet of the minority is one I shall advance as a fact, without any expectation of provoking much agreement: every really good hunting dog I've ever known has been the pet of the man he hunted with. The rest are an army of lost dogs.

Let me cite the revolting case of Eddie-Joe X., whose dialogue in the following should be read in a mean, midsouthern accent:

A mutual, nonhunting friend whom I am visiting has arranged for Eddie-Joe to take me out for quail; we are driving in Eddie-Joe's car. His dogs, two wan pointers called Jake and Birdie, are, of course, in the trunk; my dog, thank heavens, is five hundred miles away. I have protested, as we got in, that there's no need to shut the dogs away on my account, hell, I don't mind them climbing on me. Eddie-Joe's reply has been a sour look, which conveyed considerable doubt that he and I were going to get along.

Now, as we drive, perhaps considering his obligation to the friend who arranged this hunt, Eddie-Joe decides to be ingratiating:

"That son-of-a-bitching Jake dog, back there. I got him right at the end of last season. He's a real dog, but he's a stubborn bastard if you let him get by with it. He'll chase fur, and there's only one cure for that."

"This looks like bird country all right," I say, hoping to be spared the particulars of Eddie-Joe's prescription.

"Let him get on a rabbit in the brush, maybe forty, fifty yards out and shoot him in the ass with birdshot."

"You've done that?" I ask. I have heard other rabid pharmacists prescribe corrective shooting, but never met one who'd say he'd actually administered the dose.

"Hell, yes, I let go a blast at him," Eddie-Joe says. "We were hunting through the woods, hunting singles, and I don't think any of the shot got to him. But he came back in right now."

"How was he afterwards?" I ask.

"You won't see him chase fur," Eddie-Joe says.

He is absolutely right. No one will ever see old Jake chase anything again. He slinks along, not always in front of us, tail down, looking over at us from time to time, not so much (I fancy) in the shy hope of being approved of as simply to keep the fount of correction located at all times.

Yet there is something of the bird dog he once was left in Jake. When he scents quail in the air, he does quicken, and his tail comes up. He leads us into a rather steep draw, false points, moves forward stiff-legged, points, moves—this is the behavior, if I am any judge, of a dog working an unalarmed covey which is strung out, feeding, walking along. Birdie, the other dog, who has less experience but more training, stiffens into a point, backing Jake.

As I am about to observe that these must be moving birds, two of them rise, whir away; then another; then half a dozen from various points in the draw. Eddie-Joe and I both fire, late and disconcerted, missing what seem easy enough shots but are actually the most unlikely kind—the shots one takes without being quite set for them. In the serene, philosophical moment which follows such a display of skill, Eddie-Joe screams:

"Did you see him blink that point?" And runs at Jake with the intention of kicking him. Jake, who has been kicked before, apparently, and has some curious objection to it, crawls under a bush, and Birdie, the other dog, gets knocked off balance as surrogate, by Eddie-Joe swiping side-footed.

Eddie-Joe has had Birdie just two weeks, he tells me, and right now's the time to stop her from picking up any bad habits. She's a young dog, and quite well trained; she makes the next point for us, half an hour later, and this time the birds are properly coveyed up. Old Jake, I notice, doesn't back her. He just lies down, panting, while Eddie-Joe and I walk in. The covey goes up and this time Eddie-Joe shows me how to shoot, dropping two birds neatly. I make my customary covey rise score, a hit and a miss, so we have three quail in front of us now, lying out in the grass.

Birdie, steady to wing and shot, is still holding her point, and is praised for the achievement with the soothing words, "Hunt dead, goddamnit!"—as if her waiting for the command were a fault rather than a virtue some trainer has spent many weeks of patience (and, perhaps, love) to develop. By now Jake has slipped by, is out hunting dead, and retrieves one of the birds for us. He brings it to me instead of Eddie-Joe, and I risk patting him for it. He goes out to resume searching; Birdie has found a quail, and holds it in her mouth, looking over at us, a bit uncertain just what's wanted.

Eddie-Joe informs her: "FETCH!" loud enough to make *me* jump. "What the hell's the matter with you? FEH-ETCH!"

When I jumped, Jake scurried away. As for Birdie, she sees Eddie-Joe running at her, and a good bit before he arrives she puts the bird down and backs away from it.

He picks it up. "Hunt dead," he commands. "Come on, you dogs, there's another bird out here."

I hand him the one Jake brought me. "Here's your other one," I say.

"Didn't you get a bird?"

"No. No, I missed."

"Could've sworn you got one," Eddie-Joe says, and we move towards the next field, where the singles are scattered. The dogs seem happy to be leaving.

By the time we have shot a single or two, and chanced onto another covey while looking for more, the hunt has gone on for just over an hour, covering about a two-mile circle around the car. Birdie, who is still eager, has probably run six or eight miles as Eddie-Joe and I walked the two, and Jake, in spite of his moping, must have covered four. Birdie, eager though she may feel, is beginning to look exhausted, and Jake is pretty much dragging himself along. I understand that their thinness is from underfeeding, not exercise. These dogs don't get out of the pen from the end of one hunting season till the beginning of the next.

"Dogs are starting to settle down and work careful now," Eddie-Joe says, throwing a clod of dirt at Jake to get him moving.

"I wish I could say the same," I say, angling us towards the car. "Guess I'm out of condition."

"The hell you are?"

Actually, I feel great. I love this country and I love these birds. It's the first real quail shoot for me in a long while, and I've carefully arranged to keep the whole day clear for it.

"Want to rest a while?" Eddie-Joe says.

"I'm sorry Eddie-Joe," I say. "Guess I just can't take it. I'd like to go back to town."

"Well, I'll be go-to-hell," Eddie-Joe says, and tries to cajole me, but I insist I've had enough.

In the disgruntled silence on the way back to town, I ask the one question which could induce Eddie-Joe ever to speak a civil word to me again. It's not that I feel any great civility towards him, but I want to confirm a hunch.

"What'll you take for Birdie?"

"Hell, you want a dog you better buy Jake. You can't keep up with her."

"That's my business. Is she for sale?"

"Any dog's for sale," Eddie-Joe says. "Last week it would've cost you five hundred for her, but you saw how she was about

123

retrieving. I don't know. What'll you give? See, I know a man's got some year-old setters. . . ."

I can't really buy the two exhausted dogs lying in the trunk, though I wish I could. Well, it'll protect one of those setter pups from what happens when an Eddie-Joe ventures into trying an untrained dog—the pup's allowed to hunt once, makes a few zealous mistakes, and after that is tied in the yard where he learns to bark. But I've learned what I wanted to know, which is that Eddie-Joe's a shopper and a swapper, who will go through several dogs a season, ruining each in turn. Eddie-Joe is a composite, too, of course, of some number of men that I've encountered— but every characteristic and attitude with which I've endowed my composite is prevalent, and often stoutly defended as correct.

There is all too much resemblance to all too many people, living and dead, in my composite, and that is really why I can't buy poor old Jake and young Birdie—if we rescued them all, at a dollar a dog, it would still run up around a million.

One can err, I guess, in the other direction, and I suppose I have. I've hunted the same dog for ten years now. He is my old Weimaraner, Moon, of indifferent conformation and average breeding. He is a house dog, and because of it he knows me well enough to know precisely what he can get away with as far as obedience goes.

On the other hand, he has never been out of condition; a dog whining in the kennel can be ignored, but one living in the house, bugging you to exercise him, cannot. You find that you are making time, somehow (or your wife is), to give the dog his daily run, and I cannot see that the daily walk you must take after him does you anything but good.

Though Moon was beautifully trained at one time by Chet Cummings, an absolutely first-rate professional up in Litchfield, Connecticut, I have been too soft-headed to keep him properly in hand. He is still reasonably steady to wing, but at the sound of a shot he charges off like a berserk locomotive, and I no longer try to control this. Instead of a pattern of precise control, what Moon and I have worked out is a high degree of compatibility, based on our mutual pleasure in what we are doing—he knows his part of it, rough though it may be around the edges. And it can be said that very few of the men who have hunted with Moon and me more than a time or two have failed to inquire if there weren't some way to get one of Moon's pups. Since this can't come from admiration for a polished performance, it must come from seeing how much Moon and I are enjoying one another— and this enjoyment, I am convinced, comes from nothing more than the fact that Moon has been a pet, played with and catered to, since the time he was a pup.

Admittedly, this can get to be a bother. Moon sleeps on beds, is often reluctant to yield a favorite sofa corner to a guest, and must be figured on like two extra persons when we are calculating the seating capacity of the car. He is, in his resting behavior at home, particularly fond of goose down; we own four goose-down pillows, and Moon can generally manage to preempt one, particularly if forestalled from settling onto the goose-down comforter with which my wife keeps warm; I have often speculated on whether, if I should sometime manage to shoot a goose while hunting with Moon, he would try to retrieve it or run over and lie down on it.

Let me acknowledge that there are occasional private dog owners who operate like professional trainers and handlers—that is, they provide well-kept, thermally sound kennels, feed intelligently, and keep their dogs in training and in condition in hunting season and out. Such a hobbyist, assuming him to be a reasonably gifted trainer with time to work at it, would certainly produce a more finished hunting field performance than I get from Moon. Whether this perfectionist would get as much pleasure out of hunting his dogs may well be a matter of temperament—some prefer hunting with a close friend, some with an absolutely efficient guide.

Some say, "I love to watch the dogs work"; others like to go hunting with their dogs.

The sort of devoted and successful amateur I've described— a briefer and more abstract composite—may argue that good hunting dogs are ruined if allowed to become pets, then, but he and I will be talking about different things. As for all the others, who support his view without following his practices, I can only say that it seems to me that we have the whole licensing thing backwards. It isn't dogs who need licenses, it's owners, and if I were your Commissioner, there'd be damned few issued.

First published in Esquire
under the heading
"Outdoors," February,
1965.

Closing Days
(The Last Column)

C losing days of our hunting seasons are like the last, late
hands of poker, after most of the players have left the
game. The crowd is not rowdy any longer, nor is it a crowd.
Some losers are playing through to the last hand, desperately
drawing the worst cards of the evening. There are only one
or two winners left, playing for conscience to give the losers
a chance, or because they've become a little compulsive, or
sometimes out of an odd kind of nostalgia—the evening
started so long ago, and so much has happened since, that is
is pleasant to muse now over hands that don't matter very
much.

It seems to me that I have hunted on the final days of duck
and pheasant seasons in states of mind like all of these.

To have been a loser, that is to have had a poor season

when shots were scarce and generally missed, and to try to re-
deem it all somehow on closing day, is to court long odds. I
remember a duck season when I'd done poorly and, for some
reason, been unable to hunt the few days just before the last one.
It was during those days that the weather turned cold, and,
friends told me, many ducks came down into Iowa from the
North. I pushed aside some rather pressing things to get out that
morning to the pond where my decoys were, only to find it
frozen. There were ducks in the sky, miles away, and I thought
of breaking the ice—though it was more than an inch thick—and
trying to call. Then I looked again at the decoys; there were
nearly two dozen of them, the cardboard kind, and I saw that
being trapped in the quick freeze had crushed more than half of
them into grotesques, squeezing them at the water line so that
the soft upper bodies mushroomed fat and elongated over the ice
and the heads went off at strange angles. It seemed to me that
it would take a pretty neurotic wild duck to land among these
creations, if I freed them, so I sat on the bank, loaded my gun,
and had a pretty good time shooting the heads off my decoys, the
sound and the unsound alike, one by one. It was such a poor hand
that it was a relief to fold it, take my losses and go home unen-
cumbered.

I have, like the winner who stays out of conscience, taken
people out on closing day, hoping to show them birds, and with
absolutely predictable results: no matter how I try to arrange it
otherwise, the shots that come along come my way. My friend
is blanked, and I am left uncomfortably with triumphs I should
rather have avoided.

I have been the compulsive winner, too, unable to stop though
I've really had enough of hunting and enough success; this would
have to be the equivalent of crowding one's luck, but I suspect
my metaphor breaks down a little here. I have no clear recollection of a closing day which led to some sort of disaster, even a

mild one—except that perhaps it is a bad thing to go out hunting, and have moderate success, at a time when the genuine enthusiasm for it is past, for the risk is surfeit. Surfeit with hunting, I would guess, will not come all at once, but will accumulate as a kind of fatigue, held in suspension as it gathers. Then there might come not a moment but a time when the bulk of it would outweigh the pleasure of hunting, even at the start of a season, and the gun might be left in the case, the dog let sleep. If one is constituted as I am, then hunting is so far one of the few profound pleasures which the world offers, and it is stupid—could be disastrous after all—to risk its eventual loss. For I can think of nothing which might replace it.

It was, however, as the nostalgic winner that I closed out last pheasant season. I had had two fine months of it, by then. They began with a fair opening, with out-of-town guests I was fond of, and a very good first week; a big crop of birds. Then I'd had to work through the annual period when my shooting goes bad (it lasts at least a week—I'm damned if I know why—and the difference between a good pheasant season and a bad one is whether I start to hit again. Last year I did, fairly quickly).

There was a time, after I came out of my shooting slump, when I put myself on a rather absurd but somehow pleasant program, described by a slogan: one hour, one bird, one shell. Under it I could permit an hour's hunt, portal to portal, on any given day, even though I was working. I had some birds saved up, here and there around the country, and would drive to and hunt just one of my coverts; generally, I confess, I carried half a dozen shells and would try for birds till I got one or until the hour was up; but there was a string of four splendid days in a row when the program went according to slogan—it was some of the best hunting I'd ever done.

During the final month of the season my work let up, and I met a farmer named Vernon Zach, with whom I had some wild, all-day hunts. Vern knew the southern part of our county, where I had never hunted, and we spent our days tearing around at considerable speed in a variety of cars and trucks, hunting hills and thickets which were strange to one or the other of us, showing off what places we knew and improvising hunts through others we'd spot rushing by, hunt and never be able to find our way back to again.

When Vern couldn't make it, I'd go out by myself, my passion for it at a real pitch, or with another farming friend named Hal Larew. Hal was almost as bad as I was about being willing to drop whatever he was doing to shoot birds—he knew places, too. The three of us together, with our pool of coverts and our mutual enthusiasm, generated a small storm of late-season pheasant hunting that filled freezers and put unexpected birds on Christmas dinner tables all over town.

Closing day came on New Year's. It had been a quiet New Year's Eve, in my house, and the day was bright and cold. There were patches of snow on the ground, but in general the walking looked dry.

Vern drove into my yard with his sixteen-year-old boy, Larry, a little after lunch. We hadn't hunted in the week since Christmas, and Vern said:

"I thought maybe you'd like to close her out."

I said that was just what I'd like to do; there was no urgency, I'm sure, for either of us, in the idea of gettting a few final birds. It was more a commemorative impulse that took us out, and we were the only hunters that I saw that day.

There were two places we wanted to try, places we'd speculated about and never got around to. One was my choice, a small, swampy cornfield at the edge of a big marsh. I thought there should be birds in the marsh grass and there were, lots of them; all hens. Moon must have pointed more than a dozen. Coming out, I swung away from Vern and Larry to run the dog through a little, weed-choked waterway inside the cornfield itself. There was a cock pheasant there all right, but he didn't wait for Moon to point. He burst out in front of the dog and straight at me, saw me, and swerved. He was still too close when I took my first shot, and missed. But there was plenty of time left for the second shot; I remembered to slow myself down, made it very deliberate, and dropped him in the corn stubble.

"Well, we're not skunked are we?" Vern said, in a leisurely way, when I brought my pheasant over.

"I really thought we'd have more shooting here," I said.

We smiled, and agreed it didn't matter. Larry, a boy who has gone on to study wildlife management at college, checked my cock's spurs and wings, and said he guessed it was a two-year-old. The spurs were thin, but nearly an inch long and sharp as locust thorns.

"Let's try the hayfield in the bottom, down near my place," Vern said, and we strolled to the car, not saying much but in no hurry, either. The season had about an hour to go.

The sun was low when we stopped again; the hayfield was big, a good thirty acres. Along the left side of it was timber, and facing us, across the field, a weedy edge of high growth. A dirt track ran along the edge to our right—the north edge. We were facing west, into the sun.

"Will they be along the timber, or the high growth?" I asked.

"Could be anywhere," Vern said. Larry is a quiet boy, and said nothing. We two old adult pheasant hands worked out a plan: Vern would take the car and drive around, using the track, to the north end of the high weed growth. Larry and I would start the other way, following the dog, go down the edge of the timber, turn north and work up through the high weeds to Vern's stand. It was a good enough plan, and left only the east edge, from which we started, unhunted and unguarded. Why is it that one's starting point never seems a likely place for game to be, or cross?

I don't know. There's always a place to which it looks as if one ought to move.

Vern reached his corner; Larry and I began our drive. And I still wonder how many birds we walked straight away from. They were all cocks, too, grouped together in their winter flock, and what happened was this: Larry and I finished the timber edge, raising nothing, and turned towards Vern through the weeds. The dog, who'd been ambling, began to seem a little birdy. He kept straying, though, away from the fence towards the center of the field; I kept calling him close. If we had chances, I wanted Vern to share them.

When we'd come to a point perhaps eighty yards from his father, Larry suddenly said, "Look back there." Over to our right, and behind us, two birds got up and flew away east. Almost immediately another rose, halfway between us and Vern; it was the only one we saw in range, and Larry had a high crossing shot at it which he made beautifully. It was with the sound of his shot, and the warning of the rising bird, that pheasants started to cascade out of the field in numbers that were hard to believe. I don't know if there were twenty or thirty or forty of them, rising from the hay, far out on our right, one after another, and streaking off east with the winter sunset making their backs glow and their tails stream light. Their combined cackling was like a great laugh at us, and we all three watched more in fascination, really, than in frustration that we hadn't thought to leave a shooter at the east edge—what shots, right and left and overhead, he might have had. But it didn't matter. It was the right way to close the season, with a kind of good-bye to all those gaudy birds, the feeling that is the opposite of surfeit: see you next year, boys. Have a good winter, and watch out for foxes. There are dozens of hens in the marsh where the little cornfield is—court them well, come spring.

First published in The
American Sportsman,
*Fall, 1968, under the title
"The Seventh Covert."*

Something New for the Old Gun

This morning I drew a small, rough map of the six dream
coverts. I had to draw it because I woke last night, at
whatever time it is one wakes, and realized that there are six
of them now, six splendid, impossible hunting areas which
exist in the night. I'm not sure which I'd been dreaming of,
just before I woke, but I lay there and counted and located
them in my mind, and realized for the first time that they
form a landscape in which each is related geographically to
the others, around a point called The Town.

Even by daylight, sitting on the bed drinking coffee, I was
still not totally certain that I hadn't experienced these places,
or some of them, somewhere, sometime, and I said to my
wife uncertainly:

"Have I . . . I've never hunted anywhere but here, have

I? In Iowa? And that one fall in South America, only it was spring . . ."

"You've made trips to hunt in a number of places," she said, crisp but not unhelpful. She'd been up a few minutes. "You hunted in Virginia as a boy, and in Florida for about ten days one fall."

"No. I mean, spent a hunting season. As a grown-up, where I became very familiar . . ." I let it go there. Coffee could do what winter daylight couldn't—convince me, in its heat and bitterness, that something as real to my dreaming as, for example, The Lotus Stretch (southeast of The Town, on this morning's map) is not actual.

Now I am in all ways a skeptic about dreams; I am too much a child of this Freudian century to think that there could be anything revealed by amateur interpretation, and too late a child of it to have total faith in the professionals. Yet I have faith enough to feel that raw dreams, offered without some clinical understanding of the dreamer, are not often interesting. But if I may speak only of the surfaces of my hunting dreams, which are so plainly wishes, it will serve a purpose of comparison: added to my six dream coverts now is a seventh, something new and as they say undreamed of, which is real. It is a place, and provides a kind of hunting, very like the dreams. It is a farm I saw not many weeks ago, in Wisconsin, belonging to a man I will call Fred Halsey; there are two kinds of game bird on it which I had never tried to shoot before, ruffed grouse and woodcock.

Let me, then, describe the map I drew this morning, and how it relates to real landscape: its center, as I have remarked, is The Town, but The Town is not really Iowa City. In Iowa City there are harshly lighted store fronts, vehicles moving, people standing or walking, even at three or four in the morning—The Town is a soundless place of sleeping houses and empty streets, lighted by a soft, general glow, through which I move with stealthy

for Ophelia

speed. The River runs through The Town, but is not the Iowa
River; The River is clear and flows gently between fragrant,
wooded banks. The Iowa, our all-American actuality, runs
muddy, at currents and levels manipulated by an oversized Corps
of Engineers' dam upstream; its banks are undercut and eroded,
its bottom trash, and it doesn't smell too good.

Southeast of The Town is The Lotus Stretch; it is privately
owned, and for some reason I am the only person who ever hunts
there. Below the buildings (I am not sure what goes on in them,
but there has never been anyone around since the night I was
told I was free to go in) The Lotus Stretch consists of an infinite
series of interlocking sweet-water canals. The water is partly
grown over with blooming lotus; there are low dikes with paths
along the middle and waist-high growth on either side of the
paths along which I can walk forever, jumping ducks of surprising brilliance who never seem to see or hear me coming; apparently they feed in the lotus. (Southeast of Iowa City, as a matter
of fact, there is a pretty good, cornfed duck area called The
Conesville Marsh. Probably I was on my way to that crowded
public shooting ground and missed a turn, the first time that I
found The Lotus Stretch.)

Just south of The Town is a place called Where Streets End;
it is amazing to me, even in dream, that no one but me takes
advantage of the fact that here, one bend of The River downstream from the railroad bridge, still within The Town limits, the
hunting is infallible. The River flows between two handsome,
wooded bluffs. The boughs of great trees reach out from the tops
of the bluffs to touch each other across a mild expanse of water.
Sunlight filters in, and drakes wheel through it as I stand on a
sandbar, unconcealed, dropping them neatly to the sand beside
me with a weightless gun that never misses. In reality, the Iowa
River does flow, just south of the city, under a railroad bridge;
it might be well, for the sake of credibility, to be able to re-

produce the precise truth, which is that one bend downstream from this bridge the river runs between low bluffs, on one of which stands a slaughterhouse; on the other is the Iowa City dump. The dream is based, apparently, on a sandbar much farther down the Iowa where I did stand one season, morning after morning before the Engineers' dam was built. It was not a completely unattractive place, but the ducks rarely came by.

Over west of The Town, curiously enough, is Lambertville. The reason this is curious is that Lambertville is a real town in New Jersey, across the Delaware River from New Hope, Pennsylvania, where I went to prep school for a time. Lambertville, as a dream covert, and I have no idea why this should be, is a marvelous, secret place for quail. You go up a steep hill, on a dirt road, and there is an abandoned farm there where the sun shines and the coveys are innumerable. (It was in Lambertville that we used to go to the movies from school, with or without permission —the pictures I can remember seeing both had Dick Powell in them. One was *Flirtation Walk* and, I think, co-starred Ruby Keeler; and the other, *The Big Broadcast of 1933* had Jack Oakie in it. There *is* a steep hill in Lambertville but the road up it, I'm quite sure, was paved.) Sometimes the return from Lambertville in the dream—for these dreams really do recur—is murky. Sometimes the bridge back across the river to safety must be attempted by a young pedestrian balancing naked on the icy, tubular supports under the roadway of the bridge; it is cold, lonely and embarrassing up there, over the roaring river. Precarious, too. Someone is coming the other way—is it Jack Oakie?—there is not room for us to pass one another and I fall and wake, never succeeding in getting back from Lambertville. But that is where the quail are.

Another sometimes murky place is the one east on my map, from The Town, called Trout Country. I'm not sure why it belongs, really, with all the bird-shooting places; doves fly there, but I am generally equipped with a fly rod. In Trout Country there is a stream which switches back and forth in a series of long S-curves down an extensive hillside, and generally I can catch fish anywhere along it. But sometimes, I must admit, the water is cloudy in Trout Country, even curiously foamy, and at other times there is a persistent, spectral fisherman who manages to appear at each of the best spots just as I am about to reach it. But when the dreamer can manage, Trout Country can be as inviting a place among the six dream coverts as any—as solitary, as loaded with game, and as accessible; and one night soon I must remember that the doves are there, and take my gun.

Except for The Lotus Stretch, which is my favorite, the best of the dream coverts are the two which lie north of The Town. One of these is Point of the Roads, and is plainly the intersection of routes 218 and 153, north of Iowa City and very close to my house. I can see it from my bedroom window, a rather busy intersection with surrounding agriculture fields, a couple of small roadside homes, and a good complement of billboards. Among the billboards is one which swings around in the wind on some sort of swivel, advertising the services of Mr. Edwards, a well-digger, and to reach the dream covert one has only to step past this revolving sign to find the fields regrown in timber, and a pothole there: again, how can no one know of it but me? The pothole is so close to the road, behind its screen of trees, that I can sit there and see cars go by, full of other hunters on their way out to places farther on, from which they will flush ducks, and all the ducks they flush will fly back, coming in by tens and dozens to this very handy place. On certain cold mornings, just before or even after the alarm, I have been able to stay cosily in bed with a dog at my feet, shooting these Point of the Roads ducks from under the blankets as they glide past the open window.

The sixth dream covert is a little farther north, and as infinite as The Lotus Stretch. It is called The Big Hill Country on the Far Bank, and to get to it one has only to go north across The River. It is a continuum of wooded slopes and meadows, through which one drifts up and down, never getting lost among the trees or winded on the hills. There is a meandering creek one meets from time to time, where ducks rise away from the feeding trout, but the Big Hill Country on the Far Bank is best known for the dependability with which pheasants rise in its fields in front of the dream dog, who never misses a point or fails in a retrieve.

The dream dog's counterpart, for the trip to the seventh covert at Halsey's farm, had quite a different function. He is a year-old springer spaniel, a breed which incidentally isn't required to point, named Bix. His retrieving is going to straighten out, he hunts very well for a first-season pup, but as I think back on it, it seems to me that poor Bix's real contribution to the trip was to act as an absorbent for whatever real-life murkiness came along. It is, perhaps, no more than a way of thinking to make one's dog a surrogate, but ways of thinking have their own reality. Therefore, I do not hesitate (or not for long, anyway) to point out that Bix, a beginner at bird work as I am at trout fishing, is at a point in his dog's life which is a fair parallel to that stage of early adolescent human development I was in during my year or two in prep school, across the river from Lambertville.

Things began to get murky for Bix, I suppose, when he found himself being urged onto a scale at the local airport, to be weighed as excess luggage. He was quite obliging about getting on; he even sat, stayed and was praised for it. When I called him off he made a quick dash over to the crate he was to travel in; he had reason to be suspicious of it, for I had practiced loading him into the thing at home, and he hadn't much liked the confinement. So he ran back to the scale, jumped onto it and sat down again, courting further praise. With which the hateful crate moved towards him, its dog-consuming mouth open wide; forces transferred him to the interior, the mouth closed, and the whole thing began to move on rollers, dog and all, towards a tiny doorway into a room full of suitcases. Bix called for help, but his master did not respond.

His master, as a matter of fact, was pleased and relieved at the way things were turning out. Instead of having to comply with a darkly anticipated welter of regulations concerning certificates, loading forms, consignment slips, surcharges and special taxes, in order to take the dog along, I stood and watched the ticket agent make a simple calculation. He added the weight of dog and crate to that of my gun and suitcase, found the total to be thirty pounds or so over the luggage allowance, and wrote the charge on my ticket: $3.14. I'd been prepared for twenty.

In the room beyond the tiny doorway, Bix in his box was being put onto a cart; strange voices belonging to unseen men told him he was a good dog, but, as he could see peering out his wire window, the hands and arms connected with these voices were remorselessly piling suitcases and mail bags around him. The cart began to move, out of the dim room and into a windy, barren space where something roared, louder than a hundred trucks. He was moved closer and closer to the roaring; then, abruptly, it stopped. In the silence, after a time, his master's voice spoke, but instead of words of comfort it said:

"Oh, be quiet, Bix." Then he and his crate were lifted, tilted, shoved into a new dark room, and the suitcases followed like live pursuers, sliding in and around him. The door closed. The roar began again, louder than ever; the room grew cold and began to vibrate. There was nothing to do but chew for it.

Having seen to Bix's loading into the baggage compartment of the plane, I climbed aboard. There were many seats, few passengers. The others were in business suits, fussing with top-coats and briefcases; I wore an insulated jacket, whipcord pants and leather boots, and being in rough clothing gave me pleasure.

I carried my shotgun on, in a take-down case, and the stewardess, a small, pale girl with dark hair, asked nervously:

"Is that a gun?"

"Yes it is," I said.

"It isn't loaded, is it?"

"No ma'am," I said, playing the reassurance role with quiet enjoyment. "It isn't even put together."

By the time his master and Fred Halsey received it from the plane, Bix had half the woven wire chewed away from the window of his crate, and the strips of molding which were supposed to hold the wire in place were nothing but splinters on the floor.

I let him out immediately, right beside the plane, and he capered around in such big happy circles that I had to catch him again, and snap on the leash to keep him from capering into an idling propeller. Fred drove us on up to the farm, about an hour from Madison where he lives; the farm is used as a weekend place, but it's an easy drive from the city. Again, I can report nothing but agreeable sensations for my part—Fred, though a relatively slight acquaintance to begin with, turned out to be as easy to talk and listen to as I had hoped. He is a few years older than I, interested and knowledgeable in many things about which I am interested and curious. For Bix, I am pretty sure, both the drive up and the night in the farmhouse extended the ambiguities he'd been experiencing since leaving home: there was another male dog with us, a handsome English setter called Jiggs. At Bix's age a strange male dog produces a remarkably confusing choice of attitudes: is the creature to be fought, played with, fled from, ignored or mated? It was a question of propriety which, in the thirty-six hours of our visit, Bix never could decide.

In the morning we got up at a comfortable time, seven or seven thirty I think. The day, while not bright, was at least quite calm so that we wouldn't need awkwardly heavy clothing. The land, out the window, looked sandy; there were evergreens and, near the house, a springfed pond full of clear water. Fred came to stand by me at the window, and pointed:

"Just past the pond is a stream," he said. "We'll go down along it through the meadow, one on each side. There might be a bird, but you see where the woods start?"

"Yes," I said. It was the place four or five hundred yards down, just the place, as a matter of fact, where one would turn and start hunting along the edge or back through the field again if we were quail or pheasant hunting.

"There's where we ought really to start seeing birds," Fred said. "There and beyond it."

The stream, when we reached it, was small and clear, varying in width from eight to fifteen feet with a steady, moderate current. Fred crossed on a log, and we started down along it; there was tall enough brush on the banks to hide us from one another much of the time, and Fred was out of sight when something happened right out of the Lotus Stretch. I saw, through branches, a disturbance in the water of the stream, something heavy-bodied swimming downstream and disappearing. I thought it might be a muskrat. In the moment before the dogs noticed and came rushing back, I stepped around a little bend, came out on a short stretch of cleared bank, and three ducks rose. They had seen not me but the dogs, racing back from downstream, and their flight brought them directly back over my head at a range of fifteen yards—not an easy shot for me, but an exciting one to try. I didn't try it, nor did Fred; I'm not sure why. Probably in his case because ducks weren't what he was hunting; in mine it was that I was so intensely surprised to see them there at all. There was a shallow place, with stones to step on, just below where the ducks had been, and I felt I had to find out about this creek. Fred saw me coming, and was waiting on the other bank.

"You saw the wood ducks?"

"Yes," I said coming off the final stone to join him. "Couldn't believe it."

"They're here most mornings."

"In the stream?" I asked. "There isn't a pond, or marsh?"

"No. In the stream. Sometimes there're mallards here, too."

I looked down through the water. There was no sun to mar its perfect clarity with reflections. "Fred," I said. "This isn't . . . a trout stream, is it?"

"Sure. There are some trout in it," Fred said.

"And the road: is it really right back there, visible, where I see the phone pole and the hedge running past the house?"

"Yes. That's the road."

We started to stroll along; the dogs were capering, rather than hunting, and I had one more question: "You have much trespass problem?" I asked.

"No." Fred said. "This isn't a major trout stream. The only reason we post around here at all is deer hunters. In grouse and woodcock season, I have the place to myself, and most of the other places around here, too."

Just as he said this, a bird went off. It went off like an alarm-clock buzzer with a whistle attachment, startling, and at first, without specific location.

"Behind you," Fred said, and I looked back to see something disappear, quail-sized, brown and determined. "Woodcock." As he made the identification, another rose with the same sound, directly in front of me, and I could see that it was larger than a quail, and longer-winged. I tried to get my gun up but the bird was into the bushes across the stream, and rising above them, going away, before I could coordinate. Now, as its silhouette became clear, with sky for background instead of brush, I became aware of the absurd length of the bill, more than twice as long as the head was thick. In this characteristic it was quite like its cousin, the Wilson's Snipe, at which I'd shot for years, but three times the size and with quite a different way of flying. Snipe start off low and twisting, and then zoom upwards with a wing stroke which seems almost to flicker, like a bat's. This woodcock made a straighter take-off, its wings propelling it more smoothly, into an almost vertical climb; but what was unique and—yes, dreamlike—was something else, a comparison which came to mind unbidden and seemed for a moment literal: it was not a bird but a comic, irascible little man with his arms stuck out and flapping, long-nosed and goggle-eyed, climbing crossly through the air away from us.

With which, though a long shot was, at the final moment, possible for me, I couldn't shoot. "Sorry," I said, lowering my gun, confident enough that this bird which could look like a quail, a snipe and a little man would eventually settle down to looking like itself. "I guess I should have tried."

Fred smiled. "You'll see a lot more woodcock than you'll shoot at, if the birds are down. And it looks as if they are." He had explained to me, driving up the evening before, that woodcock, in their migration down from the Canadian breeding grounds, come into a strip of woods by night—the hunter may go out one morning and find none at all, and on the next they can be everywhere he steps.

They were down. It was a considerable adjustment for me to make, as we worked slowly down along the stream, pushing our way now through alder thickets, to realize that there were birds here by the dozen—that one could let ten go up without taking a shot and still count pretty confidently on seeing ten more. In quail and pheasant hunting there is a covey or a cock every hour or two, on a good day; the shots are open, and one feels a miss keenly, for the chance to shoot again may not come for a long while.

But with woodcock, I soon realized, missing is part of what builds into a general exhilaration. I tried my first shot shortly after we got into the thick part of the woods. I was just through freeing my sweater from some kind of thorny branch, and where Bix was, just in front of me, looked even thicker-grown if not as thorny. The bushes under which he worked were dark-stemmed, almost black, and very fully branched out though the leaves, whatever they had looked like, were now gone; Bix was beginning to get, I could tell from the way his body tensed and his tail swung, a strong, exciting scent for which nothing in his experience prepared him, though everything in his ancestry insisted it was relevant. The very name of Springer derives from woodcock hunting, and this first experience of true odor for a dog who had smelled and pursued everything from field mouse to barnyard goose must have caused powerful atavistic stirrings. When the bird went up, out of the thicket, he made no move to chase as, in his half-trained way, he will much of the time after pheasants; he stood, looking up, and I have the conviction, yearning. I should have shot it for him, and Bix, hearing the gun go off, was sure I had; but I was late that time, and late the next, shooting just as the birds swerved out of sight, rattling the branches behind them.

The fifth woodcock, and we hadn't been hunting more than half an hour, I had no shot at; I could only see him along the trees, going away. The sixth I might have tried if I could have squeezed just a little more nimbly between two little pines—I could see the bird in the clear for quite a stretch, maddeningly enough, for my head was free; it was my arms, my gun and my legs which weren't yet past the obstacle.

Then I had a relatively open shot, one I felt I ought to make, and missed that, too. Then the land mine went off. It exploded with a rush of sound and air, ten feet to my right, hurtled for a dark place in the branches, and had disappeared before I could even think about raising the gun, leaving me nothing to do but the idiotic thing—chortle, and call over to Fred:

144

"There went a grouse, I guess."

"I heard him," Fred said, appearing suddenly out of the tangle beside me. "Which way'd he go?"

I pointed towards the dark place.

"Sometimes they don't go too far, and you can flush them again" he said. He blew loud and long on the whistle around his neck and, in a moment, there was the faint tinkle of a bell. He blew again, and the bell came closer.

"Your dog?" I asked. I had heard of woodcock bells.

"He'll be in in a minute," Fred said. "Have you gotten any birds yet?"

"No. Four trees," I said. It would be hard to explain why, instead of feeling frustrated and impatient with the mishaps and difficulties I was having, I found it all pleasing and funny; it was in large part because I liked being in the woods, though, and the rest was seeing all those birds. "I'll have one soon," I predicted. "How about you?"

"Just one," Fred said. "I've shot at five."

Now Jiggs came up, trotting and tinkling, and Bix, for once, knew how to react. A dog with a bell on was just about peculiar enough to bite, and Bix assumed a fighting crouch, raised hackles, and prepared to pounce; any oddball that would wear a bell couldn't be much of a fighter, and I'm sure Bix found it really perplexing that his attack should be met, turned, his ear seized and that wretched bell banged into his nose.

There was a hauling apart and scolding of dogs, and we went on after the grouse. We didn't find him, but we did get into an area away from the stream where the brush changed. It was lower and leafier here, with an occasional hardwood tree—an oak or hickory—and with even occasional open spots of wiry grass. They were full of woodcock. Fred shot two more, to add to the one in his game pocket, and I missed two.

"That's ten shells," I said.

"You'll have to forget about getting on the bird and swinging with it," Fred said. "Just raise up and fire. Snap shoot."

Now I might say that for me, snap shooting has always been a most tempting sort of fault. Unless I think not to, it is always my tendency to mount the gun, go bang and see if anything falls. You can't shoot pheasants or waterfowl this way, and there aren't too many quail situations where it works—so I have had to learn deliberation (and as often as not, I overcorrect, deliberating too long). I took my release quite happily, and, on the next bird, I had the shot touched off before the gun was really settled on my shoulder. I wish I could say the woodcock fell. He didn't. Only my shoulder took a pretty fair jolt, from the gun's having been held too loosely, and I thought—it may have been the one rueful moment of the day—"Easy there, snap shooter, not that snappy."

Then, on the twelfth try, I got a woodcock. Bix found him, in one of the more open spots; he rose, I fired and missed, and the bird went out of sight with Bix after him behind an oak tree. Then they came back in sight, on the other side of the tree, and the bird swung down what was, in effect, a corridor among the branches; and I was standing in the corridor, with my gun already mounted. It was a lovely, easy shot, and the woodcock fell, almost on top of Bix's head.

A warm, dead bird? Huh? Under a dog's nose? Why? All morning Bix's master had been shooting off his gun, apparently in a spirit of contributing to the fun of running around in the woods, by making some loud noises. This obviously could not now, so late in the game, have resulted in a warm, dead bird under a dog's nose—and an odd-looking, odd-smelling one as well. Bix supposed he might pick it up—but what if that were the wrong thing to do? He looked up and saw his master moving towards him, shouting encouragement—was he being encouraged to go on hunting, or to retrieve? When in doubt, sit; Bix sat. Then he peered down his nose and saw that somehow the strange bird had gotten into his mouth; he threw it from him with a toss of the head and, as I came up, scampered off to find another live one.

After that I settled down to a kind of rhythm of four or five misses and a bird hit. It seemed to me that the technique was less a matter of shooting than of how one walked—if I kept moving this way and that, always with an eye to where the lanes of fire opened up briefly in the foliage, then there was a chance that one of these crazy birds would appear suddenly in the lane as I reached the right position for it. When I could work this out, a snap shot might get me a woodcock; when I couldn't work it out, I'd get to shoot another tree. The excitement, as in no hunting experience I'd ever had before, was very nearly continuous; and now and then the pitch would go up from hilarity to madness when, as I tried to crash into position for a woodcock shot, there would come the totally unexpected pitch and boom of a grouse —from the ground, from under a bush, even once from the branch of a big pine tree.

Snap shooting got me no grouse. Fred Halsey insists that they are a slow-flying bird, compared even to a pheasant, but in my half-dozen chances that day, I was never on one before he disappeared. When I finally did shoot a grouse, it was not a grouse shot—I was standing with Bix in a clearing, waiting for Fred and Jiggs to come out of the brush. I heard the roaring take-off, and heard Fred fire. Then, way overhead, I saw the bird sail across, and I shot as one does at ducks or doves at long range, tracking and leading; and, feeling unentitled, got him.

My actual bag for eight hours of hunting was that grouse, and five woodcock. Fred did a little better on both, but didn't hunt as long. He had a pump to fix in the afternoon, and sent me and Bix out alone; we were glad to go, though we were almost totally ineffective. It made a difference only of one woodcock bagged, but there were many seen, a dozen anyway, it was quiet in the woods, and the sun, which had come out about noon, reached in to us at times. There were pine needles and damp leaves underfoot, and the only real sound was the rush of the creek; sometimes I cared whether or not I managed to get a shot off. Sometimes I didn't try. There was a combination of serenity and excitement that shooting in open fields could somehow never have, and the one bird I got was precisely the one I needed. For Bix found him, and raised him up, right in front of me; the woodcock went up vertically from his thicket, changed direction and skimmed across the creek. I shot, quite nicely for once, and the bird fell, thirty feet away, on the opposite bank. Bix marked it, Bix leapt into the water and swam the creek; Bix brought it to me, through the current, without hesitation or confusion.

It was the right note to end on, so, though there was still an hour or so of hunting time left, I unloaded my gun and we walked back through the woods.

I bought the dream dog dreams for the trip home—Fred knew a vet on the road to the airport, where we stopped and had Bix tranquilized.

After I saw to his loading, saw him dozing comfortably in his crate among the suitcases in the luggage compartment, I shook hands with Fred, and put all the fervor I could into the promise, lightly demanded, to come again. Then I got aboard the plane.

This time the stewardess was blonde, rosier-cheeked and better rested than the last one, but she looked with the same suspicion at my take-down case:

"Is that a gun?"

"Yes it is," I said.

"It isn't loaded, is it?"

"No, ma'am," I said, finding it proper and pleasant that this conversation should recur. "It isn't even put together."

3 "We have friends, but they are quite diverse..."

Take Latin in high school? Remember that essay of Cicero's we had to read, *De Amicitia?*

I don't. I wish I did, because now I want to write a paragraph or two of my own on friendship, and it would make me feel elegant to be able to throw in a phrase or two of Latin from memory. Put me right in the line of classical commentators.

Line is correct. From the information I have just now cribbed from the Britannica, Cicero cribbed *De Amicitia* from a Lesbian named Theophrastus. No, I mean a man from Lesbos who did pretty well for himself, coming into the Athenian intellectual hive from out there on one of the islands, and winding up as Aristotle's successor. King bee.

But I don't know if Theophrastus lived in the country

149

much, or practiced journalism, so I don't know how it might have affected his ideas on friendship. As for Cicero, in addition to being up to his wrinkled neck in politics at a dangerous time, he seems to have earned quite a few sesterces as the F. Lee Bailey of his day. He had at least two villas, at Tusculum and Formiae, in addition to a 3 1/2-million-sesterce place in Rome, right on the Palatine. He bought the house from Crassus, whom he hated, and after a while it was destroyed by another enemy named Clodius (and after that Milo killed Clodius, but not on Cicero's account).

Anyway, it's hard for me to imagine what Cicero did at those country villas—probably watched the slaves work, took baths and had a stateless Carthaginian girl rub oil on him afterwards, lovely and sad. He never quite earned a triumph, but the Senate gave him a nice *supplicatio* for a good year's work out in Cilicia, and flatterers called him "Father of His Country" for a few months . . . I don't seem to be having much luck trying to move into line with Theophrastus and Cicero. I know what it means, all right, when Plutarch says Cicero was always in money trouble. But I don't know what it meant to live with the foreknowledge he must have had at the age of sixty-three, after long service to the State and to the bar, that when Antony's boys caught him at Caieta, the only parts of him that would ever make it back to Rome again would be his head and his hands. December 7, 43 B.C.—1984 years before Pearl Harbor to the day.

I wouldn't know how to interpret what a man who lived that life said about friendship even if I could remember it.

Perhaps this, though, from a letter of F. Scott Fitzgerald's? "It was fun when we all believed the same things. It was more fun to think we were all going to die together or live together and none of us anticipated this great loneliness . . ."

That is the burden of expectation we put on friendship, in our early twenties. The expectation lessens as we grow older, and grow married and grow children.

For a middle-aged man living in the country, it is only his family that is going to live together and only for a while; but because of the family there is not (except when the man is nostalgic for his boyhood, or his might-have-beens) Fitzgerald's great loneliness.

Most of those I think of as my close friends do not live nearby. We seldom see each other casually, without prearrangement. I suppose we do, pretty much, believe the same things, but that seems rather beside the point—we feel we can count on one another in certain ways, for certain things, and hope we'll never have to. We hope the conversation next time we see one another will go on as if the conversation we've been having this time had not been interrupted (time to go to the airport). We will be relieved if it happens so.

Sometimes it doesn't.

My point is that living in the country cuts down the opportunities for the enjoyment of old friendships, as well as the opportunities for making new ones. This is not a complaint, only an observation. You will simply not see a lot of people. Weigh this as you consider buying the farm up the road.

You will have neighbors, and there is still a tradition of interdependency in terms of helping out. There will be local political matters, small dealings, some entertaining back and forth, some outdoor recreations. But this probably won't lead often, if only because people in the country have morning chores, to long evenings of booze and pleasantry, exchanging comfortable male-chauvinist information about Cicero's latest acquisition:

"You heard Terentia carry on about it? Thirty years married and he divorces her for a fifteen-year-old chick."

"Publilia? What's she like, anyway?"

"Delicious little bundle of arms and legs, with something warm in the middle, the way Terentia talks."

"That ain't the way Tiro tells it."

"Cicero's freedman?"

"Yeah. He says as far as Publilia and the old beagle goes, it's more the money than the bunny."

"Nice when they're packaged together."

"'S'to it. 'Nother touch of this Johnnie Walker Black Mead, from Britannia?"

"Can't resist. Those funny little blue monsters really know how to put the alky in the amphora, don't they?"

We are struck silent for a moment, thinking of Tullia, Cicero's daughter, whom we both half-loved . . . three times married and dead before she was thirty-five, that wild, beautiful girl . . .

No. There's sociability and mutual respect, but not the sense of a common past with neighbors in the country, unless of course you grew up on the place yourself. And even if you did—in the seven years we have lived here, seven places have changed hands of the eight nearest us, and the ninth is empty since its owner's death. So: we have friends. They are quite diverse. But, though this is essentially a group of portraits, I haven't written about them here, with, I say in sorrow, one exception.

Friends do figure elsewhere in the book, of course, sometimes under their own names, sometimes in comic disguise.

The exception is Nick Goldman, for whom I wrote, but have not previously published, an epitaph. We were friends, insofar as two men can be who have twenty years between them in age, and start as teacher and pupil.

About the other four of whom I have written in this section, two I met on assignment, Charles D'Olive for *Esquire* and Norman Borlaug for *Life*.

Spending a day with Mr. D'Olive, a World War I aviator living in Waterloo, Iowa, whose tale had not been told before, had the same kind of pleasure in it as finding something really nice in the attic. It was a day of drinks and reminiscing which we both enjoyed; we saw one another afterwards a few times just for sociability. The piece about him is "Memoirs of an Ace," third in this section.

Life and I never seem to get our gears moving at the same speed, and they didn't use the piece about Dr. Borlaug, an Iowan who won the Nobel Peace Prize. I have rewritten the sketch of him for this book, making it less formal and three times as long so as to be able to fill it out and describe a later meeting. Our first talks took place in a series of wheatfields in Mexico, but for the last we were home again, and I was no longer a certified interviewer, only a concerned acquaintance. "Peace Prize for a Fighter" explains my concern.

There had been an odd continuity about my going to the Toluca wheatfields. They are in the great Mexican archaeological region, though somewhat north of where I've worked; five years earlier I had interviewed another, quite different American scientists in Mexico about grain. He was Richard S. MacNeish, not a bad name to drop if you find yourself among archaeologists, who will refer to him as Scotty. The work he showed me was in caves, not fields, where he had been excavating in search of the origins of corn. It was an interview I undertook without assignment; my strong impulse to do so reflects the delight any migrant to Iowa would feel in bringing home new information about corn. It was published in *Horizon,* and I re-used some of the information from it in my last novel; I've put it first in this section though I'm not sure I could explain why.

These three, then, were men met in the normal line of an author's work. If further acquaintance sometimes developed, I was no more than an interviewer when we met. But I was never a disinterested interviewer, partly, I suppose, because I am not a disinterested man; even more, though, because two of my men were rural Iowans and the only things I am raising on my farm which are really important to me are a couple of rural Iowans.

This leaves me with one more relationship to try to define, and

it's going to be difficult. It's the one I have with Senator Harold
Hughes of Iowa, the central figure in the piece called "A Jaguar
Hunt," and a man for whose elections I've worked, first as Senator, later—until he withdrew—for the Democratic nomination
for President. It will clarify things for me to say simply that I
hope to be working for that very high, but to me not inconceiva-
ble, goal again.

First published in
Horizon, *Spring, 1966,*
under the same title.

The Corn of Coxcatlán

When I arrived in the Tehuacán Valley of Mexico, in the spring of 1964, I already knew that it had been the scene of an archaeological discovery no less exciting to professionals than the Dead Sea Scrolls or the Ruins of Troy.

In terms of something to exhibit, photograph or write headlines about, the object concerned was certainly unimpressive: a piece of dried vegetable matter, less than two inches long—finger-shaped, withered, but looking considerably younger than its age, which was about seven thousand years. It was a cob of wild corn, almost certainly an extinct plant, gone perhaps as long as Moctezuma or the last Inca, probably much longer, and far more crucial to the cultures they inherited than any king or emperor. With its discovery in Mexico were settled scientific controversies about form, existence, evolution and place of origin which have been going on for more than three hundred years.

The final and successful search, which had been preceded by many others, covered twelve years intermittently and began with a botanist and an archaeologist drinking tea together at Harvard; by the time they were done they had brought in something like two dozen other distinguished scholars, from foundations, universities, and government departments in three countries—the United States, Mexico and Canada. And they had spent around $100,000 of foundation money. It seems fitting that this marshaling of funds and intellects should have been directed, not towards finding lost gold or buried cities, but towards solving the problem of the origin of corn, a plant very nearly as important to our political and economic life as it was to the pre-Columbians. And fitting or not, such a project is quite representative of the direction of archaeology today, away from a quaint, rather greedy past of palaces and gentlemen adventurers, towards a disciplined present of highly technical research into the details of daily life among the ancients by sophisticated scientists, specially qualified to conduct it.

The botanist involved in the corn find is Paul C. Mangelsdorf, head of the Botanical Museum at Harvard, whom I have not had the privilege of meeting. The archaeologist, a man in whose acquaintance I feel considerably honored, is Richard S. MacNeish. This account will necessarily be weighted by Dr. MacNeish's point of view, not only because it was he whose work I saw and with whom I talked. This will be so as well because, little as I know as an amateur of modern archaeology—the nineteenth-century treasure hunts might have suited my capabilities better —I know nothing at all about botany.

But there are books and articles for the man who knows nothing at all. The ones I have relied on, quoted from, summarized, and sometimes paraphrased in trying to understand the story and write this report, are three: Dr. MacNeish's "Ancient Mesoamerican Civilization," an article published in *Science,* February 7, 1964; Dr. Mangelsdorf's "Domestication of Corn," from the same issue of the same magazine; and, for background, an engaging text called *Indian Corn in Old America,* by Paul C. Weatherwax; it was published in 1954, usefully enough, just after the initiation of the Tehuacán Project, and in it Dr. Mangelsdorf figures as a young Turk, propounding brilliant but perhaps outrageous theories. How precisely vindicated one botanist might now be in the other's eyes I had better not try to say.

Dr. MacNeish, who is called Scotty, came to his role in the corn problem rather haphazardly. In fact, as he describes it, there has often been a haphazard element in the way he has made his life's commitments.

"I became an archaeologist in the eighth grade, in White Plains," he told me. "We were supposed to be making notebooks on ancient art that spring. I was pretty busy playing baseball and put it off till the last minute; then I picked the Maya for my notebook, because they were Indians. I found a Morley article on the Maya in *The National Geographic,* cut the pictures out of it, and got the first A I'd ever got in school.

"I was taken to the Chicago World's Fair, happened to go through the Mayan temple there, and was able to collect enough literature so that the Maya became the basis for every paper I had to write in high school."

By the time Scotty MacNeish was ready for college, archaeology had become as sincere an interest as athletics. He went on summer expeditions as a worker, boxed and ran track events at Colgate in the other seasons. At the end of his sophomore year, he made his choice: he transferred to the University of Chicago, which offered little chance for development to a Golden Gloves champion (New York State Regional), but had the only anthropology program MacNeish could find which included undergraduate fieldwork in archaeology.

MacNeish first got to Mexico in 1948. "People had been saying for years that there must be some connection between the ancient Mexican cultures and the South-Eastern Mound Builders in the lower Mississippi Valley. This left a huge, unexplored gap —the Gulf coast of Texas and the whole Mexican state of Tamaulipas. If there really was a connection between the Mound Builders and Mexico, there would have to be evidence in the area between them. I got a grant to survey it."

One of the frustrations of an American archaeologist's life is that there is so much to be done, spread out over the geographical immensity of two continents; having seen the huge, undug northern Gulf area, noted various kinds of occupation evidence (including pre-ceramic, which is to say very early), MacNeish next found himself, because of conditions attached to a fellowship he applied for, making an extensive survey of Iroquois pottery which took him frequently across the Canadian border.

"One morning I was talking with Douglas Leechman, of the Canadian Museum," he recalls. "As much for conversation as for anything else, I was describing my interest in the Tamaulipas-East Texas gap. I was comparing it to the Mackenzie River basin, in the Northwest Territory. It was generally assumed that everybody migrated down through there, but no one had ever dug along the Mackenzie to check the assumption. Another gap, you see? At noon that day I met Mr. Leechman again for lunch, and he started right out by saying, 'Mr. MacNeish, we like your project.'

"I probably said, 'Huh?'

" 'Of course, you couldn't start digging in the Mackenzie Basin before summer,' he said."

At this time, the fall of 1948, MacNeish was busy with a number of things. He had his Ph.D. dissertation to hand in at Chicago, a course or two to finish, reports on various field projects to write, and work to do towards getting a new grant so as to be able to return to Mexico. Except for the grant, these things went pretty well, moving the curiously interested reaction to him in Canada to the back of his mind.

"When the grant hadn't come through by the end of the year, I borrowed a thousand dollars from my sister and went back anyway," he told me. "My heart was in Mexico. I dug caves in Tamaulipas, early man sites, and found a great deal, including the first pre-ceramic corn in Mexico among the other food remains. The corn seemed incidental to me—interesting, but no more so than other things. I was just finishing up the season there when a set of civil-service blanks arrived from Canada, inviting me to apply for appointment as Archaeologist to the Canadian Museum.

"I filled them in, sold my jeep, flew to Canada on a Friday and was sworn in. I left for Edmonton the following Tuesday to organize my first Northern digging. One of the last-minute things to be done before leaving Mexico was dispose of the stuff I'd found in my caves. Various objects were left for appropriate people, including the corn, which was left for a man named Mangelsdorf who, I understood, was a botanist working on a Rockefeller grant, classifying the various races of corn as part of the search for corn's origins."

As he went off to start work in Canada, MacNeish had only a sketchy idea of how complicated and controversial the corn problem was. To begin, as botanists had to, with modern corn—and I quote from the Weatherwax book: "From the standpoint of human interest, an ear of corn is a masterpiece of perfection, but biologically it is a monstrosity."

This is because, in its cultivated and only current form, the plant cannot propagate itself. The ears, which contain the seeds, are, of course, enclosed by husks, and there is no way for the seeds to scatter. If all corn planting were to cease, for some reason, there would be a few years of skimpier and skimpier volunteer crops; then the plant would disappear altogether.

The wild ancestor must have been different, at least in this respect: how should this difference be described? Might wild corn still exist somewhere? Did corn, perhaps, evolve not from a wild ancestor at all, but from one of the other wild, botanically related plants still known to exist? How did corn evolve under cultivation, and was it really of American origin? The questions were not unlike those relating to human evolution and the debate aroused by them, if narrower, was sometimes just as acrimonious.

When botanical historians turned to sixteenth-century records, they gained only more confusion. Though Columbus himself brought back the first grains of corn, he did not distinguish it much from other grains already known in Europe, such as the grain sorghums. It was a time, of course, when no one really knew what the explorers were finding; scientific opinion, as the 1500s developed, was uncertain whether it was concerned with new continents or new shores of Asia. The impression got around quite generally that Indian corn was of Turkish origin, and it wasn't long before some Renaissance botanists were confidently illustrating in their herbals not one but two kinds of wild corn—one from India and one from Turkey.

During the sixteenth century there were widespread and generally unrecorded introductions of seed for the new crop. One of the more fateful of them, so it is theorized, for the false lead it would provide four hundred years later, was an introduction of Brazilian corn by the Portuguese into the back country of India. There it persisted, even reverting towards a more primitive state, until early in this century, when its rediscovery gave the Asian-origin thinkers (a group as stubborn as Baconians) something to get excited over.

One of the reasons, as a matter of fact, why it took another year or so after the Tamaulipas dig for MacNeish and Mangelsdorf to meet was that the latter was in India, for a while, studying the crude corn found there. (He concluded that it was a primitive race, all right, but of cultivated corn—not, at last, the wild plant.)

Meanwhile, another archaeological corn find had preceded MacNeish's, though not in Mexico, by a few months. This was corn found in Bat Cave, New Mexico, by Hubert Dick, in August of 1948. "Accumulated trash, garbage and excrement in this [Bat] cave," Mangelsdorf notes in his *Science* article, "contained cobs and other parts of corn at all levels, and these cobs and parts showed a distinct evolutionary sequence. At the bottom of the refuse, which was some two meters deep, Dick found tiny cobs, two to three centimeters long, which were dated by radiocarbon determinations at about 3600 B.C."

These little cobs, though not yet those of wild corn, were assumed to be pretty close to it. They were a popcorn—that is, the kernels would explode when heated—and at the same time what is called a pod corn—that is, a kind in which each kernel is enclosed in what botanists call glumes. One has had vestigial glumes, when eating corn, stuck between one's teeth. With this information to go on, Mangelsdorf crossed modern popcorn with pod corn, producing a hybrid. Then he kept back-crossing the hyrid with popcorn, until he had achieved a pod-popcorn whose husks would open at maturity. This, he felt, was reconstructed wild corn; it could reproduce itself handily and served, as Mangelsdorf says, a "useful purpose in showing the archaeologist approximately what to look for."

By this time—it was 1950—MacNeish was pretty well absorbed by what he was finding in Canada. In his first seventeen days of survey in the Mackenzie River basin, he had located twenty-three archaeological sites, largely with the help of bored bush pilots. Just after his arrival, one had flown him to a lake with a nice beach on which they had found some spear points.

"It was the best fun the pilot had had in months," MacNeish says. "As soon as word got around that I was a guy who knew how to find arrowheads out in the bush, I could get myself flown anywhere I wanted to go."

There were excitements like canoeing down the river from Fort Providence through unexplored country with an awesome guide called One-Eyed Lafferté, and problems like excavating in permafrost, where the heaving up of ground overnight completely reverses the stratigraphy, putting the bottom occupation layer on top. But in 1951, wanting to write a report on his Tamaulipas work, MacNeish spent his vacation in Mexico, trying to learn what had become of the things he'd dug up. The answer, it turned out, was nothing. Through some mix-up, the things were intact and undistributed; he decided to pack up all the vegetable remains and bring them back to the States for dating, and for dispersal to the various sorts of experts.

In this connection we may note the low-comedy aspect of the sort of digging he'd engaged in: when a desert, or very dry cave, is dug, the organic material which has been beautifully preserved often includes specimens of human feces, thousands of years old. The individual entities of this material, which can be analyzed to provide very useful information about ancient diet, are called coprolites and, says MacNeish: "They look exactly like what they are. I'd separated the material I had to bring through customs into various boxes—matchboxes, many of them. Separate ones with squash for the squash expert, seeds for someone else, avocado pits for yet another man, corn for Mangelsdorf—the coprolites were to be analyzed by Dr. Eric Callen, of McGill. I put them in some of the largest matchboxes—kitchen-match boxes."

With all these various specimens packed in a large carton, MacNeish flew across the Gulf to re-enter the United States and go through customs in Florida.

"What's in the carton, Doctor?" said the customs inspector.

"Archeological vegetable remains of various kinds," said MacNeish.

"I'd better have a look," said the inspector, and, confronted by different-sized boxes within the carton, inevitably picked up one of the larger ones.

There was a long line of travelers standing behind MacNeish, watching, when the customs man opened the matchbox, reached in, and held up the thing contained. There was a shout of laughter from the watchers.

"All right, all right," cried the inspector, dropping the coprolite. "Can't you see it's very old?"

Samples of the material retrieved were sent for dating to Dr. W. F. Libby; the corn, once again, went on its way to Mangelsdorf; and MacNeish returned to his Northwest Territory excavations. When he got in from the field, he says, there were two letters waiting. One, from Libby, said: "Your corn has a radiocarbon date of 2500 B.C., plus or minus seventy-five years." The other, from Mangelsdorf, said: "Yours is the most primitive corn yet found"—that is, it was less evolved, though dated later, than Bat Cave corn.

"I switched the letters," MacNeish told me. "I sent a copy of Libby's to Mangelsdorf, and vice versa."

These documents had barely had time to reach their destinations when there was a phone call from Mangelsdorf.

"When can you come to Harvard?" he asked MacNeish.

"I've got work to do here," MacNeish said. "And we haven't funds for that kind of travel."

"I'll get you permission to visit," Mangelsdorf said. "I'll get the money, too."

The directors of the Canadian Museum were cooperative, and MacNeish was allowed to fly to Cambridge. The first thing he found was that his corn samples were quite jumbled up, as far as chronology went. Some of the directions for their arrangement had been lost.

"Can you lay them out according to the levels at which you found them?" Mangelsdorf asked, and MacNeish said he'd try. When he was done, Mangelsdorf asked:

"Do you know anything about botany?"

"No," said MacNeish.

"You've put them into a precise evolutionary sequence," the botanist said. "From a primitive race of corn through several stages to some of the hybrids that are still being grown. We've got to get more of this stuff."

This was when the two sat down to tea—served in corn-shaped cups, MacNeish recalls, with corn wafers to eat. Professor Mangelsdorf's scientific devotion to the plant is not unlike the somewhat religious devotion shown by many Mexican Indians who still, out of reverence, plant certain fields in Nal-Tel and Chapolote, two of the ancient races of corn, alongside more modern and productive strains; one is even reminded of certain Texas cattlemen, who keep the long-horn steer from extinction in much the same spirit.

"When can you go back to Tamaulipas?" Mangelsdorf wanted to know.

"At first I thought he was kidding," MacNeish says. "I told him that I was certain I could find more ancient corn down there, but that I'd require three years and twenty thousand dollars to guarantee it. Paul insisted that money was no problem.

"I was staying at Clyde Kluckhohn's house in Cambridge." Kluckhohn was one of the most celebrated of Harvard's anthropologists. "I went back there, had supper and went to bed. It seemed to me I was tired, from the trip and the day's work, but instead of going off to sleep, I pitched and tossed and drove jeeps around in Tamaulipas.

"Finally, I got up and went to the portable typewriter in

164

Kluckhohn's kitchen, and began to develop a description of a project. I worked on it till seven thirty in the morning. At eight thirty I met Paul for breakfast, and gave him what I'd written. He read it, we talked about details, and by ten o'clock he was saying, 'All right, let's get you some money.' He had all sorts of blank applications to various funds lying around, and he started filling them in, asking for a couple of thousand here, a couple of thousand there.

"In 1953 I made a quick trip to Mexico to get permits and arrange for a digging season the following year. In 1954, in November, we went down and began to survey. I heard about a guy who'd found a cave on his ranch and dug a mummy out of it, fifteen years earlier. I found him on Christmas day, and he offered to take me out the next day, the twenty-sixth, to look for the cave. He was very helpful, but wasn't certain any longer where the cave had been. We went out on horseback in the rain, looking for it; no luck. Went out again the next day, same rain, same horses. We rode to the top of a mesa, as we had the day before. My rancher kept saying it had to be there somewhere, but we couldn't find it. We were about to turn back, as a matter of fact, when a couple of cowboys came along and asked what we were looking for. When we told them they laughed. We'd been riding back and forth in front of a clump of cactus that hid the entrance all day long.

"Anyway, there was the cave. I went in. The floor was full of looters' holes, and there were corn cobs lying all around the edges of them. It was my twenty-eighth day of survey, and I had corn.

"We cut roads, built a camp and hired a crew. It was the richest place in dried plant materials I'd seen yet, not just corn but beans and pumpkins and gourds—all of them primitive, all to be studied by the bean expert at one place, the pumpkin man at another, the gourd man at a third."

But the corn remains, though profuse, were disappointing. They were not earlier than the 1951 samples; they were later. At the end of the season, on his way back to resume summer digging in the North, MacNeish conferred with Mangelsdorf again. There had been a new development: a researcher named E. S. Barghoorn had made microscopic studies of dirt taken from a drill core which had gone down seventy meters, in the Valley of Mexico, and which showed some pollen identified as that of wild maize going back perhaps eighty thousand years, to the last interglacial period. The Valley of Mexico is in the center of the country, considerably south of Tamaulipas.

"Paul thought perhaps we should be looking as much farther south as the coast of Peru," MacNeish told me. "I still liked Mexico. So we split the difference. We tried Guatemala and Honduras in fifty-eight. In fifty-nine I moved back north a little to Chiapas—found pollen again there, and we found corn, too. But it wasn't any earlier than what we had already."

Still it seemed likely that somewhere between Chiapas—the most southwesterly state of Mexico—and Tamaulipas, the most northeasterly, would be the site where corn was first domesticated. The area of search was narrowed down to just a few hundred thousand square miles.

Actually, of course, it was much narrower. Wild corn was a grass, probably a highland grass; but for there to be any chance of finding it preserved, it would have to have been a desert grass as well—for only in the driest caves are ancient vegetable samples found. The Valley of Oaxaca was the next possible place to be ruled out moving up from the South, the Valley of Puebla the next to be ruled out coming down from the North. By the time MacNeish had surveyed them, and decided the caves were not too promising, there were not many major, dry highland valleys left; one was that of Tehuacán.

It is a valley seventy miles long and twenty wide, where rain falls seasonally, during four months of a normal year, so that the annual total of moisture is low; there are strong springs in the Valley, though, to help extend the growing season by irrigation. Thus, although it is a desert most of the time, Tehuacán agriculture might be compared to our own in the Northern states—that is, it must take advantage of a short growing season terminated regularly by radical climatic change—dryness there, wintertime here.

Mexico has considerable public interest in its archaeology. In 1961 a questionnaire had been sent out to all the country's schoolteachers, asking them to make local inquiries and report on all the sites that townsmen knew of. When MacNeish arrived in Tehuacán, a pleasant resort city in the center of the Valley, he was given access to this formidable collection of raw documents —formidable because the Valley is quite literally covered with archaeological sites of all periods, the remains of five thousand years or so of precolumbian occupation. Among the hundreds reported, MacNeish was interested, of course, primarily in caves. He was loaned a 1942 army command truck and a soldier to drive it with which to check some out.

"One of the schoolteachers had reported on hearsay that there was a cave near Coxcatlán, a tiny desert village. After I'd seen thirty-four others, we got to that one. We hired a local guide to take us to it, but it was just a little cave. I told the guide we wanted something bigger, and he knew of another. We went there, made some test holes and found some preservation, but it didn't seem to be quite what I wanted. Meanwhile, though, the guide, who was enjoying the off-season wages, thought of yet a third cave, a big one, and took us there. It was an eight-mile walk from where we left the command truck; took us two hours. But when we arrived, it looked right; it was a good big cave, the thirty-seventh I had looked at.

"The guide became a digger, we hired a couple more, and

went back the next day. We took off a layer of goat dung, I laid out a trench. We went down four occupation levels and found a sandal, primitive-looking and quite well preserved.

"I decided this had to be it, and I had the boys start making a road so that we could drive in closer. We started digging in earnest, then, and began to get into stuff—potsherds and so on. By the third day we were through the ceramic remains and into loose gravel which seemed quite sterile. I figured we were about to get to the cave floor, and that I'd drawn another blank.

"But on the fourth day, when we'd dug through the gravel, we hit a layer of ashy soil and in it there were artifacts. Chipped stone things. Pre-ceramic.

"I was out of the trench, sorting them, when a digger called, 'I found a corn cob.'

"I ran over to the trench. They were pretty well down—I was looking at the tops of their heads. 'You sure it didn't fall in?' I asked. There was plenty of corn lying around on and near the surface. He said he was sure, and I got into the trench. His cob of corn was about the size of a cigarette.

"I looked all around for rat holes it might have slid down. There weren't any.

"Then I took the pick and started digging myself, and within an hour I'd found two more cobs, half the size of the first one. We went back to town, I bought the boys a beer, and wired Mangelsdorf: 'We've hit corn.'

"I sent a sample by air express, and it got lost. I wrapped the other two in foil, put the foil in a plastic bag, and the bag in a box, and flew up to Harvard with them myself.

" 'These are the earliest yet,' Paul said when he saw them.

" 'They ought to be.' I said. 'Everything at that level looks very primitive. I've got some wood from the same layer—let's get it over to Michigan for dating." The radio-carbon dating method requires organic substances, for it records the remaining

for Ophelia

radioactivity contained in all such materials; this property leaks out, decade by decade, and the rate of loss being known the method can determine age by measuring what's left of it. The process is also expensive: the hundred and four radio-carbon dates eventually accumulated for the Tehuacán project cost fifteen thousand dollars.

" 'Your corn seems very close to wild,' Paul said. 'Is it a big cave?'

"I said it was, plenty of it left to dig, and that I'd been hearing of others.

" 'We've just been practicing,' Paul said. 'Now we're ready for the big leagues.' "

The conception and organization of a large, interdisciplinary scientific project were fascinating to MacNeish. Instead of packing up materials for experts to study at home, they would now bring the experts themselves to Mexico. Instead of using one's own car or jeep, or borrowing something locally, the expedition would buy whatever vehicles and equipment were necessary. There would be a headquarters building leased, with its own kitchen and living quarters (though later, when wives of the various associated specialists began to come along, it was found better to live outside of headquarters; besides, what had started as bedrooms were soon crammed with findings of all kinds, from bones to textiles, undergoing classification).

The first choice to be made was that of a sponsoring institution, and while Harvard was willing and inviting sponsorship by the Smithsonian considered, it was decided that the best strategy for approaching the major foundations would be through a smaller entity which wasn't currently asking for anything else. Someone in the professional peer group—it was Gordon Willey of Yale—encountered at a conference, suggested the R. S. Peabody Foundation for Archaeology, at Andover, Massachusetts. It was very small, had a solid record of achievement and publication, and

169

nothing currently on hand. Its directors, Douglas Byers and Frederick Johnson, were experienced fund-raisers and administrators, and could give help in the field as well—Byers with geographical investigations and Johnson with dating problems. Under their guidance an application was made to the National Science Foundation for funds for three years of excavation and study, estimated at $65,000.

Well before the time when the grant was officially announced, there was reliable word that it would be; MacNeish resigned from the Canadian Museum, took the title of Research Associate of the Peabody Foundation, and began recruiting a field staff (which eventually consisted of Frederick Peterson, an energetic Mexican specialist, as assistant director; five fully qualified archaeologists directing five digging crews; and a Sorbonne graduate named Antoinette Nelken in charge of the laboratories). Since the payroll, including guides and diggers, often included fifty people working at various sites and surveys around the area, MacNeish found himself with complex executive duties, during the next three years, along with field supervision. (Being a man of impressive physical as well as mental energy, he solved the problem of how to divide his time, according to his colleagues, by getting around to sites during the day and working at the executive matters most of the night.)

The original grant from the National Science Foundation covered only the first projected year, and was $8000 less than MacNeish and Mangelsdorf felt they needed for twelve months. Supplementary funds had to be raised, and were got from the Rockefeller Foundation. Thereafter, the first year showing success, the N.S.F. supported the remainder of the project and will finance the publication (in six volumes, by twenty-one authors) of its findings.

But nowhere within this extensive publication, I suspect, will one be able to find, in narrative form, a description of the exact, climactic moment when the first cob of wild corn was found; nor can I supply it. It was not an object, like a golden idol with ruby eyes, which the archaeologist uncovers, and holds up, saying: "Here. We have found the treasure." Nor, as I understand it, could the botanist, had he been on hand when the first particular relic of wild corn was picked up to be wrapped in foil, have recognized it for certain.

Instead, from extensive excavation in five different caves, came 12,857 intact cobs. A number of these, marked as coming from the earliest occupation levels, are found to date between 5200 and 3400 B.C. After careful laboratory study, the botanist concludes that among these earliest cobs are many of wild corn, giving six reasons which I shall paraphrase from Dr. Mangelsdorf's *Science* article: 1) The cobs are uniform in size and other characteristics, as is true of most wild species. 2) The cobs have fragile spines, as do the seed-heads of many wild grasses, which break easily so that the seeds may scatter. 3) The glumes are long and must partly have enclosed the kernels, as they do in other wild grasses. 4) There are sites in the valley well adapted to the growth of annual grasses, which competing perennial shrubs appear to shun. 5) There is no evidence from other plant species unearthed that agriculture had yet become well established in the period to which the cobs belong. 6) The predominant corn from the next phase (3400 to 2300 B.C.), in which agriculture definitely was established, is larger and more variable than the earliest corn.

Accepting this, we learn that a mature ear of wild corn, the seedhead of a tall annual grass, was about as thick as a pencil and an inch and a half long; it was only partly enclosed by the leaves which we call husks, had a tassel growing out of the top, and was located at the top of its stem; it usually had eight rows of brown or orange kernels, an average of seven kernels to a row; each kernel was partly enclosed by chaff, and the food value of the

171

whole ear was probably less than is contained in a single kernel of modern field corn.

The men of seven thousand years ago—*homo sapiens,* whose forebears had almost certainly spread down gradually from Asia through earlier centuries—harvested wild corn in season as part of their subsistence pattern of hunting and collecting. These men lived in caves, finding food nearby during the wet season; they roamed, hunting and collecting and very nearly starving, when it was dry. The population estimate for the entire 3400 square miles of valley in the pre-agricultural time is dramatically lonely: there were, before 6800 B.C, as the original population, three "microbands"—family groups probably—of four to eight persons each in the whole area.

In the period 5200 to 3400 they were just beginning to domesticate the plants they had been using wild—corn, chilis, avocados and gourds. Whether similar small groups in other valleys were starting to plant the same seeds at more or less the same time is not known yet, though it is known that there are similarly early domestications of other plants (". . . pumpkins . . . in northeastern Mexico, sunflowers in the southwestern United States, potatoes and lima beans in the highlands of South America," as MacNeish reports) in other regions. The Tehuacán population increased by ten times, to between 120 and 240 persons—and instead of occupying seasonal camps, the building of villages, then towns, then cities and temples, would now begin to be possible. The stone tools and pre-ceramic containers found with early domesticated corn were still crude, but, as Dr. Mangelsdorf points out: "Man's cultivars are artifacts as surely as are his weapon points and pottery."

As for corn, as soon as these early men began to plant it, they began to improve it, possibly by watering it, certainly by removing other plants which would compete, so that corn grew larger. Then, in the period between 3400 and 2300 B.C., corn began to hybridize with either or both of two closely related and still extant plants, one or another of which recent botanists (Burbank was one) thought must be the actual ancestors of corn: teosinte and tripsacum. Both are forage grasses, with tasseling seed heads; both are native to some parts of Mexico; and both continue to reproduce in their wild form. It was the hybridizing, certainly inadvertent on the part of the growers but fortunate for its effect on the productivity of individual plants, which consigned wild corn to extinction. Clouds of windborne pollen were produced by the hybrid corn; it could not have taken very many centuries before the remaining stands of wild corn were fertilized by this pollen and grew as hybrids the following year—to cease reproducing the year after. If there were isolated patches of wild corn left, which Mangelsdorf feels unlikely, at the time the Spaniards arrived, "then it was almost certainly rapidly extinguished . . . [by] the numerous types of grazing animals [introduced]: horses, burros, cows, sheep and—worst of all—the omnivorous and voracious goats."

It makes an affecting image: a sixteenth-century colonist's goat on top of a hill too steep for even the wind to climb, mildly chewing up the last, sweet ears of wild corn left in the world. But one may see their like in the project headquarters at Tehuacán (or in the series of actual-size photographs accompanying the *Science* article), and though there were differences in size and yield and many external characteristics, the little cobs are unmistakable. An uncoached layman, should he be shown one and asked to guess what it was, would call it corn, I feel quite certain, with no hesitation at all.

173

First published in
Esquire, *under the same*
title, in August, 1964.

Memoirs of an Ace

On September 12, 1918, Charles D'Olive, a twenty-two-year-old flier from Alabama, shot down his first German plane. The next day, September 13, in an engagement which officially lasted twelve minutes, he shot down three more. After that, as he says, he cooled off. On October 18, while flying support for the battle of the Argonne, Lieutenant D'Olive shot down his fifth and final German plane, possibly shared another, and was himself shot down.

In 1962 Mr. D'Olive, by now a sixty-six-year-old business executive living in Cedar Falls, Iowa, was driving home from work, listening to the NBC Monitor radio program. It happened to include an announcement that the final day was at hand when veterans of World War I might ask to have their service records corrected.

"I knew there was something I wanted corrected," Mr. D'Olive says. There is still in his voice a good deal of the soft, pleasant bounce of Deep South inflection, though the accent has been modified by many years of living in the Midwest. "When I got home I dug into a footlocker where I'd put all my service papers." In it he found and read the citation for his Distinguished Service Cross, awarded for having shot down the three planes on September 13. He also found the official confirmations issued him for planes shot down: these showed one confirmed on September 12, and one on October 18, but only two for September 13.

If the confirmations were correct, he was one plane short of having been an ace; and indeed, according to *Air Service Information Circular* (*Heavier Than Air*), Volume 1, No. 7, dated February 9, 1920, only seventy-one aces are listed and Mr. D'Olive is not among them. He is credited, in this list, which is the score sheet for all the men who fought that first, tentative air war, with four planes only.

Either the D.S.C. citation or the confirmation list was wrong, and Mr. D'Olive knew which. He had known for forty-five years, more or less, that he was the seventy-second ace, and he had reached the age when men want the histories of their lives set straight. He decided to write to Washington, pointing out the discrepancy. He got forms requesting corrections from the Veterans Administration, and sent them along with copies of the relevant documents and a letter asking that they be checked.

"Do you suppose that the official confirmation for my other plane is still lying around someplace?" About a week later a letter came saying please be patient; we'll try to find out.

Most men's days in war are, like the days of courtship, relatively brief, eventually remote, but always vivid. Mr. D'Olive, who seems considerably younger than his present sixty-eight years, remembers quite precisely what happened on each of those three days of distant violence when the Fokker D7's went down under his guns.

"Things get a little fuzzy back there," he said once or twice, but I hope that when I am sixty-eight I shall remember as well. Though his hair is white, Mr. D'Olive has the eye and stride, the ruddy cheeks and firm waist of a man much younger; he has not let the executive life keep him out of the fields where he hunts, or off the streams where he fishes. He receives visitors in what he calls, with a certain twinkle, his "bragging room"— a room with a cabinet of fine guns, a swordfish sword, a tarpon tail, the horns and hides of American big game, and the autographed photos of some of the other young fliers with whom he served in the A.E.F., men who stayed on in the Air Force: Lieutenant General Ennis C. Whitehead, Major General Frank O'Driscoll Hunter, and General Carl Spaatz.

Charles D'Olive was born, he told me, on July 10, 1896, in Suggsville, near Mobile, where the family had lived for more than a hundred years. The name appears on early maps, spelled of course with a lower case d, d'Olive; no one can be sure when the change was made or why.

From a photograph he showed me of himself, taken in the summer of 1914, I imagine him to have been both a sensitive and a spirited boy; he had just finished hoboing through the wheat fields, and was ready to return to Mississippi A. & M. (now Mississippi State) for his junior year in engineering. His father, a lumberman, had moved the family up to Mississippi for the yellow-pine harvest.

When he graduated in 1916, after three years of a military regime modeled on West Point (though with no resulting commission), he chose a field to go to work in which must have seemed as new, and in some ways doubtful, as rocketry is today: he went to work for the telephone company.

"That was Southern Bell," he said. "They made me traffic manager at Memphis. And there I was when one day in March, 1917, three airplanes landed in the infield of the County Fair racetrack."

They were Jennies, Curtiss JN 4 D's with OX 5 engines, and they comprised the equipment of the 4th School Squadron of the Signal Corps' Aviation Section; Memphis, one supposes, must really have turned out to stare at them.

"The war started for us then, in April, and I thought I'd go back over to the fairground," Mr. D'Olive says, "and see if I couldn't enlist with them. I had a knot where I'd busted my thumb, but I kept it in my pocket where the doctor wouldn't see."

He got by the physical examination, was accepted into the little outfit (there were four or five officers and four or five enlisted men), and asked the captain in charge where to draw his uniform.

"Why, we don't have uniforms," he was told. "You might want to get yourself some overalls."

"Yes, sir." It must have seemed pretty strange, this being the real Army, after four years in a military college. "Where's the barracks, sir, and the mess hall?"

"Those are two more things we haven't got. You just go on living at home, and report out here in the mornings."

Private D'Olive explained that he was a long way from home, was, in fact, living in a boardinghouse which cost more than the thirty dollars a month he'd be paid.

"Good Godalmighty, I never thought of that," the officer said. "Well, we'll make you a sergeant and you'll get seven-eight dollars a month. Will that do it?"

"Thank you, sir," said Sergeant D'Olive.

In the next few weeks, he was put to work making hinges for toolboxes, and only once got to ride in a plane. His clearest recollection is of Pop Geers, who trained trotters at the fairground, being delighted to have the Jennies take off and roar around over the track. It got the horses accustomed to strange sights and loud noises.

About the time Charles D'Olive finished with the hinges, orders came for the outfit to dismantle its three planes, pack them in crates and load them on the train for Chicago. The cars were put off on a siding at 85th Street and Crawford Avenue, near what was then Ashburn and is now Cicero Field.

"It was just a piece of prairie, with one dilapidated hangar, already years old," Mr. D'Olive says. "It had been the exhibition field where the old barnstorming pilots kept their Curtiss Pushers —Walter Brookins, Alvin McCauley, Pop Dickinson and Katherine Stinson.

"We dragged our crated planes through the mud to the hangar and put them back together. Shorty Schroeder and I moved into one of the Jenny packing crates; we hung a tarp over the front for a curtain, and put in some hay to sleep on. Shorty was a self-taught pilot, who'd been Katherine Stinson's mechanic. Later he got to be a major, and after the war was chief test pilot for the Army Air Corps—set an altitude record of 38,000 feet in an open-cockpit plane."

In Mr. D'Olive's analysis, the little group around the Jennies at Ashburn Field at that time—the spring of 1917—were like a bunch of rather serious hot-rodders, interested in mechanics and technique but basically attracted by the speed and adventure of flight. He had another ride or two, but still hadn't really started learning to fly when one day two new Jennies arrived.

"That made five. As far as I know, the first cross-country formation flight in history might have been when the squadron flew those five Jennies down to Rantoul, Illinois, to open Chanute Field. We waited for a clear day so we could follow the railroad tracks down. That was navigating by the iron compass, but of course it was all contact flying in those days."

Things began to get organized. At Chanute Field a group of overage civilian pilots, the old barnstormers again, had been signed to contracts as instructors, and Sergeant D'Olive was among those who were allowed to take lessons.

"We were the eager ones. Those old county-fair pilots weren't all that crazy to be up in the air every chance they got. Days they didn't feel like working, they'd come onto the field, hold up a handkerchief, kind of flutter it around, and say, 'Boys, it's too windy to fly today.' And back to town they'd go.

"They gave us our dual-control instruction, and they got us going. My instructor was Harry Powers, and it wasn't too long before he had me soloing. The day you soloed, you were an automatic first lieutenant.

"I had about ten hours of solo flight there, and I loved, it. I think we got a bigger thrill out of flying than kids do today, all cooped up in a little cabin with a rulebook to follow."

In the fall of 1917, Lt. D'Olive was ordered overseas, spent seventeen seasick days crossing to Liverpool, and was sent on to the Third Aviation Instruction Center at Issoudun, France. Here the instructors were French, combat pilots who had been wounded, generally, and the planes were Nieuports.

"The Nieuports had rotary engines," Mr. D'Olive told me. "The whole darn motor turned around, not just the propeller. It was like trying to fly a gyroscope, and we had to learn all over again."

The most difficult thing in a Nieuport was to taxi it in a straight line, and the students were started in *rolleurs*—planes with the wings clipped off; it also got them accustomed to controlling a two-piece throttle: one piece fed gas and the other air.

179

"When you could handle one of those things on the ground, they'd let you fly again."

There were three Nieuport models: twenty-three-, eighteen-, and fifteen-meter. The new pilots started on the big ones, the twenty-threes; when they had solved handling the rotary engine in the air, they graduated to the eighteen-meter, which was snappier, and finally to the fifteen-meter, the smallest and fastest of all; it had been the standard French fighter plane early in the war. In one of these, Lt. D'Olive learned aerobatics.

"It was winter, and kind of cold. They had some big oil cans set up on the field with fires going in them. We'd stand around the oil cans, keeping warm, and watch the instructors do stunts —but not my instructor.

"Mine was a tired old pilot named Didier Masson. I think he'd been with the Lafayette Escadrille, which was an outfit made up of American volunteer ambulance drivers who decided to switch to flying—and this little Masson was of French extraction. He had him an easy chair and a stripped-down fuselage—even the wheels were off it. Nothing but the body and controls.

"He crawls in there, and announces that he's going to teach us ze *vrille,* or spin: 'One, close ze throttle. Two, kick ze rudder. Three, pull ze steek back in ze corner. All right? Now, to come out of ze *vrille:* One, straighten ze rudder. Two, put ze stick back in ze middle. Three, slowly open ze throttle. Now you go do it.' "

Having gone and done it, the student knew the fundamental aerobatic maneuver. The others were learned through a process of somewhat competitive experimentation:

"It was like a bunch of vaudevillians, with different tap routines. You'd say, 'Hey, watch this,' and you'd take a plane up while the others stood around the oil cans and watched you. When you came down, the others would say, 'How'd you do it?', and you'd explain, maybe boast a little, and someone else'd say, 'Okay, now watch me.' And he'd go up."

From Issoudun, Lt. D'Olive went on to Cazeaux, early in 1918, to gunnery school.

"My roommate there was Quentin Roosevelt, T.R.'s youngest son, who was shot down and killed a little later at Château-Thierry. Quentin was flying a type-28 Nieuport, which was the first fighter plane that American pilots used.

"But we were still on the fifteen- and eighteen-meter Nieuports at Cazeaux. We'd chase balloons around and shoot at them, or work on ground targets, and there'd be a towed target now and then.

"Our instructor there was a captain, a White Russian and a brilliant mathematician. After I'd been there a while, and seen Quentin and some of the others leave for the front, I told him one day: 'Captain, sir, I want to get the hell out of here. I've done a lot of shooting now, and it's getting repetitious.'

"He told me he'd think it over, and next morning in class he made us a little speech I've never forgotten." Mr. D'Olive paused, smiled, and went on; his rendering of a White Russian accent, recollected after forty-five years, wasn't much different from his rendering of a French one. "The captain said: 'One member of zis class have requested most emphatically to leave so to join friends who are going to ze front. Zis request is denied. Ze front, it's different—ze target have very disconcerting habit of shooting back at you.' "

Most any veteran of any war could guess just about what must have happened after gunnery school to a man who was genuinely eager to see action: Lt. D'Olive was ordered back to Issoudun, as a dual-control instructor on eighteen-meter Nieuports.

"It was twenty or thirty hops a day around the oil cans," he says. "Then there was combat school, and duty as a ferry pilot. But finally, in August, 1918, I was ordered to Paris, to Orly Field, to draw a type-13 Spad and fly it to the front. That's

181

properly written S.P.A.D., of course, and it was the plane every-body flew from then on. It had a 220-horsepower, Hispàno-Suiza V8 engine, and a geared prop, and it carried two .30-caliber machine guns.

"I got mine, flew it to Voucouleurs, and landed in a pasture behind the U.S. 1st Army. There were canvas hangars there, back in the bushes. It was the base of the 3rd Pursuit Group, commanded by Major William Thaw, who'd been commander of the Lafayette Escadrille.

"There were four squadrons in the Group. The 103rd was the parent squadron, and used the Lafayette Escadrille Indian head for its insignia. I was assigned to the 93rd, commanded by Major John Huffer; we didn't have an insignia yet.

"There were three flights to a squadron, seven planes to a flight, and a hundred eighty enlisted personnel."

The last big German push of the war had been stopped at Château-Thierry in the summer of 1918, but there was still a big salient at Saint-Mihiel, over which the 3rd Pursuit Group flew. Pershing wanted to straighten out the line.

"It was a little bit vague, really, just what we were going to do to help, but we'd take off and fly over the lines, maybe try our guns on ground targets and get shot at by antiaircraft.

"By September eleventh I'd done enough of that to be getting a little skittish. No, hell, I was scared. It was getting serious. But we wanted an insignia for our squadron—we'd look at those beautiful Indian heads that the 103rd had, and we wanted something like them.

"Now Major Thaw'd announced that we were to be the Indi-an-head group; each squadron would design its own particular head. But before we could paint them on the planes, some man in the squadron had to get a Hun. Of course the mechanics started betting on whose pilot would be the first, and that brings us to September twelfth.

"That morning at two there was a terrific artillery barrage. It woke me and kept me awake; I'd never heard anything like that. We got up early. There wasn't much point staying in bed.

"There was no briefing particularly. We were told to fly a certain area, a sort of aerial patrol. The particular purpose was never clear, but if we saw ground targets we were to shoot them. If we saw troops moving, we were to report it. If we had a chance at an enemy observation balloon, and were feeling brave, we might go after it. Mainly, we were up there to keep German planes on their own side, away from *our* observation balloons—they were really quite important, because they did the target-spotting for the artillery. They flew at two thousand feet, protected by machine guns and sometimes by us.

"There were three of us in the flight that morning, me and a boy named Rummel and a boy named Cox. We got separated from Rummel, and we were flying along, Cox on the left, me on the right.

"We went over a little puffball of cloud, and I looked down and there was a Hun below me, on the right edge of the cloud. Cox flew on; he never saw him.

"The Hun never saw me either; he must have been looking down at troops on the ground. I dived through the cloud, caught up and came up underneath him. I saw the crosses on his wings, raised my nose a little, and when I was lined up with his propeller I started shooting.

"I think he must have been killed by the first burst because the plane went straight up, fell off, took three turns and hit the ground.

"I flew back to the base, feeling pretty good, landed, had a drink, and wrote my report. It had to be confirmed, of course, before we'd get our insignia, but my crew started getting ready to collect their bets and throw a party.

"The confirmation procedure was this: you'd write the report, giving time, place, altitude, how the plane fell and whether it was burning. You'd hand it in to the adjutant, to compare with other pilots' reports, to be sure there were no conflicting claims. If there weren't, he'd write *Confirmation Requested* on the report, and then send it on to Colonel Mitchell, in command of the whole Air Force. Now somebody else had to have seen it—a pilot from another outfit, or someone in the artillery or infantry, or a balloon jumper. They reported whatever planes they saw shot down—that was what we had to have instead of camera confirmation, like they did in World War II. If that second report came in all right, confirmation was granted.

"That confirmation came in all right, of course; I don't recall just when. I'll tell you what I do recall—it was right after I finished writing my report that I got scared. Really scared. We didn't have parachutes, or anything like that, you know. I didn't sleep much that night either, and the next morning I was up early again. That was September thirteenth, the three-plane day."

We must deal, to some extent, in probabilities to fill in that day, until we come to the fight itself. If routine was followed, Lt. D'Olive and his fellow fliers were up at six thirty and had breakfast at the squadron mess. The food, for which they paid out of salary, was good, but it's likely that Lt. D'Olive wasn't too hungry. There was most mornings, he recalls, "a kind of paralysis of the solar plexus" which killed appetite, and he may well have had a nip of brandy before breakfast, to relax it.

There was, probably, an uneventful patrol flown that morning, and when he came in from it he must have joined the other returned pilots, standing around on the field, waiting for their friends to come in and report what had happened.

In the afternoon, and this is no longer conjectural, it was overcast when Lt. D'Olive and his flight took off again.

"I went up into the overcast and couldn't find my bunch," he says. "I joined up with two pilots from the 103rd, a kid named

Jones and a kid named Furlow, and sort of tagged along with them.

"We were flying in a little V, and the first thing I knew we were being shot at. Ever been in the butts on a rifle range? That's what it sounded like, and it was too damn close. The boy in front on my left burst into flames; that was Jones, and as I went by the burning plane I could see the mud streaks on his tires. A moment later, a German dived between me and Furlow, on the right.

"The German turned in front of me. He was about a hundred feet out there, at three-fourths deflection. I cut at him with tracers; that was really what you used, not the sight. There were four solid bullets and one tracer every five rounds, and you watched where the tracers went.

"The German rolled up. I kicked the rudder and went up under his belly, shooting tracers into him, and he went over on his back and out of my sight.

"I was getting too low by then, and I started to climb. Right away I saw there was a dogfight on the left, above me—Furlow I guess—and I saw another Hun heading to get into it. I came right up under him and fired; on the first burst his propeller flew apart. He turned over, and went down, and burned where he hit.

"I started climbing again, but I hadn't got to more than five or six hundred meters when I realized there was a third Fokker D-VII shooting at me. I'll never know where he came from. I tried to turn inside of him. He tightened up and slipped off, into a half spin. We were both almost stalling, but I was in slightly better control and was able to shoot first. I hit the cockpit, and saw him throw up both hands, and saw him hit the ground. This is all supposed to have taken twelve minutes, but I don't believe it took more than three or four. Remember, we were going a hundred thirty miles an hour each; take that, times two for two planes, and you know how quick it's over.

"But there's an effect of everything slowing down, just as

you're ready to shoot—maybe you know it from bird hunting. Those planes seemed to be standing still in the air. I could see the stitches in the pilots' helmets.

"Well, by the time the third fight was over, I had one gun empty and my engine was overheated, so I headed back. And I remember when I landed, my crew came up, as they always did, and someone said:

" 'Anything happen?'

"And I said: 'I've been in a hell of a fight.'

"There was a boy named Ros Fuller, about as close to me as anyone. That evening he came over to get me to tell him about it, and we had some drinks. I don't remember anything he said or I said. Ros was killed later. Roswell Fuller.

"Well, let's see. Furlow got credit for two planes in that fight, and I got credit for two. I handed in another report asking for confirmation of the third, and forgot about it. But two or three days later, Major Thaw said to me: 'Charley, that was pretty good shooting,' and Major Huffer put in for the decoration for me. The citation says Furlow and I took on five Germans, but I believe there were more of them. I don't think we got the whole fight.

"Jones, the boy who burned, was from Glencoe, Illinois. After the war, I went to see his people, and I didn't want to tell his mother that he burned. I decided I'd tell a little lie, there, and I said I'd seen Jones jump out of the burning plane onto a pretty green field. That seemed to comfort her. I got to know the family after that, and along about 1919 or 1920 I was there for dinner, when along came an Army colonel with a package. He said, 'Mrs. Jones, I was an infantry captain under that fight, and I saw your boy jump out. Here are his tunic and his wallet.' So I wasn't a liar, after all."

Burning was the great fear for those early pilots. Simply going down might not be too bad; there was a good chance of survival, if you landed on your side of the line, and actually forced landings were fairly common. There were various mechanical difficulties which could cause them, not the least frequent of which was having the synchronization fail slightly so that you shot your own propeller off. When this happened, you landed as best you could, got a ride back to the base, and were probably sent to Paris to pick up a new Spad. Lt. D'Olive went through four Spads, he remembers, in his twelve weeks of combat, all carrying the number 24, and the particular Indian-head insignia which he had won for his Squadron on September 12.

"After September thirteenth, I wasn't so eager. As I said, I cooled off. We flew, of course. We shot up some roads. I made passes at balloons a time or two, but I never got one. You had to bunch your shots to knock down a balloon—a few scattered holes weren't enough to let the hydrogen out. There was a special balloon gun, an eleven-millimeter cannon, that you could take with you.

"The great balloon killer was Frank Luke, Jr. Is his name forgotten now? He really got a pile of them before he was killed. The balloons were so valuable that that ring of machine guns on the ground could put a real curtain of steel around one. Frank Luke was a nut. He'd go right in on a balloon and then, when he'd hit it, he'd dive down and chase the gunners away from their guns.

"Eddie Rickenbacker, of course, was the ace of aces on planes. We were together, the day before the war ended, being decorated, and we got to talking about how it was that he could have shot down so many more than any of the rest of us.

"I remember saying, 'Rick, I think it's a matter of fear. You're a little older than the rest of us, you were in the second Indianapolis 500 race, you've taken chances a lot more times. You know what the rest of us can't realize—that the odds start fresh again every morning. You can get your goggles shot off one day, and still know that you start with the same chances the next. I don't think the rest of us have really learned that.'

"But going back to late September, we rigged up some twenty-pound bombs—you could put four of them on a Spad. We'd go over and drop them on troops. When the troops would scatter, we'd fly at them and machine gun them, and they'd shoot back. I'll tell you what else I rigged up: I had me an iron stove lid, wired to the seat, right where I sat. But I was never hit from the ground.

"I got run home a few times, all that kind of stuff. It was cat-and-mouse deals a lot of the time. You'd see a plane under you and start to get on him, and suddenly realize there were ten or fifteen more up above, coming down to get on you. I got pretty good shots at three or four, but none fell."

Soldiers of the Second World War often have anecdotes to tell about a figure like Eisenhower or MacArthur; my older brother tells about Ike. I can throw in a remark or two about Montgomery, though I never really saw him. When this happens, my father may counter with a story about General Pershing, on whose staff he was as an air adjutant. Mr. D'Olive's Pershing anecdote comes during the month when he had cooled off:

"I was walking back from a forced landing one morning, through a field, when I walked up a covey of about fifty quail. They were getting ready for the Argonne push then, through the forest, and they were issuing sawed-off shotguns to the troops because there'd be Heinies hiding in the bushes. Well, I went back to the mess and I got hold of a boy named Shelby, a Mississippi bird hunter, and we got hold of two of those sawed-off pump guns and went back to the field with some purple number-eight shells we bought in town. We didn't have a dog and after the covey rose I went walking up singles one way, and

Shelby went the other. I was going toward the road, and two birds got up. I got the right-hand bird, and swung, and got the left-hand bird, and I was picking them up when I noticed a big Cadillac—and General Pershing.

"He got out, and said: 'Young man, that's the way to hit them.' He sat on the running board, and we talked about bird hunting and I invited him to a quail supper at the mess. I think he wanted to come, but he couldn't, so I gave him nine birds.

"You know, about a week later I had a date at a hospital at Vittel, where H.Q. was. I was meeting a kid there, and I flew over and landed at a real muddy little field. I was covered with mud when I walked into H.Q., and just then General Pershing came down the stairs. He didn't remember me, I'm glad to say, and he didn't say a word, but the look he gave my muddy boots is the worst bawling out I've ever had."

On September 25, the Third Pursuit Group with its four squadrons moved up to Lisle-en-Barrois, near the Argonne forest. The barrages came nightly now, and the pattern of air activity changed.

"Hermann Goering's outfit and others were pulled down from the British front. Those guys were pros. Twice I tangled with Ernst Udet's blue-tailed Fokkers, and I got licked both times.

"By October 18 the ground troops had begun to break through a little. That day every U.S. plane that could fly and had a gun on it was ordered into the air, in a great, loose formation.

"There were two hundred seventy-eight airplanes. There were our Type 13 Spads. There were two-seater Breguet observation planes. There were two-seater Salmsons, and even a few British De Havilland 4's—they were two-seaters, too, made in the U.S. with U.S. Liberty engines, and we called them 'flaming coffins'; they had a big gas tank, placed right between the pilot and the observer. The Salmsons were the best of the two-seaters; I never saw one burn.

"October 18 was the first time I was ever aware that there was a major air-force target. 'Go bomb this area,' they said. 'Tremendous troop concentration.' Almost all of those two hundred seventy-eight planes had bombs to carry to the target, fifty miles away; nearly all had a fight that day.

"When they saw us coming overhead, the Heinies on the ground sent up a column of stuff like AA shells with tracers in them. It was strange-looking stuff. It spun off like fireworks, and all exploded at the same altitude. Maybe it was some kind of a signal, because right afterward everywhere you looked there was a German plane.

"Chet Wright was leading our flight. I was the last plane on the left, and I looked down and saw five Huns under us. One turned in under me; I dived, turned quicker, and got ahead of him. He came in view under me, and I was almost directly on top when we leveled out. I started firing and saw my tracers going over him; I lowered my nose and they started in a line down the center of the plane, and he rolled, out of control, and went out of sight.

"There was a fellow named Goulding in a dogfight above me, and I went up to get into that, shooting a few rounds, and maybe shared his Hun. He started to spin right away. Now you can tell if a guy is spinning on purpose or is really out of control, and I was watching to see what this Hun was doing when I had a funny feeling.

"I looked up and here came this guy, two hundred feet away. Instead of turning in toward him, which would have been safest, I turned away, and he shot three times. That's the mark of a good pilot, he doesn't waste shells lining you up; he only shoots when he's on. He hit both my wings and the gas tank and a hung bomb that hadn't released. Every shot was right in line with where I was sitting. He was using a seven-millimeter bullet that exploded on contact, and the next thing I knew fragments from one of them had penetrated my gas tank and killed the pressure.

"I had enough momentum to complete the roll I'd started, and I turned on a little emergency gravity gas tank, but I'd slowed down so much that he was out in front. I shot as I saw him go by, but didn't do any damage, and he pulled over by me. He had me then—but he didn't shoot again. He waved to me and flew off. I never knew why."

Mr. D'Olive and I talked about it for several minutes. Did the German pilot who was (like the one Lt. D'Olive may have shared with Goulding) out of Goering's group hold fire because he saw that D'Olive's plane was already done for? Was he being chivalrous? Or did he see, as seems most likely to Mr. D'Olive, other American planes diving at him and decide to get out while he could? In any case, the crippled Spad made it back to the American side of the line, and Lt. D'Olive managed to land and catch a ride on a motorcycle back to base.

"I took four or five days getting a new plane after that, and I got transferred to the 4th Pursuit Group, 141st Squadron, where I trained new pilots. Dick Shelby went with me. Hobey Baker, Princeton football and hockey player, was Squadron Commander.

"We got in a fight one day with three Huns below, but then we saw ten more above us and got the hell out.

"One day Dick shot down a Halberstadt two-seater, the kind we called a newsboy, because they used them to drop propaganda, and then pretty soon the damn war was over."

On November 10, Lt. D'Olive received his Distinguished Service Cross; Rickenbacker and others were decorated in the same ceremony.

After the war was ended, D'Olive was sitting in the tent at Toule Airdrome with Shelby, roasting chestnuts and drinking

191

French beer, and waiting for orders to get them home.

"Hobey came in. He had orders to go home, and was kidding us about it.

" 'I'm going to hop over to Nancy and pick up my new uniform,' he said.

"Shelby said, hell, if the war was over, let's not fly any more. Let's take the Cadillac, but Hobey said no, went out and got a plane and took off. His engine slugged down right over the hangar, and he tried to turn back. He knew better than that; it's a cardinal rule that when you have engine failure on takeoff, you land straight ahead, regardless of obstacles. When he tried to turn back the bottom dropped out. He may not have fallen ten feet, but with all the weight of the plane stopped like that in the air, it killed him.

"I didn't fly again till 1930."

That was in the Air Reserve, which Mr. D'Olive joined briefly, finding some pleasure in qualifying for the then modern planes. But his growing business, first as a consulting engineer, then as a manufacturer, took him away from that Reserve group, which included some old war comrades, and he let his membership lapse.

He married, he had a daughter, and he moved, six years ago, from Winnetka, Illinois, to Cedar Falls, where he is Vice President of the Chamberlain Corporation. Sometimes, on a charter flight, he will take the controls for a little while, but he doesn't really miss flying.

I suppose I was trying to get him to say that he did miss it, trying to urge on him a nostalgia for his war which I never felt for mine. It's our fathers' wars, I guess, that we're nostalgic for, the wars we thought about when we were boys.

"Sometimes we acted kind of crazy, if you like," Mr. D'Olive says. "Sometimes when we couldn't get a pass to Paris, we'd get lost and land there. And there were some nuts in the outfit." But his summing up is more judicious, and quite unemotional: "Most of the time we were serious-minded, when we weren't scared. And even if we didn't always know what we were doing, you'd have to say it had some importance as a springboard for what they have now."

We relaxed from the long session of storytelling; we had a drink, and talked about hunting dogs, and then I asked about the letter to the Veterans Administration.

"I was down in Georgia at our branch plant when the final reply came," he told me. "My daughter Susan called me up from home, and said: 'What do you know, Pop? Those dopes in Washington found your third plane on the thirteenth. History just caught up with you; you're an ace.' "

He patted his Weimaraner, and sipped his drink. "Well, I'm too old to get a real, belly-deep thrill out of it," Mr. D'Olive said. "But I'll confess to a tingle."

First published under the
same title in The
Atlantic Monthly,
February, 1973.

Peace Prize for a Fighter

My country neighbors, in this part of Iowa, felt that our community was honored in the fall of 1970 because I was sent to Mexico to meet Norman Borlaug.

They were really pleased about it—Earlis and Lucy Rohret, substantial farmers by whose family name the next road north has been called for several generations. Orval and Claretta Yoder, who have the Windham Garage, where cars and farm machines get fixed. Mac McKinney, who grew corn in Tipton until he decided it would be more fun to run a tavern. And Bob Asquith, the Soil Conservation Service technician. It mattered less to them than to me that I was the least prepared of any of us to meet Dr. Borlaug—I was a book writer, professor, buyer of much bad farm land; the man who didn't want the road paved; and the only one around who

for Ophelia

had never heard the new laureate's name before it was announced that an agricultural scientist from Cresco, ninety miles
north of here, had won the Nobel Peace Prize.

Norman Borlaug had been part of my neighbors' Iowa farm
pride for a long while. His picture appeared on farm magazine
covers, his name came up in sermons at church. His work with
wheat breeding was as familiar to them in technical detail as, say,
the prose of Hemingway or Faulkner is to me, and the international consequences of Dr. Borlaug's dedication were clear to
them and frequently discussed. When he got the prize, they had
a true share in it, for he was a product of the way they lived and
raised their children, a personification and perfecting of their
values, one of themselves raised to the level of great man.

The Des Moines Register, recognizing this, gave it the excitement
of an eight-column banner headline, all across the top of page
one: IOWA'S OWN MAN OF PEACE.

An editor at _Life,_ making the same connection, phoned to ask
me to try writing the story, which was why I was going to Toluca,
the old Mexican market town, near where some of Dr. Borlaug's
wheatfields were.

In town, and at the university where I work, we were ignorant.
The Humanities knew nothing of him. A friend over in Botany
knew in a general way, but said: "Why Borlaug? There are quite
a few fine plant geneticists around in Agriculture."

Agricultural science, you see, spoken of as if it weren't quite
a science—in the same way that ag school is inflected to indicate
that what it offers is not quite education, and agricultural life
spoken of as if it is not quite contemporary American life.

Only at the Law School, where some of them get abroad to
work, on loan to foreign governments on things like agrarian
reform laws, did they know much about Norman Borlaug, and
their knowledge was political: "Sure. He's one of the Green
Revolution boys." They would not have understood as com-

195

pletely as my neighbors all that was implied in what Ed Well-hausen said to me, ten days later when I visited him to finish my research in Acapulco. The director of CIMMYT, for which Norman Borlaug works, Dr. Wellhausen is a great corn scientist, and he put the matter with absolute simplicity: "We are all proud that agriculture has been honored at last," he said, neither a young nor a well man any longer.

What agriculture had done to deserve the honor was, if I could believe what I learned in those ten days, genuinely awesome. And obviously whether I believed it—there are experts who do not—was beside the point; two pretty impressive bodies did. One was the Norwegian parliament, which awards the Peace Prize (Alfred Nobel thought Norwegians more peaceful than Swedes). The other was UNESCO which, in the same week, awarded its science prize to CIMMYT itself, by unanimous vote of five scientist judges, one of whom was Russian.

CIMMYT is an acronym for a string of Spanish words (*Centro Internacional de Mejoramiento de Maíz y Trigo*) which translates International Center for the Improvement of Corn and Wheat—though all its fields of interest still wouldn't be represented if you expanded it to CIMMYTAPEA, adding *arroz, papas* and *economía agrícola*. If you understand what is meant by the Green Revolution, think of CIMMYT as the high command; think of the Rockefeller and, more recently, Ford foundations moving diplomatically and financially in its support like a couple of sovereign nations; and think of the collective wisdom and experience of American farmers as having established, through the generations, its basic revolutionary doctrine.

Here, as simply as I can put it, is the achievement of the Green Revolution: you recall the Malthusian catastrophe, that demographer's nightmare in which world starvation results from overpopulation, and we all go down together? It happened. It didn't merely threaten, it started happening about twenty years ago,

196

beginning, of course, in the most overcrowded and farmed-out places. India, for example, which had always had cereal grains to export, began importing them. So did Pakistan. The third horseman of the apocalypse was in full canter there, and damned if mankind didn't shoot him between the eyes, under the direction of CIMMYT, and with Norman Borlaug organizing the ambush.

That's what the prizes were for.

Here is an excerpt from one of Dr. Borlaug's letters: "*. . . that the masses should starve and die, slowly, peacefully and gracefully. . . .* Do you think for a moment they will die peacefully? *. . .* a biologist knowing anything about animal behavior can't be that naive. *. . .*"

Whether his correspondent was convinced, the Norwegian parliament agreed.

But it took me a while to understand that, just as it took me a while to feel that I understood the man himself. I flew off to Mexico with only one thing clear to me: any guy who'd got a Nobel Peace Prize for wheat breeding was going to look like Albert Einstein, talk like Albert Schweitzer, and have tame birds sitting on both shoulders.

He looked like a Viking prince, a light, muscular, compact man, with thin, white-streaked Scandinavian-blond hair, tough hands, and blue eyes that had seen a lot of weather.

In our first interview, we were both walking and he was working as well, part of a crew selecting plants from a couple of hundred acres of experimental wheats, pulling them up by hand from the hard Mexican soil.

"Could I think of you as a kind of county agent to the world?" I asked, thinking of the extension men at home who visit and advise.

He was attracted enough by the phrase to pause.

"Well," he said, "I do think I'm able to talk to farmers. I have a sense of what they're thinking, how to show them things, even

197

when I don't speak the language." He smiled, an odd, pursed-lipped smile in which his mouth contracted slightly as the teeth showed. "But no. I don't think that's it."

He gave me a glance that offered to fight this one out, words, fists or free-style, and said flatly: "We move governments."

He was speaking for hundreds of urgent, selfless men, and perhaps standing for them too, a brilliant, aggressive, 152-pound wrestler, challenging history's heaviest menace in a Little League baseball cap, with that rough, puckered smile and his boots full of wheat chaff. If, for my own convenience as a writer, I needed to use him to particularize, I was learning that there were many others: Robert Chandler in rice, at the IRRI in the Philippines. Ernest Sprague and Dr. Wellhausen in corn. John Niederhauser in potatoes. Bob Osler in subsistence farming. Frank Zillinsky in triticale, the first man-made grain—one produced, that is, by geneticists manipulating genes instead of by evolution. There are man-made forages, the sudangrass-sorghum cross for example, but the parents were genetically close. Triticale, Dr. Borlaug told me, a wheat-rye cross, is something more like breeding a dog to a cat. It was first produced fifty years ago, and what the CIMMYT men have finally done is to overcome the problem of sterility in triticale—its high protein and productivity will make it miraculously useful as a cereal grain and for feeding stock, a rival to high-lysine corn, which designates the breakthrough in that plant family.

There they are, spread around the world by the great foundations, and many others whose names I don't know, trying to keep the world from starving to death until a way can be found to check the deadly, spewing glut of human population—if it can. They are an unlikely band of heroes, living in comfort they seem neither to notice nor disdain, working with immense sums they neither question nor exploit, scientist-salesman-administrator-superfarmers.

Their story, or that of the representative whom the Nobel people had chosen from among them, began for me at Cresco, Iowa, where I went for a day, just before the flight to Mexico. And from Cresco to Saude, Iowa, eleven miles away over dirt roads.

It was impulse that took me there, but the impulse seems sound. More than is true in most American cases, Norman Borlaug's character can be found in his ancestry and in the geography of his boyhood.

The Borlaugs and the Vaales, his mother's people, have been an odd, shining Norwegian combination of teacher and fighter through four American generations. His maternal grandfather, Ole Vaale, is still remembered as a country wrestler; all the women taught.

Northeast Iowa, where they settled, is a cool land of timbered slopes, clear water and white clapboard buildings. The landscape in the loveliest in the state, and the heavy clay soil the most difficult to work.

The buildings of childhood were grandfather's house, where one was born. And then a newer house, not a large one, which father built as the family grew, on adjoining land. The church, white clapboard, too, out along the dusty road, counts quite particularly; it is Saude Lutheran.

There was a crossroads store, a mile from church, closed now, the false-front building still standing, but the one-room school, Oregon Number 8, has been torn down. There you and your siblings, your cousins, and neighbor children—eighteen or twenty at a time, of varying school ages—went to learn the first eight grades, together in the same room.

The teacher was most likely an older, girl cousin. The community had sent her on to Cresco, where the high school was, to take what was called Normal training, and then come home to teach until the next bright girl was ready.

"I'd have one grade at a time—two or three children—come up to the front of the room to recite with me," Sina Borlaug Watson told me. Mrs. Watson, Cousin Sina, has remained a teacher. "I'd give the others seat work to do. There wasn't any homework. At home they had chores. Both Norm's sisters took the Normal course and came back to teach in Saude.

"Oh, but those children had spark. Children don't have it today."

I asked about the hickory stick.

"Oh no. There wasn't any need. Hardly ever."

But when there was, her Cousin Norman told me later in Mexico, the teacher's authority was never questioned. "There'd be very big boys, eighteen or nineteen, finishing eighth grade. Not because they were slow, but because they only went for a few months when they couldn't be working on the farm. And some little tiny girl, maybe younger, but through high school— when she reached for the switch the big ones got it harder than anybody else, and stood for it, too."

This was still during the first day's interview at Toluca. We had broken for lunch, and were in the seed shed. Dr. Borlaug always brings more than he can eat, and has surplus cookies and sandwiches to hand around. He is also the man who automatically takes over making mechanical adjustments on the seed-sorting machines, ties the strongest, fastest knots on seed packages; so there'd been an interruption in our conversation while he got his shed crew's morning problems straightened out.

"Your Uncle Ned gave me some biographical notes he'd written about you," I said. "I thought you might like to have them, and I've checked a few lines I'd like to quote."

He took them with a different smile, not the puckered one which is a competitor's challenge, but a wide, friendly one.

The lines I wanted to quote, in Uncle Ned's seventy-five-year-old handwriting, read:

Now summers I had a threshing rig. I paid Norm a dollar and a quarter a day, but when we took a break I had to wrestle with him. And at home when they finished chores, his father had to go wrestle with him in the hay loft. Norm was very impatient with his Uncle Oscar's slow, old-fashioned methods of farming, but when it came to milking cows, Norman was slow as mud himself. He was very hard to wake up in the morning. . . .

"Those cows drove me off the farm," Dr. Borlaug admitted.

Off the farm meant going from white clapboard to red brick: Cresco high school. In dry and clement weather he slept at home, operating the family Model T as a volunteer schoolbus for the neighborhood. When winter closed in, he boarded in town, population then and now four thousand.

From grandfather, father and uncles, imagination is caught now for the first time by men outside the family on whom to fantasize a future. For Norman Borlaug they were Harry Schroeder, who taught agriculture and was a man of deep humanitarian convictions. And Dave Bartelma, who was principal of the high school and its wrestling coach.

Farm strong, light, fast and hotly aggressive, Norman Borlaug played football, baseball and, of course, wrestled. He graduated in 1933, the middle of the Depression, and saw no chance to go to college.

"I cut fenceposts for fifty cents an hour, and ran a trap line," Dr. Borlaug told me. "And I saved about a hundred dollars."

Then, after a year out of school, word came, nothing like today's athletic recruiting. There was a Cresco boy on the Minnesota football squad. "I can get you a job for meals and a place to live if you want to wrestle at Minnesota," he said. A job for room and board wasn't an inducement to choose Minnesota over some other place; it was the opportunity to go to any university at all.

"I went, with another Cresco wrestler, Irwin Upton," Dr. Borlaug said. "We did well enough as sophomores so that Minnesota sent for Dave Bartelma to come coach the University team."

It was quite a team. Once or twice, when they clearly had their opponents overmatched, Coach Bartelma would put one on for the spectators:

"Let someone else wrestle their hundred-fifty-pound man, Borlaug," he'd say, creating a metaphor for his star's future. "You try their heavyweight."

I'd heard the story before I went to Mexico, and now I asked about it.

"Were you able to pin one?"

"Oh no. It happened twice, and I won both times, but they weren't very good heavyweights. A good one would have killed me. I'd go in, try to move fast, stay behind him. Put my scissors on him, and keep moving. But they were much too strong for me. I just had to try to out-maneuver."

Taking various semesters off to work, he learned forestry, a profession of service and, I recall from my own Virginia boyhood, some romantic appeal, which would keep a man outdoors.

"One day we were making sections of pine, trying to draw the blue stain of a pine fungus, when a man with a pipe stuck his head into the classroom, came in, and looked at some of our work. After a few minutes' looking, he walked over to the blackboard and said, 'Well. I think you people are just atrocious anatomists. You've got the fungus all right, but you've got the wood all wrong.'

"He spent about ten minutes showing us how we should be drawing the pine. Then he said, 'Well, I've taken up too much of your time,' and left. None of us knew who he was."

It was Norman Borlaug's first encounter with E. C. Stakman, a towering contemporary figure in plant pathology.

"Stake's really one of the old school. After that, as an under-graduate, I never missed his lectures whether I was in the course or not. He's a tremendous speaker, a philosopher, a historian, at home in every discipline of science."

American education went like that once: white clapboard, to red brick, to university granite, and men each place on whom to model a larger image of your life. Before Stakman, Norman Borlaug hadn't thought much about graduate school.

I wondered if I were hearing some echo and development of Dr. Stakman's style in the next few paragraphs Norman Borlaug spoke. We had left the seed shed, and were waiting for a truck, standing among some wheat plants. He was smiling, not at me but at the wheat; I hadn't really started asking about the Green Revolution yet. We were getting to know one another.

"Plants can talk to you," he said. "Laugh at me for saying it if you want, but plants speak, very softly, and you can learn to hear them. They tell you how they feel, or that it's a little cold for them this morning, by the way they stand. They say, 'Couldn't I have a little water, please?' or 'Hey, it's beautiful today. I feel great.' "

I confessed I had a feeling of individual personality about the three young apricot trees I'd planted at home—that one is sturdy and self-reliant, another tries too hard to please me, and a third is heedless and wild.

"Of course," he said. "And if you studied them, I'll bet you'd find the differences are genetic."

I said I wanted to believe that. That I knew a biologist at home who felt that our elms would never succumb to Dutch Elm disease, because they were so prolific—the genes to fight it were going to show up as they never had in the American chestnut, a much less varied and vigorous species.

"That assumes that there'll be a mutation," Dr. Borlaug said. "It may or may not happen. The resistant elms are on other

continents. But, look, a couple of years ago I went to a conference of forest pathologists on the West Coast. They know I like
to keep in touch with forestry, and they often invite me.

"They were facing Western white-pine blight. The white pines
were dying like the elms, like the chestnuts. But out of every
thousand, they said, they were finding one or two that would
withstand it. I suggested the foresters might have a fossil gene
that was still active. Millions of years ago, when the white pine
was native to Siberia, and in migration across what's now the
Bering Strait, it could have carried resistance to this blight. It
proved out. They found prehistoric Western white pine, frozen,
in Siberia.

"Let me tell you why I made that guess. There is corn in Africa
now, old American corn species carried back on slave ships that
were returning empty four or five hundred years ago. That corn
hadn't known certain American diseases for centuries, until some
material from this continent reached there—perhaps from an
airliner flying over, dropping out corn cobs, after lunch. Quite
a few African corns became diseased, but the old slave-ship species still carried their genetic resistance to American diseases that
hadn't been present before in the African environment. You see,
if we can put together what we learn in one field and apply it to
others, we can get answers.

"So we might say, if plants can do that, then we should make
our experiments in manipulating mutations, for example with
radiation, much more imaginative than the things they're trying
to do now. We could free our sophisticated researchers—for
example, with radiation genetics a physiologist might be able to
produce a mutant alfalfa bacterium which would form its nitro-
gen-bearing nodes right on a corn root. Then you'd have corn
that would produce part of its own fertilizer." He waved at the
truck which was arriving now. "The Atomic Energy Commission's got so damn much money," he concluded. "And I've got

a crack plant physiologist here. Maybe I could get him a grant to work on that."

His mind had gone casually from prehistory to the future in about two minutes.

That afternoon I learned at least about the first part of Norman Borlaug's contribution to the Green Revolution—there are three, altogether, more intertwined than I shall try to render them. And I will save discussion of the ways in which his achievements have become controversial, and the result of that on Dr. Borlaug's life, for the end, though some of it may be obvious enough as I go along.

First then: through the years, and incorporating (as he would insist on my saying) the work of many dedicated wheat breeders, Norman Borlaug changed wheat from a tall plant with a fragile stem, which would fall down in the wind and rain, to a thick-stemmed, heavy-headed dwarf which would convert irrigation water and intensive chemical fertilization into grain instead of taller straw.

He bred resistance into it, to rust and other parasites, and though this had certainly been done before, found a remarkably simple way of beating evolution. Wheat rust is capable of mutating annually, all by itself, so that a wheat that has been resistant one year may be susceptible to a new mutant rust the next. But in Mexico, Dr. Borlaug realized, he could produce two crops of new seed a year, by simply taking advantage of the fact that there are two geographically distinct growing seasons, one in Sonora, the Mexican wheat belt, and the other near Toluca, which is much higher and has different rainfall and temperature patterns.

"We've got to keep moving," he said, as he explained that to me. "We can't stand around and preen like peacocks while the sky is falling."

Most recondite, and most important in its world implications, Dr. Borlaug bred into the new wheats a quality called "day-length insensitivity," which means that the highly productive, disease-resistant varieties may be used at many latitudes, regardless of the hours-per-day of sunlight, so that there is no time-consuming need for developing special wheats for each locality.

What goes on, then, first at Toluca, then with the Toluca seed at Sonora, then with the Sonora seed back again, is that 4500 to 5000 new seed-producing varieties are planted and tested, and the best of them put into production for seeds to be shipped around the world every year. The breeding, the very first step in producing all this, is a kind of sacrament. Here is how you do it:

Choose a plant of ripe wheat which pleases you, in lineage and individual quality, and sit by it. Carefully open each kernel of the head, probing in with needle-nose tweezers, and remove the little male parts, discarding them—eating them, even, if unconsciously you are moved to. Now, with very sharp scissors, cut the top from the case which encloses each of these newly emasculated kernels, rendering the whole head green, exposed, moist and sticky. You must cover it—her now—with a little glassine envelope, and clip the envelope at the bottom with a paper clip, for in this condition wild pollen might find her before the mate is ready.

Choose a head of wheat from another plant, robust, of complementary ancestry, and cut it off with a short section of stem. Again with the scissors, extrude the male parts by shearing off the top of each encasement.

You have just created male and female.

Stand the male in the sun, or, if the sun be weak, circle him with the warmth of your hands, careful not to touch. In a moment he will begin to swell visibly, and yellow filaments will push out of each opened sheath. Quickly: cut the top off the glassine envelope which shields the female. Blow it open into a cylinder. Holding him by the stem, turn the male upside down, and thrust him completely into the envelope. Rotate, swirl, shake—and in a moment a cloud of yellow pollen will emit millions of fertile spores, filling the envelope, clinging to the receptive female. She is bred.

It takes only one spore to fertilize. Throw the male aside. Fold the top of the envelope down. Put on a paperclip. Next couple.

The following morning I had breakfast with the Borlaugs at their home in the Lomas, an upper-middle-class residential section of Mexico City, and we talked again of Minnesota and the Depression. Mrs. Borlaug was a stately matron now, her two children grown, married and living in the States. When she met Norman Borlaug, she was Margaret Gibson from Oklahoma, living at the same Minneapolis boardinghouse and, like the wrestler who wanted to go to graduate school, earning her keep by waiting on tables.

"We worked an hour for breakfast, didn't we?" she asked him. "Three prunes, a piece of toast and coffee."

"And glad to get it," Dr. Borlaug agreed. "Even so, the landlady was going broke. She'd grind up the meat left on the plates at lunch and make hash for supper."

"There were ten people waiting" Mrs. Borlaug said, "for every job like that."

Their dates, on cold Minneapolis winter nights, cost twenty cents. "An egg sandwich to share, and two cups of coffee," she said.

"And we'd make it last from nine to midnight, at the Greek restaurant."

It was pleasant to hear them reminisce, there in what for her had become an empty house, over tropical fruit and eggs and sausages, he in a strong tenor with a slight suggestion still of Scandinavian cadence, she in a voice no less deep which still carries a suggestion of the Southwest. To enjoy conversation was something young people learned in the thirties, and it was plain she was enjoying it now for he is seldom home, and when he is works seven days each week, from first light to last.

"When was the last time you spent a morning here?" she asked, and he shook his head. Probably about the last time he got out his bass rod, for he likes to fish, or his waterfowl gun. "You can't do those things," he said, no simple wheat breeder after all, "when you're riding around the world on airplanes all the time."

They both read constantly, compulsively even. "But," he said, "you read ten books to my one."

"You don't just read books, you study them," she replied. For whatever it's worth, I can report that Robert Ardrey's *Social Contract* was the book on the seat of the car in which he was generally driven to Toluca each day. That morning, since we were going down late, he drove the car himself, his strong hands very firm on the wheel as he went with the wild Mexican traffic, using his three speeds resourcefully, changing lanes as frequently as the other drivers but always with care, so that I was able to make notes on the rest of what he and Mrs. Borlaug had told me.

He'd got his B.A. in 1937, and started work for the Forest Service. Then, much more decisive, she'd got a job proofreading for a publisher, so that he could quit the Service and start graduate study. He did his M.S. and Ph.D. in three years, working on a forestry problem for the first, shifting to plant pathology and working with flax for his doctoral dissertation. He was hired out of school by DuPont, and was working in its laboratories when the war started. Cresco boys were being drafted to fight, but DuPont wouldn't let the Cresco fighter go.

"I'd get myself reclassified to leave, and the boss would get me classified right back in again," he said. "We were fighting a tropical war for the first time, and ours was the only laboratory equipped and staffed to work on the new kinds of problems that came up. Rot-resisting materials, insect control, things like that.

Once I had three generals in my lab, yelling about some piece of research on materials for the tropics . . ."

Henry Wallace, another agricultural scientist, was Vice-President in the first years of the war; our Mexican allies were having severe difficulties with their corn crop. Wallace took the problem to the Rockefeller Foundation, and the Foundation sent down experts to make a detailed survey of Mexican agriculture. One of them was E. C. Stakman, and one of the recommendations was that a plant pathologist be hired to work on the tortuous genetic problems of Mexican wheat which, though there was land and water available, was so weak and susceptible to rust that thousands of tons had to be imported.

That was the job that was waiting for Norman Borlaug, whenever DuPont might let him go. "Even though I'd never farmed wheat or worked with wheat—except for a time in graduate school, when I had a job going to the wheatfields with garbage cans to collect rust for the men who were doing wheat work there."

But Henry Wallace, who interviewed him and noted his almost intemperate impatience to get to work outdoors, agreed that Borlaug might be the man.

Norman Borlaug arrived in Mexico brash, energetic, ready to start driving for solutions, and found himself in that sea of mud produced by his life's most persistent enemy, bureaucracy.

A short-tempered young man who needed physical work outdoors as much as he did food and sleep, Dr. Borlaug found himself instead confined to offices, to poorly organized agricultural stations staffed by the nephews of dignitaries.

He wanted to set up experiments directly on farmlands. "The best farmers would hardly shake hands with us," he said. "They thought agricultural scientists were parasites on their taxes. After a few months I used to think, 'If I could only have my job back at DuPont.' But I had to show them something."

Henry Wallace, meeting him again, was amused: "Are you still as aggressive as ever?" he asked.

Twenty years later, the farmers who wouldn't shake hands named a street after him in Ciudad Obregón, in Sonora; Mexico's production of basic foods (wheat, corn and beans) was up 300 per cent; and he was still as aggressive as ever. At an international genetics meeting, he wrote this into a scientific paper on wheat-breeding and delivered it poker-faced: "I suggest that you direct your efforts to save our civilization through the establishment of an irradiation genetics program designed to develop a new race of *homo sapiens*. This new improved race of man should have the enzyme cellulase in his gut which will thereby permit him to eat, digest and grow fat on the mountains of paper and red tape which are being produced in ever-increasing quantities by the world's planners, bureaucrats and the press." And went on to suggest that this be "tightly linked to the following three additional genes . . . 1. A gene for compassion which seems never to have existed in the wild (normal) type; 2. A gene which will provide massive doses of common sense, since the original gene for this character has been badly eroded and lost its effectiveness in the wild type . . .; and, 3. A gene which will assure a low level of human reproduction. Again . . . a gene that has never existed in the wild type. . . . Man has repeatedly bred himself into misery and famine."

Fortunately, among the administrators of the program which he'd joined in Mexico, there was both compassion and common sense enough to know that if you've got a firebrand, you can light a fire.

"Norm came storming in saying, 'All I want is land, sunshine and water,' " one of them told me. "So we let him have it. He took his sleeping bag and camping equipment into Sonora, and started breeding wheat."

Today he loves Sonora, and is nostalgic for the years he spent there. "I carry an American passport," he said. "But I have many countries, especially Mexico. And really I am Sonoren. It's wide open country. Mesquite. Cactus. At first I found the desert frightening, empty by daylight. Now I think it one of the most peaceful things in the world, especially at sunset when the wildlife starts coming quietly out . . . and the people feel for the land as people did where I grew up."

He and Margaret raised their children there, and with them whole teams of Mexican Little League ballplayers, for he was not a Schweitzer, but the man who brought Little League to Mexico. Nor did tame birds sit on his shoulders; his ballplayers began as little kids hired to chase birds away from experimental seed plots. He has seen one become a big-leaguer, several go on to become scientists, but he still broods—though he denies it—over a referee's decision that cost his Sonora Little League team a decision in the Mexican semi-finals, one year, years ago.

He'd wanted land, sunshine and water. He began to want something else: young scientists from foreign lands to train. He got them, internes from Latin American and Asian universities, with good minds and social consciences.

"But they'd never had their hands dirty," Dr.Borlaug said, and he set about the training with the same coach's combination of discipline and inspiration that he'd given his kid ballplayers— and it all went back to Dave Bartelma, the high-school wrestling coach, and maybe his father in the hayloft:

"Dave used to say that anyone found smoking was off the team," Dr. Borlaug remembered for me. "And for a lot of them, they'd been doing a man's work on the farm and smoking like men since they were twelve. It wasn't for conditioning, Dave said. 'If you aren't willing to give something up, you're not willing to put anything out.'

"When I started Little League in Sonora, I'd tell the boys, 'Bed at eight-thirty.' Their parents would tell me they couldn't keep those kids *out* of bed. We'd play games at low altitudes, in hotter climates, and I'd say: 'Once the game starts, no liquids.' There'd be my little kids sitting very straight on the bench, pointing out some player on the other team with a Coke, and my kids would say, 'Look, Dr. Borlaug. That boy's going to make himself sick.' "

The young scientists who began to come to him from foreign agricultural schools were generally upper-middle-class boys with some sense of idealistic commitment. It is sometimes objected that he takes them all—plant physiologists, pathologists, theoretical geneticists—and turns them into wheat breeders, but Dr. Borlaug sees it differently. The true need in his mind is for tough, disciplined men, above politics, loyal to science and humanity—for after the training comes the third of his achievements: production campaigns.

"We've told the FAO, whoever sends them: we don't want numbers, we want leaders," he said, about the time we reached Toluca. "We want to produce a combination of technical excellence, across all disciplines, the courage to say what needs to be said at the right time in the right place, and a sixth sense for human feelings. So we try to give them a philosophy about work, both as scientists and as men. Then we toughen them up.

"First there's about two weeks of seminars on the philosophy of research, scientific obligation. Then we stretch their backs."

They go to work in the fields, either in Sonora or Toluca, side by side with Norman Borlaug, who never tires.

What they must do is plant by hand the 4500 to 5000 new varieties of wheat developed for the current year, or about a million and a half individual seeds. This must be done with both speed and care, working from sunrise to dark. As soon the last seeds are in, the first have sprouted and the real ordeal begins: every one of the 1,500,000 plants has to be inoculated by hypodermic containing wheat rusts in solution.

for Ophelia

There were dignitaries in the wheat fields at Toluca that second day, being told about the training program, and Dr. Enrique Rodriguez, once a trainee—now staff pathologist—explained and pantomimed inoculation for them. Being on the staff means he works right along with Dr. Borlaug and the internes.

"It's muddy by the time we inoculate," he said. "Hard to walk." He began to slog, slip and stoop his way along. "The plants are only a few inches tall, and each gets two shots with the hypodermic." He squatted, rose, squatted, leaned over. He showed us how the back begins to hurt, the legs. "By evening . . ." He grinned and became a man dragging himself to bed, muttering rebellion.

Not all of them last.

"You see," Dr. Borlaug told the dignitaries in his fluent, unaccented Spanish. "We have methods of selecting plants, and also methods of selecting scientists."

Those who survive develop enormous *esprit.* Around the CIM-MYT office, "los de trigo"—the wheat team—are known for their closeness to one another and the fierceness of their loyalty to Norman Borlaug.

It has enabled their work to survive disasters like the scattering of a whole year's production notes—105 pages—by a whirlwind one year. Only five pages were ever recovered, and a year's time lost.

It has also produced martyrs, for one year the valley where the seed was stored flooded unexpectedly. Two of the wheat team made a raft, fitted an outboard to it, and were making trips to the storehouse to save the seed, taking it out through a hole in the roof. In the high wind, their raft upended, and both men drowned.

But most of the disasters inherent in field science can be taken more lightly. There is a moment I always enjoy when tough, American intensity slides into pragmatism, conceding the irrepa-

213

rable. "Almost twenty-five years to the day," Dr. Borlaug told me, "after the *remolino*—the whirlwind—that scattered our notes, another came along like an anniversary present and hit the bundles of seed wheat we'd untied for drying. Oh, they were all mixed up. The boys were pretty upset, so I said, 'Well, we'll just name this batch Whirlwind '69, and send it on out.' "

Norman Borlaug grinned, took a helmsman's squint at the sun, and I noticed that his forearms bulged like Popeye's. "As long as we've got a chance, we're sure as hell going to keep on trying," he said, and that seemed to set up our last day's interview, which took place in the office he avoids, its desk piled with letters and telegrams of congratulations from all over the world, most of them unopened.

"There's one here from President Nixon," he said, but couldn't find it for me to read.

"Tell me about the Green Revolution," I said, but of course by then I knew a good deal of what was meant. Country by country, in the famine belt, the CIMMYT men had mounted national production campaigns, making vast use of those three factors, of which I've already partly described the first two: there is adaptive research, fitting the new-style seeds and production methods to the particular country. There are the young scientists, trained now and sent back to prepare localities like humane secret agents. Then comes the salesman, the evangelist, Johnny Appleseed in suit and tie, to inspire prime ministers and cabinet officers and get it rolling. The goal for Norman Borlaug is always a 100 per cent increase in national wheat production in the first year.

"The very first attempt must be a success," he said, "or the game may be over. You've got to throw the long bomb and score the first time, because there won't be any second time."

He was comfortable talking sports jargon, and it made me think of the tone of service-club lectures, back in the midwest;

and then of one service club in particular I'd been asked to speak to once, a branch of the Optimist Club which meets at 6 A.M. in Iowa City, and calls itself the Sunrise Optimists. Dr. Borlaug, as an emissary, would be pretty much of a sunrise optimist himself, I thought, and imagined him talking to discouraged heads of state, charging them up, getting them going—"We move governments," he'd said.

Not always, of course. There have been failures, one particularly which still disturbs him and which, I think, he considers a failure of personal diplomacy. But his staff has asked me not to name the country where that took place. They are optimists, too, and hope to have another try there.

There have been stunning successes.

"The so-called Green Revolution," Dr. Borlaug told me in the office that day, glad enough not to have to start opening and reading all those letters, "started with the worst administrative decision ever made. That's exactly what they called it in New York.

"Ed Wellhausen was away from Mexico, and they'd made me acting director. We'd finally negotiated orders for three hundred and fifty tons of Mexican seed wheat for Pakistan and two hundred and fifty tons for India, and we'd finally arranged for enough acreage in those countries to make a massive demonstration.

"The seeds were to be shipped by American freighter from Los Angeles, and my colleague Ignacio Narvaez went up there to supervise loading. It would unload first at Bombay, then in Pakistan.

"We almost missed that boat. It was the time of the Watts riot, and the trucks were held up. Fortunately, the boat was, too. Finally, on a Friday afternoon, Narvaez called up to say he'd got the trucks through the police lines to the dock, and I had just time to reach the bank before closing with the letters of credit from India and Pakistan to get money to pay the Mexican Seed Office.

"The one from India was all right. The letter from Pakistan had three words misspelled in it, and the bank wouldn't cash it. I knew the Seed Office would be storming for the check, ninety thousand dollars, but we had to make that boat. So I called Narvaez back and said, 'Load it. I'll fix this up on Monday.' That was the decision.

"By Monday India and Pakistan were at war, communication stopped, and the boat had left."

Bombs were falling—it was not the 1971 war, of course, but the one before it. New York pointed out that it was uncertain that the boat would be allowed to proceed from Bombay.

"I said, 'By God, I'll get the money,' and stopped answering the phone," Dr. Borlaug told me, and a month later the corrected letter of credit did come through.

Meanwhile the seed arrived in both countries barely in time for planting, with Dr. Narvaez there to supervise on one side of the battle lines and Glenn Anderson, another colleague, on the other. There'd been no chance to test the seed from the Mexican warehouse beforehand for germination. When Dr. Borlaug arrived in Asia, local germination tests were completed and plants were coming up—just 25 per cent of them.

"We sat in a miserable hotel, opened a bottle of Scotch, and said, 'What in hell are we going to do?'

"The only thing we could do was double the rate of seeding, and use up our reserve. Kick up the fertilization, and keep our fingers crossed. Fortunately, we could go from one side to the other by sea. Spring came, and it was the best wheat they'd ever seen." He smiled happily. "Narvaez and Anderson were wonderful. That's when you have to be the kind of quarterback who can scramble. When you don't have that big line in front of you."

Then: "We've made Pakistan self-supporting in wheat. India

too. If we could have gotten to . . ." (Here he named an important national leader, recently deceased.) ". . . before he died, we'd have made his country self-sufficient in two years."

Whenever he can enlist support at the top for his own, aggressive young scientists in the field, Dr. Borlaug can move, asking only for one chance, confident of being able to make his psychologically overwhelming demonstration of 100 per cent improvement in yield. The people at the top will protect his young men from the bureaucrats in the middle, he feels—but he is no longer the hotheaded, undiplomatic disrupter and by-passer of channels.

"Norman is a different man outside of Mexico," Dr. Wellhausen was to tell me, down in Acapulco next day. "He has learned to solve his own administrative problems. He's mellower, more patient, and he creates that total support in others. He's the most inspiring man to others I've ever known. Our only problem with Norman now is to develop younger inspiring men to back him up."

If he was once their problem child, he is now their giant-killer, their breakaway runner. They support him with more urbanity, perhaps, then he himself can produce; and with more energy, sophistication, and commitment to the common goal than would be conceivable in a group of men less made to the measure of this ominous age, with its several possibilities of human extinction.

For the Malthusian possibility is still here, and will be as long as population spews unchecked. "Everything considered," I have a note of Dr. Borlaug's having said, "Mexico's made a hell of a lot of progress . . . if the damn population didn't grow so fast. For example they've cut illiteracy by 50 per cent, but there are just as many illiterates— 25 per cent of sixty million instead of 50 per cent of thirty million." He blames stupid politicians chiefly. "Ayub Khan was for family planning, and it was used to destroy him politically." Then he cited with disgust another leader, whom I won't name, in another country in which the cities teem with rural poor, who have left the land that won't support them any longer. This man's campaign theme was that there were vast depopulated areas, so obviously his people in order to become great should multiply vigorously and fill the spaces.

But let me return to a letter of Dr. Borlaug's, a little of which I quoted earlier, so that I can put his case for the Green Revolution in his own words. He had received a letter from an acquaintance, mounting the standard attack on his work: that the heavy reliance on pesticides and chemical fertilizers was harmful to environments, that creating more food encouraged higher birthrates, that modern plant breeding moved towards a dangerous depletion of genetic variation in plants, that rich farmers were helped more than poor, and other such items.

". . . I will answer immediately, even though I have a thousand things to do before leaving for a long trip through Africa to fight politicians, bureaucrats, planners and scientists on food production problems. I must say it is a thankless task [he had not then won the award] for one is criticized if you don't succeed, and apparently criticized even more if you are in a small way successful. But after all, as far as I am concerned, all life is a game or challenge in which one must try to do his best.

". . . You are barking up the wrong tree. The correct tree is population growth—but why then attack the Green Revolution? . . . I know the population explosion cannot be stopped immediately . . . education must lead the way. . . . So what is to be done? Are we to sit idly by and watch the world starve? This I cannot watch!

"I have spent my professional lifetime trying to increase world food production. . . . and through this process buy time—perhaps two or three decades—in which to permit population control programs to become more effective and dynamic.

218

"Is the so-called Green Revolution expected to correct all the social ills that have accumulated since the days of Adam and Eve, and then on the Sabbath (while resting) solve the population problem as well? How stupid can educated people be? What has happened to the indispensable, rare character called common sense in the over-populated, over-sophisticated, over-computerized so-called educated American society?

". . . Food production need not be the number one problem for the next twenty or thirty years. We have bought you time. Use it wisely . . . sell the need for population control.

"I am sure my colleagues feel as I do that the most unfair of all criticism are those that . . . say we have . . . created more problems than we have solved. Perhaps we have, *but we have also generated hope where there was despair.*"

The last thing Norman Borlaug said to me before I left Mexico was, "Say anything you want about me, Vance. But don't say anything that would damage my effectiveness."

I hope that I have not, and hope I will not in the few additional paragraphs that follow.

About a year after the Mexican trip I saw him again. Since I hadn't published anything, I'd obviously had no bearing on his effectiveness, and I have no idea what his standing was and is abroad. Nor can I say that he had exactly lost ground at home, since before the prize there wasn't really any to lose. Rather, then, he had had a chance, been in a position, to have great impact on people in this country, and lost it. And I'd become too much his advocate in our few meetings not to care.

There were not, after all, very many Nobel Peace prize winners around who were first-rate speakers, inspiring men, crack scientists and experienced at moving governments.

He could, it seems to me, have had any forum in the country, up to and including an appearance before the joint houses of Congress, and it was clear that he was not indifferent to being heard; he did appear at state legislatures and at universities, asking support and understanding for his work. I think (but have no idea whether it would have appealed to him) that he might have run for very high office here—he'd have made an extremely attractive candidate. He still would.

I need to make two speculations to explain, at least to myself —and I hope, when this reaches him, to Dr. Borlaug—why he does not yet figure in the general American imagination as one of our important leaders, in or out of office. Nor would I offer these speculations—it would otherwise seem simple decency to let the matter drop—were I not convinced that the situation is retrievable, and that Norman Borlaug's may well be a voice we will learn to hear. And should.

First, I think he was too much out of touch with valid and important currents of American concern in the particular area of environment, and did not know the quality of its leadership, only that of its cranks; and I think he simply didn't take time (or maybe have time) to think through the relationship of his work to those concerns in a way that would permit him to offer us fresh wisdom from a man of demonstrated judgment and integrity, a scientist and humanitarian established beyond criticism in his field.

Instead, and this is my second speculation, he responded to the criticisms of some of the crankier environmentalists in his younger character; he reverted to being a fighter, with scores to settle.

I can see the difference, in my notes from Mexico, between the things he had to say about conservation in 1970 and those he was saying about conservationists a year later, in the fall of 1971. As a forester, he had a deep knowledge of ecology as a field of study years before most Americans had ever heard the word. His attitude in Mexico, for we did talk about it, had been judicious, humane and not without sorrow. On the North American continent—I'll have to take responsibility for this summary—he felt we still had the space, the lack of population density, and the affluence to be able to afford to concern ourselves with environmental deterioration. We could try to save our wildlife, our water, our air, our woodlands, and then function best, if we could learn to control our own population, as an example of restraint and good management to other nations. We could try to prove, for example, that breeding disease resistance into crops is better ecology and better economy than heavy use of pesticides, try to become in this and many other ways a model for what world environment ought to be.

Meanwhile, though, as far as other continents were concerned, if the tragic choice had to be made—and often it did—between, say, preserving wildlife and saving human lives, he didn't have it in him not to choose humanity. For another example, disease-bearing insects had to be controlled or the tropics would become uninhabitable—wouldn't it make more sense to support crash programs of research on how to control them with the least environmental damage than to insist on a worldwide ban of DDT? It did not seem to him acceptable to limit the alternatives to a baby dying of malaria on one side, a hawk laying thin-shelled eggs on the other.

The voice I heard saying these things in Mexico was calm, deeply thoughtful, and the things I heard it say genuinely quieted the harshness with which I myself had advocated—to stick with the last example—public flogging for chemical manufacturers. Like all extremists, I needed moderating; there were many like me, and he was someone we could listen to.

But I don't think Norman Borlaug realized we were there. He had barely begun speaking his views, after the prize was awarded, before the hotheads began to attack—as, indeed, some of them had before then. And he came out of his Mexican corner, as I should have known he would, with the puckered grin and his arms ready to grab hold and wrestle.

The occasion of our second meeting, in 1971, was the dedication, in Cresco, of a monument to Dr. Borlaug, and I heard, in his acknowledgment speech, a brief and not very careful version of what he'd been saying. Again, I'll summarize, and take responsibility for it: environmentalists were dangerous radicals. They were attacking farmers, who were his people, and he wouldn't stand for it. They were scientific halfwits, callous to human suffering, selfish in their demands for an environment which would serve chiefly their personal pleasure. He did, and when I asked later if I'd heard correctly he apologized and said it was a slip, call American conservationists by the worst of American political names.

I didn't, and still don't know what his political inclinations are, though Margaret Borlaug, at a gathering after the dedication, told my wife of having met and liked Vice-President Agnew. It did seem clear, anyway, that he was not aware that the conservation movement here is an improbable political coalition of the far right with middle-class liberals of both parties; the affluent young with the deprived old; intellectuals with outdoorsmen; suburban consumers, who have little idea what it will cost them in increased rates and prices, with our purest romantics, the hippies, who don't care. It is only a secondary cause to most radicals, who are suspicious of the accompanying population-control proposals; it is in direct conflict with the production goals of those farthest left communist countries (and their sympathizers) which have not yet industrialized successfully.

What I wanted to tell Dr. Borlaug at the gathering to celebrate the memorial was that he misread the politics of the situation—that the people he was counterattacking included, along with the cranks, most of his natural allies in the fight against the terrible, underlying problem of population glut, and that he might disregard the shrill and the embittered among them and find many people with that common sense he holds so precious.

Mostly, though, I wished he could talk with some American farmers—my neighbors—in whose defense he felt he was speaking, for they were the men whose fathers started the Green Revolution; the men who sent their sons to agricultural school, and then pioneered chemical fertilization and new seeds, mechanized farming and chemical control of weeds and insects. They made, as I had to move to Iowa to learn, America as much a great agricultural as a great industrial country, and their grandsons who are farming today are proud of that. They are, I contend, a more concerned and knowing group than either Dr. Borlaug or the conservationist-politicians realize.

To take the four neighbors I named to begin with (and I didn't set it up this way): Earlis Rohret concedes readily that meat raised naturally is of better flavor and texture than the pork he supplies—but he will also add that the pressure on him is to achieve acceptable quality and very high quantity at low cost; he feels strongly and directly a responsibility to keep this country fed—meanwhile, the condition in which he keeps his nonfarmable land is a joy to see. Orval Yoder, who has probably been more inconvenienced than anyone else by my resisting the paving of our road, since he takes care of the vehicles that use it, has nevertheless been my ally in trying to get the County Engineer to rechannel the creek for road-building in a way that will preserve water quality, though it would be more costly. Mac Mac-Kinney, before he bought the tavern, was raising 160-bushel-to-the-acre corn, but he was also planting all his fencerows to wildlife cover, though to do so takes the space away from additional rows of grain. And Bob Asquith, the Soil Conservation Service technician, has been selling and engineering soil-and-water-conservation practices all his professional life. To any of these men, food production is obviously the basic job, and they are as proud of the way they do it (maybe with more reason) as Detroit is of its cars. Nor do I know a single farmer out here who isn't eager to learn, and even try experimentally on his own to discover, those ways of supplying the national need which least damage the land he lives on and loves.

I didn't get a chance to say those things to Dr. Borlaug at the gathering in Cresco. Though we greeted one another with some affection and managed to have a couple of drinks together, our attempts at conversation were pretty constantly interrupted by old friends of his, and by a couple of anxious Madison Avenue men, employed by the chemical industry, who'd been following his speeches, hoping he'd become a soothing, respectable spokesman. I was almost sympathetic with them; they had a tiger by the tail. They wanted to hear him say moderate stuff no less than I did, though for them tact would only be a tactic.

But what I really wanted was a good deal more than moderation. I wanted to be inspired, I guess; I wanted the fighter to turn loose, turn his back on the hotheads, and start getting us sunrise optimists together again. Teach us to yell, *Sure, here's to the Green Revolution, let's go coach.* To hell with the sour apples, show us how to make it even greener—wheat green and rice green, oakleaf, pine and grass green, and even a touch of robin's-egg blue for accent. The population thing may beat us yet, but let's stop wasting time and strength, trying to beat one another.

Not Previously published.

A Jaguar Hunt

Harold Hughes first saw me about eighteen months after his election as Governor of Iowa. That was in 1964, when I appeared in his office in Des Moines, from Iowa City 110 miles away, as a constituent, one of a solemn-faced group come to demand an accounting on conservation matters.

I was just beginning to get interested in state politics, a recreational activity of middle-aged men and of women whose children are started in school, if a grim matter to asphalt contractors, executives of regulated industries and political careerists.

A year after our first meeting, I turned up jollier as one of Governor Hughes's motley hunting companions on a trip to Yucatan.

In 1967, I reappeared at the office, this time as the writer who was to do a biographical piece about the Governor for the *New York Times Sunday Magazine*—a piece which I have not reprinted in this collection, though I have reused some of the material from it. Harold Hughes had attracted national attention as the head of the Democratic Governors' Caucus; he'd been instructed by the others, who must have been relieved to have Harold to leave it to, to have a tough talk with President Johnson about the heavy Democratic election losses of 1966. ("Frankly, we took an awesome clobbering," Governor Hughes told a dinner meeting in December.) He and Lyndon Johnson had considerable personal liking for one another, but during the conversation, Governor Hughes told me, "There were no words minced." The former truck driver and the Texas rancher are both noted, in political locker-room tales, for the pungency of their language, and I asked whether Governor Hughes felt their friendship had been damaged. He started to shake his head; then he said: "That kind of strain between people has to have some effect, doesn't it?" In perspective, I suppose that meeting in January, 1967, with a strong young leader whom he liked, was the beginning of the last act of Lyndon Johnson's personal tragedy.

Harold Hughes was forty-five then. So was I.

The following year, 1968, Governor Hughes took me on as a member of the staff in his campaign for the U.S. Senate, which he won—in spite, so the party professionals out here still say, of his having nominated Eugene McCarthy for the presidency in Chicago. Since then I've either seen, or exchanged letters, or talked on the phone with Senator Hughes two or three times a year.

Somewhere, I have a letter from him, apologizing for his delay in answering one of mine, in which he remarks that secretaries had shuffled it around, "not realizing that you are a personal friend." I would feel quite content to accept the phrase, but not quite honest.

I take it to be part of the particular loneliness of public life that when a man reaches a certain level in it he can no longer make new friends in any full sense of the word, unless it be with others at the same level, and only then if both men have decided against competing to rise to the next level. For all the rest of us, he finds himself the prisoner-king of a realm of jockeys and sharpshooters, wherein the highest rank a new acquaintance may attain, except by some miracle of affinity, is something short of friendship—an honorable and useful courtier, perhaps, a favorite jester; at best a trusted counselor and confidant who, taking the risk of independence, may deserve knighthood or dismissal, depending on how things turn out. But it is only with an old friend, from the time before it all began, that the public man need never be on guard; so be it.

From the standpoint of the new acquaintance, there are things about the public man one automatically respects—his privacy, for example—except when specifically invited not to; and the invitation cannot, in the nature of things, be a standing one. There were one or two times in the 1968 campaign when Harold Hughes and I were close; but they came when he indicated a need for someone to talk to, and I was at hand, and it would have been stupid of me to presume that the tone of an evening's dialogue would carry over to our work next day.

It's as simple as this. In hot weather, and if there's no one else to do it, and no matter how big and strong the candidate may be, you carry the suitcase to the motel room. You know what breaking into a sweat would do to his shirt collar. I remember Harold Hughes saying to me quite ruefully on a day like that, as we started out campaigning, "You've got to take care of the product if you want to show it, don't you?"

Let me offer a different example: there is nothing so easy and pleasant as doing something for a friend or, on the other side, accepting it. But there is little one can offer to do for a public man, outside of plain work, which the jockeys and sharpshooters aren't eager to do more handsomely. They are always offering gifts and favors, which your public man generally finds it wise to refuse. You do not want to put him in the position, then—or yourself either—of having to inspect your motives. Perhaps I am oversensitive on the point, but however that may be, it's hell on spontaneity, making a climate of checked impulse and small constraints.

I am, then, no more than one of a number of men Harold Hughes seems to have found more useful than irritating, likes pretty well (I think I can say that), and can count on. If we have some affinity going as well, our circumstances don't bring us together regularly enough for much more than I've set forth to come of it.

Nor have I, to be wholly truthful, set forth one final awkwardness; to do it, I've got to confess that many of the times I've felt less than comfortable with Senator Hughes have had nothing to do with his position, but were rather a consequence of the personality which put him into the position. Harold Hughes is, quite simply, an overpowering man. I sometimes wonder if he realizes the strength of his own magnetism.

This is the thing I continue to ponder, for the phenomenon of human magnetism seems to me a central mystery to be solved in trying to understand how certain men alter history. It is, according to a formulation I began to make after spending my week with Norman Borlaug in 1970, a quality to which we give different names at its different levels of strength.

At a low level we call it charm. At the next we recognize it, perhaps, with an old-fashioned term like character. At Dr. Borlaug's level we call it personal authority, and at Harold Hughes's dominance.

Since I am easily charmed, respectful of character, responsive to personal authority, and can be awed (and discomfited) by dominance—yet have some rebellion in me, too, and some cynicism—I cannot guarantee that I will always like the way I behave with men who have these various degrees of magnetism. This feeling is not unusual in the men around Harold Hughes. I remember one of his staff saying to me, during the '68 campaign:

"You know, I think I'm pretty good. When I go in to make a pitch to him, I always get myself up for it. I'm going to get him this time. But he always takes me. I may get to make my point after he does, but he always has to take me first."

"God," I had to say. "He even takes me over the telephone."

Try him yourself some time.

I don't, by the way, see much reason for translating the traditional English word *magnetism* into Greek and calling it *charisma.* What's the difference supposed to be?

For a time I thought it one of the peculiarities of American politics that there was little correlation between the qualities which make a good campaigner and those which make an able executive or legislator.

This was because I failed to see that magnetism might exist at levels more potent than charm, a degree which we more often associate with harm politically than with good, learning finally to prefer the intelligent, conscientious office-holder who gets his work done. Probably it should have been obvious to me that magnetism at the higher levels is the most essential of the various qualities which combine as leadership, and therefore find myself involuntarily sympathetic with Lyndon Johnson and Richard Nixon who have seemed to lack magnetism or even to hold it in negative quantities. "When Nixon comes in green on color TV," my wife said once, "I don't even pink him." I would like to argue that one could be a great man without being particularly magnetic, and thus not much of a leader. So I don't see how it can be fairly charged, as President Nixon has been beginning with the Scranton report, with failing to provide leadership, as if he'd chosen not to; obviously, he would if he could. But whatever its origins in personal security, in ego, in great physical and intellectual energy, in moral wholeness, a grown man's degree of magnetism is probably inalterable, like his shoe size or the color of his eyes.

Harold Hughes has more of it than any other man I ever met.

2

It was very early in the spring of 1964 when I met Governor Hughes as a member of the delegation I've mentioned. Our main concern, as I remember it, was that there wasn't much being done in the way of long-range planning to expand State activity in conservation.

I'd been to the State House a couple of times before, in favor of a dove-hunting bill, so the marble corridors weren't totally unfamiliar. I knew that over to the right, as we went along, the legislature was in session, and there were a few men and women I knew at work in both the House and Senate chambers. I'd seen the draped flags of Iowa's Civil War regiments before, in their glass showcases. Nevertheless, I hushed my voice and quieted my footsteps and felt, even, some sense of wanting to hold back as we turned left, down a shorter corridor towards a small, projecting walnut sign that read "Office of the Governor."

I think it was the concentration of authority, all in one building, like a giant town hall: the Governor, the Cabinet and Department heads, the lawmakers, all working under the same gold dome. There was a lot of energy in that building, a lot of power, and my share of it—as citizen, taxpayer, voter—seemed rather insignificant.

Our appointment was for eleven in the morning, and we had

to wait; no one who gets in to see a high public official ever wants to leave.

We waited in an outer office on stiff leather sofas, and I was glad enough for a chance to recover from my mild attack of awe. It settled me to watch the secretaries typing, the staff men moving in the background from their files to their telephones to their low-voiced interviews. It was, I told myself, just a business office after all.

Dwight Jensen, the Governor's executive assistant, a slim, blond ex-reporter, came to ask us to go in. We filed past Dwight's desk, in through an open door to the large office where Governor Hughes had risen to greet us, and I was awed all over again.

At first, I think, it was the place itself, not as a room but as a location from which the power and energy of the rest of the building was directed or frustrated, abetted or countered. A governor's office was not, after all, merely like that of the president of a company I might work for, nor that of a general under whom I might have served. The large man standing by the desk had no control over my livelihood nor was I under his command. Quite the contrary: his livelihood was under my control, he was under my command in the hallowed theory of the republic.

Realizing this produced, of all things, a sort of reverence in me. Unresponsive to religion, I have apparently some capacity for spiritual feeling about the great political notions—individual liberty, common action, and that consent which a majority of the governed must always be free to withdraw, whether from a man by their vote or a state by their displeasure with its actions. So I felt the continuity of a political process in which I believed more devoutly than I knew, and this was a high, holy place. Territorial governors, early ones, fighters, corrupt and stupid men, cowards, ambitious reformers, hacks and princes we had tried in this space. A man announced that he was measured for it, and then it measured him. The way one man filled it temporarily altered only part of its dimension for the next man; the greater part established by our consent was irreducible.

I had barely time to feel, certainly not to analyze, all this when Governor Hughes spoke. He was merely acknowledging introductions, but the voice seemed to collect my feelings about the room, transfer them to the massive, brown-eyed, black-haired man, and add a hint of challenge. It was a strong, clear bass ("I can't get within an octave of baritone," Harold Hughes once told another writer), now expressing the appropriate combination of friendliness and seriousness, and at the same time making us aware that it was muted. The only other American voice I know that resembles it belongs to Johnny Cash, the country singer, but as a speaking voice Cash's is second best. As boys display their strength by rolling up their sleeves so that you'll note their biceps, Harold Hughes lets you know what's there from the sheer sound of his voice.

We were asked to sit; the Governor resumed a seat behind his desk and prepared to listen.

Larry Ladin, who'd requested the meeting and organized our delegation, was both fluent and well prepared. He spoke (in a decent enough tenor, but you can see the disadvantage), following a point-by-point outline we'd all agreed on, for about ten minutes.

During this, Governor Hughes listened gravely, with his head down and his hands on the desk. I kept looking at the hands. They were blocky, well articulated, the tone of the flesh rather dark, and ought for consistency to have looked weathered; the hands of an outdoor man who lives an indoor life.

The presentation was, at several points, critical. There were a good many complications in it as well, and Governor Hughes listened almost submissively. When our Chairman had finished, the Governor looked up, looked at each of us in turn to see if anyone was going to add details, and then replied in a way which astonished me: without notes or an outline to follow, and taking almost the same length of time Larry had, he replied without hesitation to each point, in exactly the order in which it had been brought up.

I know this because I did have a copy of the outline; I checked him as he went. He didn't miss a thing. He also chose to accept each criticism of State action or lack of it as a criticism of himself, now defending, now conceding, often correcting, in a way so balanced and full of appeal to common sense that it left me feeling as if our low-key, well-reasoned presentation had some-how been a little shrill, after all.

It was, I supposed later—at the time I was simply smitten—an advanced version of the trick one learns in writing college examination papers. You learn to repeat the language of the question, and the order of ideas in replying to it, relating all the information you can recall to that language and order at as many points as possible; so it appears that your answer is responsive and your information pertinent. But the only other person I'd ever heard do it verbally before was the smartest graduate student I'd ever had—about whom I'll be writing presently.

Govenor Hughes seemed in such full, intellectual control— the other brilliant extemporizers I could remember from business and college were men who used your question or your challenge only for a starting point, getting farther and farther from it as they went off into their private and persuasive whirl of speculation or asseveration. Harold Hughes made use of nothing more than what we'd brought in, until he had it all disposed of; then he went beyond, offering a specific plan—one which would involve us further if we wished, and conceived, I feel sure, while he was speaking—for beginning corrective action. It was more than it had occurred to us to ask for.

It was also, if you wanted to see it that way, the final score in a half-hour competition in which he'd polished us off without much effort.

It's curious. Away from Harold Hughes, I tend to forget the grasp and thrust of his intelligence, remembering instead such particulars as I took away from that first meeting: the power of the voice, the mass of the shoulders, a considerable projection of candor and conviction, and something else, some quality in the way he had listened, the feeling of a man who might spend long periods leashed in and brooding.

3

About eighteen months after that session, a photographer named Dick Swanson called me up. We'd never met, so Dick addressed me formally:

"Vance, baby," he said. "What do you hear from the *Saturday Evening Post?*"

I said nothing recently.

"Sit by your telephone. Don't leave it for a minute. They're trying to reach you. You're the only man who can do it."

I admitted I was and asked what.

"Come to Yucatan with me and Governor Hughes. The Chief. The Boss. The Big Indian and you are going to shoot jaguars, baby, and I'm going to take the pictures, and you're going to write the words."

I don't know what I said. Probably something prayerful, like "Jee-zuss Christ."

4

I really knew very little about my man, less probably than I might have if I'd simply read about him, instead of having met him and been overwhelmed. But I did know we were very different kinds of hunters: Harold Hughes enjoyed trophy hunting, and had already scored in the Boone and Crockett world, with excellent antelope and mule deer heads. I was full of fussy theories about never killing anything except for the table; I liked running dogs and wing shooting. The Governor's preference, I was ready to admit, was much more demanding—trying to locate and drop with a rifle, often in difficult country and at considerable range, a superb particular specimen of one of the species for which big game hunters compete.

As for the old *Post,* and they called not long after Dick Swanson hung up, I can only guess what kind of story they expected —perhaps something about a political figure on excursion that might call to the minds of their aging readership recollections of Teddy Roosevelt and his exuberant cult of the strenuous life. They had the wrong man for that, and the wrong hunt—the old Rough Rider's kind of expedition is about as likely to occur in this half of the century as a genuine cavalry charge.

But there's no need to measure in half centuries. Nowadays, long trips to go hunting or fishing are, by common consent, always made just a month too early or a month too late.

Try arriving someplace in October. Everyone will tell you the fish were hitting in September like they'd lost their minds. Of course, there'll be a big run in November, boy, if you can come back, and hell, you can limit out on birds then in an hour every morning, and shoot elk and deer afternoons off the front porch—meanwhile, its a damn shame nobody brought any matches, we'll just have to eat the stew cold out of the can . . . hey, stop it, are you sure? Well, cut it open with the hatchet, then.

This being the usual lot of traveling sportsmen, maybe it figured to come up double for Harold Hughes. He was by then in the middle of his second, two-year term as Governor, a 230-pound, six-foot-three hunter and fisherman out of Ida Grove, population 1095. His triumphs and adversities seemed characteristically to happen on a scale to match his build, and his jaguar hunt in the jungles of Yucatan, in late December, 1965, was almost preposterous.

In the group of men who went along was one old friend of the Governor's, Bob Barry, a Ford dealer from Hughes's part of the State. There was one other enthusiastic, if inexperienced, big game hunter besides the Governor, a young general practitioner, also from Western Iowa, named Ray Baltzell. There was Gene Keiffer, a Des Moines advertising man, who had charge of arrangements for the trip.

And there were, of course, the photographer and the writer, Dick Swanson and me. Since Dick was taking pictures and I was asking questions at the rate of about three hundred a day each, maybe we go in the mishap column.

5

There is a week which starts on Christmas night each year and ends with getting dressed for New Year's Eve, during which it sometimes seems to me the world has stopped turning. That was the week, as 1965 ended, of the hunt. Before the world got back in gear, Governor Hughes felt he could take his only vacation of the year.

Christmas afternoon I phoned Dick again—we'd been calling

one another back and forth frequently, making plans, but still hadn't met.

"Look," I said. "I can't think of any particular reason for starting off with everyone else from Des Moines tomorrow. Why don't I fly from here straight to Chicago, and join you when you change planes there?"

Dick's answer was irrefutable. "Vance, baby," he shouted, giving me name and rank again. "You've got to come to Des Moines, because that's where the truth is."

I finished packing and took a night plane west to the state capital. Dick met me at the airport, a stout, fresh-faced, thirty-one-year-old man, with light straight hair, very pink cheeks and a large, deceptively uncomplicated smile.

"Vance. Vance." He seized my suitcase and my gun case to carry. If I'd had a handle, he probably would have carried me, too. "Come on. I've got you a motel room. Listen, I've been celebrating Christmas with some Italians. That's what I'm trying to do, learn to love life like an Italian."

He was one of those whose irrelevancies become relevant through sheer exuberance—and, I'm sure, still is, though he has been a couple of years in Vietnam for *Life,* and come back, since we last saw one another; sent me some Okinawan postcards, Dick did. He was waiting for the Vietnam assignment to come through, that evening in 1965; he told me that as we sipped Canadian Club in the motel room. He was eager for Asia, for what he might learn about himself.

I was reminded by the glass in my hand, and our clear mutual relish for what it contained, to ask how much drinking it would be appropriate for us to do on the trip. The first things everybody learned about Governor Hughes were that years before, after his discharge from the infantry during the Second World War, he had been a truck driver and an alcoholic. It is an open part of his record, as is the information that, having touched personal bot-

237

tom, he rediscovered religion, joined Alcoholics Anonymous, and began the extraordinary career of public service in which have been preserved, as the remaining traits of those young days (in the view of his constituents)—a fighting man's toughness, a truck driver's forthrightness, and the compassion of one who has known and overcome despair.

There was a reminder of all that in 1972, as I revised this piece. He was appearing on a network press interview show, was asked if he'd ever smoked marijuana, and replied easily yes, he had. It was during the war. Hadn't had much effect on him, but he'd tried it several times. I remembered him saying once when we were talking personally, "I've left so many footprints, everywhere I've been. There's no sense trying to go back and cover them up. If they want me, they'll have to take me as I am, and if they don't, that's all right, too."

"The Governor doesn't mind other people drinking," Dick told me in the motel room. "I don't believe he's altogether crazy about drunks, though."

And off went Dick, determined to get to bed early. I hoped not too much life would turn up worth loving Italian style on the way; we were supposed to be back at the airport at 6 A.M.

Since the motel was just across the street, I arrived first in the morning. Second was Governor Hughes. He was wearing a raincoat over a dark suit, and no hat, his black hair worn quite full and brushed straight back. He looked quiet and self-contained, Dick's Big Indian, a chief perhaps in city clothes, keeping silent. There was no delegation to be listened to—only a couple of cab drivers, reading their papers; no meeting at which he must be the best man there—only me, and a sleepy janitor, pushing his broom slowly in the other direction. As a consequence, Governor Hughes seemed less oversized than he had last time we'd met—not deflated but drawn in, an actor off stage.

I went up to reintroduce myself, but it wasn't necessary.

"Hello, Vance. Want to put your luggage with ours?" Since he knew the others who'd be arriving pretty well, it wasn't difficult for him to know who I was, but it pleased me anyway to be recognized. I know half a world full of people who'd have let on that they weren't quite sure, and called me Vince or Francis.

There was about a cord of cased guns, ammunition boxes and suitcases, which had preceded their owners, moving toward the scales on a conveyor. I added my things. It seemed an awful lot of stuff for six men for less than a week, but we'd been advised to pack for warm days, cool nights, an official dinner with the Governor of Yucatan, and the possibility of snakes. That meant four different kinds of footgear, just to start with.

The man in charge of giving such advice was the next to join Governor Hughes and me at the almost deserted airport, Gene Keiffer, the advertising man, slim, dark and harassed. Gene had had Governor Hughes the previous year as a campaign client; another client was the state-owned sisal-growing industry of Yucatan, which ships a lot of binder twine into Iowa. In that conjunction was the origin of our trip: the invitation to Governor Hughes, who had no personal wealth with which to undertake such holidays, to hunt as a guest of the State of Yucatan, had come through Gene. I think, as a matter of fact, it had probably been Gene's idea; maybe I was Gene's idea, too, and Dick Swanson who arrived now, wearing Nikon cameras and accessories like missing explorer's gear on the necklace of an African chief.

Gene Keiffer took me aside. "Did you know we went down last year to try for jaguars?" He asked. Gene's was a soft, indoor slimness. His voice and manner were quiet, confidential, but probably not always worried. "On the night we reached the jungle, word was already coming after us by short wave radio, and then by jeep to camp. The Governor's father had died. We just repacked everything and turned around and came home. I guess that's why I'm so nervous about things this time. Here. I'll

239

hold your baggage checks. I've got everybody's. I'll take us through customs." His hands were full of travel documents. He looked tired as well as harassed, and was sensitive enough to see I'd noticed because he explained again: "I'm so nervous about this trip. I was afraid I'd oversleep. I didn't trust the alarm clock. I got up every forty-five minutes all night long to see what time it was."

Dick, who didn't look exactly rested either, was taking pictures: Governor Hughes about to depart. Governor Hughes standing with a new jaguar hunter whom I hadn't seen come in —a man of somewhat the same build and coloring as Dick Swanson, but ten years older. On second look, except for bulk and blondness, the two weren't much alike; for one thing Dick's morning malady was presumably temporary. The new man had the look of permanent convalescence some middle-aged men never lose after illness or surgery. His hair was pale blond and curly, his features delicate, his hands and feet quite small.

"That's Bob Barry," Gene told me, and went off to fuss the ticket agent.

Dick and Bob Barry were laughing at something, the picture taking done with, and I went over to be introduced. The Governor moved off to reprove Gene Keiffer about something—Gene was the sort of man who, as well as in the position which, invites reproval, and we all took turns at it conscientiously.

Bob Barry and I shook hands.

"You've seen the shamrocks on the bumpers of this man's Fords?" Dick asked me. It's a pretty well-known trade mark, for Bob Barry, who lives in a town of five hundred called Danbury sells seven hundred cars and trucks a year to people and firms around the state. I thought he looked more like an Irish poet, out past midnight without his scarf on, than like a car salesman. "Look. Barry's got shamrocks all over his luggage, too."

Bob yawned and excused himself for it. "I got up at four

240

o'clock to go to mass," he said. "Here." He offered Dick and me each a Zippo cigarette lighter with the shamrock on it. "It goes on everything." You could tell which were Bob's suitcases all right. "Look."

He opened his mouth and pulled his right cheek away from the jaw. Dick peered in and so did I. And there it was, right on the outside of the gold cap, over the second biscuspid—a little green and gold shamrock nicely worked with dental tools.

Dick seemed shaken. The sudden sight of a tooth like that is not recommended as part of a hangover cure.

"That was always good for a free one in my drinking days," Bob said happily. His voice was soft, almost whispery, but very firm—the ultimate low-pressure voice. He yawned again.

It was a sleepy bunch. Even the Governor had had to stay up late and rise early, like any executive with last-minute things to take care of before leaving town. As I stored that penetrating observation—that the photographer, the advertising man, the car dealer, and the Governor were all sleepy—behind my fearless blue reporter's eyes, the final member of our group strode in, with the proud step, bright gaze and flawless complexion of an Olympic athlete: Ray Baltzell, M.D.

He was tall as Harold Hughes, slim as Gene Keiffer, young as Dick Swanson and as between him and Shamrock Bob Barry, I'd have to say the doctor had curlier hair. Our writer out of Iowa City, being the shortest, thinnest-haired man along and a touch overweight, serves no purpose of physical comparison.

Raymond Baltzell, M.D., was a recent college tennis champion from Pennsylvania, now in affluent general practice in northwest Iowa, who rode quarter horses, bought up farm land, invested in cattle, and felt just dandy that morning, not to mention every other morning. As we walked out to board our plane, shivering in the bitter December wind, the champ was chuckling at Dick Swanson, who'd elected to strap his

Nikons on over nothing more than a summer suit since we'd be traveling South. Dick had been a little overweening, back in the airport, about how much more lightly he was traveling than the rest of us.

Ten minutes after boarding, Dick was still shivering. The loading ramp wouldn't roll away properly, and the door couldn't be closed. Ray Baltzell, M.D., rising from his seat beside Gene Keiffer to put his hat on the rack—one of those gay, almost brimless little felt numbers—said:

"Sure glad I'm not all weighed down with a heavy coat this morning," and pulled his handsome tweed snugger.

"Say miss," Bob Barry, also with topcoat on, sitting across the aisle from Dick and me, flagged the stewardess to plead for the afflicted. He indicated Dick. "Couldn't we have a blanket and a hot water bottle for the young man here?"

Dick grinned, mostly at the stewardess, said it warmed his heart just to look at Ray Baltzell's beautiful hat, and turned to stow his bulky film bag under the seat in front of us. It was my turn; I was carrying a rather awkward handful, too, a shapeless musette bag.

"What in the world have you got in there, Vance?" Governor Hughes asked. "All your pencils?"

We kept it going—needling one another as a means of getting acquainted—for a cold quarter of an hour. Finally the ramp was towed away, but nobody had got to the Governor and nobody did until we arrived in Chicago, where it turned out that the room in which we'd planned to wait for our next plane was locked. This was the United Airlines V.I.P. lounge, a kind of facility many airlines maintain at major terminals so that officials and celebrities may wait in private comfort. But the door, which we tried about eight fifteen, bore a sign which read *Open 9 A.M. to 6 P.M.*

"You see, Governor," Dick and I explained respectfully, in

242

our character as world travelers, "no very important person travels before nine in the morning."

The routing from Chicago to Yucatan, which Gene Keiffer had worked out with a travel agency, was masterful. We were flown nonstop to Tampa, Florida. There we waited half an hour, and were flown nonstop to Miami. We waited in Miami all afternoon, almost four hours. Then we were flown, absolutely nonstop, back to Tampa again.

I think we spent another hour on our second visit to the Tampa airport, before we finally boarded a plane that took us off across the Gulf of Mexico to Merida, for arrival after dark. It was Bob Barry, who you'll recall had gotten up at 4 A.M. to be sure of not missing the 7:10 A.M. departure from Des Moines, who most firmly expressed our admiration to Gene for the scheduling. Ray Baltzell had a word or two to add. Dick and I, free riders on the *Post* expense account, kept quiet about it. The Governor was patient, but beginning to be a little withdrawn.

6

Yucatan is a peninsula, but it is also the name of one of two Mexican states on the peninsula—the other is Campeche. There is a third political unit, a territory called Quintana Roo, to which we'd continue flying, changing to chartered bush planes, in the morning.

The night of our arrival, though, there was a dinner for the Governors of Yucatan and Iowa at the home of the American Consul. At the dinner, sitting at a small table with some local sportsmen, I picked up sobering information: this was clearly the wrong season for a big game hunt. There were thousands of ducks now in the coastal marshes, and sailfish running close to shore, but out in the jungle in December it was wet. The men I talked to said in Spanish, and one repeated in English in case I hadn't understood, that jungle animals would be very widely scattered. The time for hunting jaguars was in March and April, dry weather, when water holes were scarce, game was concentrated around them, and the trails leading to them could be staked out.

The next morning we were gathered right about dawn, and long before the hotel dining room opened, around a man I'll call Luis, chief of a firm I'll rename Yucatan Big Game, Inc.—I make these changes because it was hardly his fault we'd come in the wrong season.

On the other hand, it had certainly been Luis who'd directed we be got up so early, though he knew the weather report from the jungle wasn't likely to vary much from day to day: *Heavy morning fog concealing landing strip. No incoming flights possible until fog clears, probably around 11 A.M.*

I suppose he'd hoped today would be an exception; Luis was counting on unlikely exceptions more than any of us realized yet.

We went on into the hotel dining room to watch the sun come up and wait for coffee, and I had a chance to tell the others about the ducks, the sailfish and the season. But it was raw information of course, rumor even, and the Governor wasn't much disposed towards a change in quarry. Big, spotted cats were on his mind, and their pursuit was what had been arranged for; he preferred to trust our hosts, and their professional, Luis.

I don't know, by the way, what was on my mind—not cats, obviously, so much as the big, brown-eyed man. Still, I remembered that only fitfully during the trip. I guess I assumed that a jaguar would be killed, or at least assaulted, and then my story would write itself. It would be hard to say what I thought I was doing while waiting for that to happen; free-loading my writer's subconscious, I guess. Bird-watching. Showing off my Spanish.

for Ophelia

Anyway, I should at least focus on that morning we spent waiting for word that the fog had cleared, because it was one of just three times we were all six together, relaxed and in some kind of communication.

I have a note that the talk turned to the nature of some of the marginal Mafia activity around Des Moines, and that it was agreed that there was enough of it so that Harold Hughes could not unreservedly share Dick Swanson's admiration for the Italian contribution to American culture. Organized crime the Governor seemed to find not so much fearsome as disgusting. His feeling about disorganized crime was quite different.

"There are an awful lot of men in prison," he said, "who differ from the rest of us, as we were at some time in our lives, only in getting caught."

It was suggested that for these perhaps some time in prison was a good corrective. Governor Hughes shook his head.

"That kind of man," he said, "may have all the correction he'll ever need the minute he hears that prison gate shut behind him. Of course, there's another kind." He grinned, and turned to Bob Barry. "You know that framed drawing I have, by a prisoner, on my office wall?"

"Yes. He's pretty good," Bob said.

"When I went to Anamosa, I asked to meet the artist. We had a talk, and I asked him what he did.

" 'I'm a burglar, Governor,' he said.

" 'No. I mean what's your profession?'

" 'I told you, Governor. I'm a burglar.'

" 'How many sentences have you served?' I asked him.

" 'This is my third.'

" 'Well, then,' I said. 'You must not be a very damn good burglar.' "

The talk turned to welfare matters, to disturbed children. I was conscientiously trying to listen carefully and remember. Bob

245

Barry, an observant man in his soft-spoken way, noticed and said to me, aside: "He's always been that way. He can't help getting involved in other people's problems." But I didn't know how far back the car dealer's *always* went.

7

It was hot by the time we got to the Merida airport where two planes were ready, a Piper Aztec and a Cessna 182, planes as familiar to a midwest political campaigner as car models to the rest of us. The Governor looked at Dick, who'd been a professional light plane pilot before he learned how to use a camera, and they both shook their heads. Fine little airplanes, but not enough to fly nine of us—six hunters, two pilots, and Luis the big game man—along with all our luggage and equipment. The argument that followed didn't take long; Harold Hughes spoke one declarative sentence at half-volume, Gene Keiffer looked at Luis whose show it now was, and a third plane was wheeled out for the luggage.

Bob Barry, Dr. Baltzell and Luis got into the Cessna.

Gene, Dick, the Governor and I boarded the Aztec, which had two engines and would get there faster.

Anyway, it would have if it had started. We watched our friends in the Cessna taxi out to wait for us on the runway; our battery was dead.

Gene said it was just as well, because Governor Torres Mesias of Yucatan wanted to see us off, but hadn't arrived yet. I can report that he did arrive eventually. We were still there. A battery was taken out of some other plane, and checked, and charged, and installed in our Aztec, and Señor Torres Mesias spent a good deal more time smiling and chatting than he may have planned on.

As we finally rolled off down the runway, a very small thing happened which reminded me of what Bob Barry had said about Harold Hughes's involuntary concern for people. The pilot should have, but it was Governor Hughes who turned his head, worked his oversized shoulders around in the cramped space of the forward bucket seat, to look first at me, then at Dick and Gene, wordlessly—just checking to make sure our seat belts were fastened.

8

At length we flew off, over the hemp plantations, over the lovely Mayan ruins of Uxmal, and on for an hour, south-southeast. I was excited. I'd spent a lot of time in Mexico, but never been in Mayan country before. The plantations grew fewer, disappeared. Now it was rain forest down there, green and unvaried like a still sea. Gray spars stood up here and there over the rest, the tops of dead mahogany and sapodilla trees.

Mahogany was the reason for there being an air strip, for which we were headed, in the jungles of Quintana Roo. The sapodilla, Gene told me, was once important, too; its sap made chicle for chewing gum.

"But the gum companies use synthetics now," he said, and, after a while: "Look. We're here."

The plane went low over a narrow, rectangular opening in the trees, and the pilot signaled his intention to land. Below a man and a boy appeared, small figures driving smaller ones, pigs and goats, off the runway.

Gene, professionally worried about the economy of Yucatan, kept telling me about chewing gum from the single seat in the rear: "The chicle camps are abandoned now. We'll be staying in what used to be the headquarters for one."

Jeep trucks met us at the airstrip to drive us to the former headquarters.

"Camp Spearmint," I said to Dick.

"How about the Indian name? Camp Chewyerliddul Troublesaway."

It was made up of a three-room stucco building on a cleared knoll in the jungle, with big wooden doors and no windows, and some outbuildings. Two of the rooms in the main house were furnished with canvas cots; the third and largest served as dining room and kitchen. There was a shed-roofed courtyard off the kitchen where Luis, the guides and the cook would sleep.

Luis, ordering his men about, seemed fretful; he had a bad cold. Gene Keiffer, on the other hand, now that he could pass on the responsibility for the trip's success to the professional hunters was getting light-hearted.

"I rather we stay in different camp, near airstrip," Luis said.

"This is fine," Gene told him. "The Governor likes it."

"More game near airstrip. Night before last, the boys see big jaguar and plenty deer. But every day still it rains. Truck can't get through."

I'd assumed we'd be hunting on foot, but I supposed the trucks were necessary to get us away from habitation.

"We'd like to sight in our rifles," Governor Hughes said. "Can we do it here, near camp?"

"Anyw'ere."

"Won't it scare the game away?" Ray Baltzell asked.

"Jaguar travel long way every night, forty–fifty kilometer this time of year. I wish you come in April."

"Now is the only time Governor Hughes could come," Gene said.

"Oh, you'll hunt tonight," Luis said. "Oh yes. I'm feeling bad, but the boys will take you. You want to hunt tonight, sir?"

"I came to play," said Governor Hughes.

248

His rifle was a presentation grade Weatherby, a gift from his military staff—men commissioned honorarily in the Iowa Militia, in return, I gathered, for political service or large campaign contributions. The Weatherby was a beautiful piece of hardware, and I noticed that the Governor and I had a poor boy's love of good equipment in common. I was fascinated by his gun; he admired a pair of snake-proof boots I'd had custom-made by Gokey's for the trip.

Ray Baltzell had a Weatherby similar to the Governor's, but a little less fancy, and there was a 30–30 carbine borrowed from one of the guides.

However, the sighting-in was ceremonial, even a little wistful. We'd been told before we left Iowa that the hunting would be mostly by shotgun, loaded with 4–0 buckshot.

"You can see how short the ranges are," the Governor said, pointing to a tangle of laced-branch underbrush and tree trunks along the road. "It's like that, with a few small clearings."

"Do they actually hunt from the trucks?" I asked.

"That's what I wanted to know last year. Well, you see what it's like. How well could you go in there on foot?"

We walked over to the edge of the road, and peered into the brush. Even a low-built creature on four legs, I had to concede, would move slowly through that.

"It seems to me," the Governor said, "we'll just have to hunt the way they show us, won't we?"

He made an adjustment on his scope, shouldered his rifle, and began to shoot, offhand. He was a superb shot. I moved closer, admiring the steadiness of the big hands on grip and forearm, my eye wanting to squint in empathy as he lined up.

"Vance, baby," Dick Swanson said. "Either open your eye, or get out of the picture."

9

At about four thirty that afternoon, Governor Hughes and I were sitting with shotguns on our laps on a plank which went crosswise above the bed of a pick-up truck, so that our knees were at the level of the cab. Dick with his cameras, and Mario, our guide, stood behind us. Dr. Baltzell was waiting in another truck for Bob Barry. Bob was with us, conducting a *bon voyage* ceremony. Americans set peculiar store by their favorite mass-produced candies, and Bob's were a kind of licorice drop called Black Crows. I'm an O'Henry man myself, and hadn't seen one of those green-and-yellow, candy-bar-sized boxes since boyhood.

"Come on," the car dealer passed us each a box of Black Crows. "Anybody want two? I've got a whole case, now come on. Take them, Dick. You may be out a long time."

Carefree Gene Keiffer remarked that he wasn't much of a hunter, but since there was a third guide, he'd go off with him in the jeep. With that the vehicles started off fast in three directions. Late afternoon and early morning are the times for game in the jungle just as elsewhere.

There were doves flying as we went along a wide dirt road, swaying at twenty miles an hour on our perch above and behind the cab. There were swift wild pigeons. A flock of parakeets went parallel over the top of the jungle brush which grew about thirty feet high on each side.

"What's the very noisy bird?" the Governor asked, hanging on for a curve.

"A kind of tropical jay," I told him. I'd seen them in the bush around Tehuantepec, on the Mexican west coast. "I think it's a kind called magpie-jays."

"That's what they sound like all right. See the little clearing? Take the ones on your side as we pass."

for Ophelia

The clearings were places where the mahogany had been re-planted, shading out other vegetation.

"Do we really just stop the truck and shoot if we see something?" I kept asking the same question. I really couldn't believe this was our method. It was precarious where we sat, and the guns which we'd been instructed to carry loaded worried us both.

"Well, don't shoot before the truck stops anyway." He smiled then, and said to reassure us both, "There must be some place they have in mind taking us."

Suddenly I cried: "Look. Those are toucans." I'd never imagined seeing one wild, in flight—but there they went in the late afternoon sun, unmistakable, carrying the huge beaks in front of them, with more ease than I'd ever have guessed. *Picacanoa, mon viejo*—old canoe-nose. Now in the oblique light their colors didn't show much. "Governor," I said, full of information like a scoutmaster on a nature walk. "Once in Nicaragua, I held a tame toucan. That big bill is light and thin as paper."

Governor Hughes smiled sympathetically, watching me hang on, hearing more in my voice I guess than information. If we'd been more comfortable and safer, I might have tried to tell him about a patio at the hotel in Managua where I stroked a toucan waiting for a friend who was a revolutionary and who never came. There was a slim, deracinated black girl there, from the hot, neglected Nicaraguan east, who could sing in English but couldn't speak it, having learned her songs syllable by syllable from Ella Fitzgerald records, played on a wind-up phonograph in a coastal bar . . . my gun, as we hit a bump, banged against the top of the cab, and the driver stopped so fast we nearly pitched off the plank.

"Where?" cried Mario the guide. Governor Hughes's gun went halfway to his shoulder and Dick's camera out in front of his face.

251

"Hell," I had to say. "I'm sorry." A tap on the cab roof was the standard signal to stop. Embarrassed, I rapped three times, the signal for go ahead; two taps would have had the driver backing up.

We went down a hill. The road was fairly well graded here, and at the bottom beside it were four or five huts with distinctively Mayan-looking people—wide foreheads and drooping noses—by them, cooking on the traditional tile and coals.

"Barbecue time in the suburbs," Dick cried.

"Mahogany charcoal," I said. "It's in this year." And we started to climb, up a very long hill.

Gradually, as we went up, I could stop hanging on. We were losing speed. Forty feet short of the summit we stopped altogether, and the laboring engine stalled. We coasted back down again as far as the huts, tried the hill again, reached the same place and stalled.

"It's not really that steep," Dick said.

"Must be the fuel pump," said Governor Hughes. We drifted back, tried the run a third time and didn't get quite as far as we had the first two.

"Tell him to turn around and try backing over," Dick said to me, our interpreter for lack of a better. But Mario the guide, who knew some English, had understood, and told me he could fix the pump.

"Let him try." The Governor took charge. "We wouldn't want to be any farther away than this and have it fail altogether."

It was getting dark. The first of our prime hunting times would be over soon. We got down from the truck. Dick had an idea for a picture, and the Governor patiently climbed back up again to accomodate it.

I watched Mario raise the hood, and felt less patient. The jungle on both sides of the road, and the dusk excited me. I wanted to be away from the vehicle and the voices.

"Let's walk on," I said. "Let the truck overtake us. If it doesn't come by dark, we can just turn and come back to it."

"I want to try the Doc on this," Governor Hughes said. He had brought along a walkie-talkie. "If he's anywhere near camp, he might be able to get Luis to send out a replacement truck, and we could keep going."

"They're supposed to tune in and try to receive us every hour on the hour," Dick informed me. "It will be six in ten minutes. Now, stand by for an interlude of recorded music."

Some barefoot kibitzers had walked up now from the huts to offer suggestions to Mario and the driver as they worked. Four or five children had followed the men part way, and were standing silently staring at Dick, the Governor and me, doing nothing.

"I wonder if I could talk the kids into posing with the Governor?" I said, restless.

Harold Hughes, holding his shotgun, didn't comment at once. He looked over at the children, his eyes as brown as theirs. They wore rags, a couple of tiny girls, four or five years old, but no taller than three year olds back home. The others were boys, older but not much larger. I remembered Bob Barry's licorice drops, and got them out. If Governor Hughes would step over and offer them some?

"What about it, Gov?" Dick said. "Make a good picture."

Harold Hughes shook his head. "No," he said quietly, turning back toward the truck. "I wouldn't want that. You can give them the candy, if you want."

At first I thought, sure; he wants to avoid a cliché, sentimental photograph, but that didn't work. Cliché, sentimental photographs are one of the tools of his particular trade.

Then I had what felt like an insight, and while I couldn't very well check whether it was correct, thought I knew what the Governor felt when he looked over at the Mayan children—and what Dick couldn't see yet, though soon he would, I guessed, in

253

Vietnam. I thought Harold Hughes must see what haunts any man who has been a soldier in this awful century: the Arab children of Africa. The bombed out kids of Italy. Japan. Korea. The shoeshine boys and their tiny, ragamuffin sisters; the kid hustlers; the heartbreaking pests and tagalongs of long ago, corruptible in their rage to survive, courting even the small amount of heat and sugar in a stick of chewing gum.

Chewing gum for which, in some strange closing of the circle, the parents of these Mayan children, back in those war years, must have climbed and tapped the tall, straight, criss-crossed sapodilla trees.

Imagine coming a thousand miles to the jungle for sport, to find this: a gun in your hand, a broken-down jeep truck on a dirt road at dusk, and a companion urging candy on you to hand out to black-haired, ragged children.

CHA-CHA-LACA. CHA-CHA-LACA—there was an unbelievably loud burst of bird noise. The brush howled with it.

Roosting time. "Wild turkeys?" I shouted the question, above the noise. There is a beautiful, small wild turkey native to Yucatan.

"I don't know," Governor Hughes shouted back.

I trotted over to one of the kibitzers. *"Que es?"*

"Chachalaca," the man cried.

"Chachalaca," I translated for my friends.

"Is that a name or an imitation?" Dick yelled and, then, as the noise died away, Governor Hughes said:

"I remember from last year. They're considered a game bird, as a matter of fact."

We looked into the brush, but could see only shadows; it was quieting down, though every now and then a single bird would give that clattering call.

"Quiet, birds. We've got to try the radio," Dick said. It was just six.

"Hunter One to Hunter Two." The Governor spoke into the transmitter. "Hunter One to Hunter Two. Come in, Doc."

He held the set to his ear.

"Any answer?" Dick asked.

Governor Hughes shook his head. "Hunter One to Hunter Two. Come in, Doc." He listened and shook his head again. "These things should carry ten miles, anyway . . . wait." He listened. "Someone's receiving us."

"The doctor?"

"No. I may be on an army band."

"We're near the Guatemalan border," Dick observed.

"Harold Hughes to Ray Baltzell. Come in, Doc."

"We can't be far from where they trained for the Bay of Pigs," I said.

"Someone's on here," the Governor said. "But it isn't Ray."

"Careful," said Dick. "They might invade."

"Tell them we're sending air cover this time," I suggested.

"Hunter One to Hunter Two . . ." He listened. "My God, you'll never believe this."

"Is it in Spanish?"

"Aviation band, I'll bet," Dick said.

The Governor grinned. "I'm being received all right," he said. "My party can't quite make me out, but she just explained, 'I'm at the Holiday Inn, but I'm going for groceries now.' "

We couldn't get Dr. Baltzell and Bob Barry, ten or fifteen miles away, but we were in what seemed to be taken for ship-to-shore conversation, hundreds of miles away across the Gulf, probably, off Louisiana or Florida.

"Sky King to Penny," said the Governor. "Damn it, Come in, Penny."

255

10

Our truck hobbled back to camp, where we waited for another to be got ready, Dick and I drinking beer and the Governor coffee. It was quite dark; I realized I was very tired, and, rather hoping more truck hunting wouldn't be possible after all said: "Maybe we'll get caught up on sleep tonight. Wouldn't be bad."

Governor Hughes said flatly: "We're not going to get caught up on sleep this trip," and the lights went out. Luis's generator had failed. "You know what, Dick and Vance," said the bass voice reflectively in the dark, "I think one of us is a jinx."

After a time, by candlelight, Luis appeared to croak in his failing voice that the next truck was ready: "You want to hunt tonight some more? In the morning, I get a shot for my cold. I can take you myself."

"If Mario's ready," said the Governor, rising and picking up his gun. "I came to play."

This time we were directed to wear headlamps; again we sat on a raised plank but now the truck went without lights, and we shined the lamps up into trees and down into bushes. We saw nothing but owls' eyes, and got nothing but cold. Around midnight, after two uncomfortable hours, we turned back and found the rest of the party at camp when we arrived.

Bob Barry and Ray Baltzell had done some shooting—long-range, at wild turkeys, at dusk. Missing. I was sorry. I was eager to see a wild turkey. Not long afterward, they'd shot at a tapir —a creature I had seen before, but never very close. A tapir is a thick-skinned ungulate, about three feet tall, six hundred to eight hundred pounds with coarse, sparse hair—about the closest evolution came in our part of the world to giving us a rhinocerous, and quite inoffensive.

The first hunter to bring game into camp, anyway, was asleep already—Gene Keiffer, the indoorsman. With his burden of care lifted, he'd shot a chachalaca on the wing from the moving jeep, his guide was telling Mario with admiration, and had mowed down an enormous pheasant.

But there are no pheasants in Yucatan, and my curiosity about what Gene had shot was frustrated in the morning—the cook had dressed the bird already. I'd been first up, best-rested I suppose, and while the others were dressing I did get to look at Gene's chachalaca. It was a dingy, olivaceous bird with a green tail, not much larger than a pigeon. I asked the cook if I might clean it, which seemed to be about as peculiar a request as he'd ever had; I wanted to see if I could figure out how it made so much racket. It took no figuring—do you know that two- or three-inch hollow tube of hard tissue in the throat of a chicken, with which it clucks? There's a tube like that in the chachalaca's throat, too, but it goes on and on, for eight or nine inches, from the throat all along the breast bone to the vent.

Then I was called and we were rushed through breakfast— fried venison steaks and tortillas—and into the trucks again.

We started off talking about the tapir. Mario wanted to know if we'd like to try for it.

"Do they eat them?" Governor Hughes asked. I relayed the question and translated the answer.

"No. He says low-class coastal savages eat them over in Belize. Apparently it's poor meat."

"Is a tapir any sort of trophy?"

I answered that one on my own, saying they were slow, and harmless and kind of silly looking.

"I wouldn't want to shoot anything like that," said Governor Hughes.

"That's a relief to us slow, harmless silly-looking types," said Dick. This morning's road was narrow and full of stones, and just then Mario, who was riding the truck's running board, slapped

257

three times quickly on the side of the cab. The driver gunned the motor and we grabbed handholds—I nearly lost my gun doing it. I looked forward as soon as I recovered.

We were speeding towards four big, blue-black birds on the road, tall as geese. We came within range, and the truck made a skidding stop. I looked for a fast way down, and Mario yelled, "Shoot!" I got excited, and shot from my perch, at one rising on my side of the road, by then about fifteen feet off the ground. He was just above eye level and gaining speed, about twenty-five yards out, and I made what should have been a routine shot poorly, behind him. The bird flew off over the brush.

Harold Hughes dropped his onto the road. It struggled up, mortally hit, and began a staggering run, but before the Governor could shoot again Mario had jumped off the running board and was chasing it down on foot. In a moment he had it and came running back, the bird expiring in his hands.

It was more a moment of embarrassment than triumph for us —I'd missed, and it had been hardly more than a potshot for the Governor—but Mario seemed jubilant. He was quite an agreeable fellow, around thirty, with long hair and a mustache, and very much hoped we were having a good time.

"Faisan," he cried proudly, holding up the bird. "Faisan real de Yucatan."

We got down and I reached for my bird book. The royal pheasant of Yucatan was, of all things I never expected to hold in my hand, a Great Curassow, a bird three times the size of a ringneck pheasant with a yellow knob above the beak and a crest of feathers like a delicate black fan rising from his head.

I had a little bird hunter's adrenalin up by then, and proposed going into the bush to try to flush the other curassows, for they hadn't flown far. Mario insisted that it wasn't possible, and we went on. The only other incident of the long morning was a stop to look at tapir tracks near a water hole, where Governor

for Ophelia

Hughes found a paw print, like a house cat's but bigger than a man's fist. Mario said that jaguar would go 150 pounds.

Governor Hughes seemed no more eager to leave that area than I'd been to leave the place where great curassows flew, but somehow we were herded back onto our precarious plank, bumped here and there some more along other roads, and then back to camp for lunch.

II

Luis, the boss hunter, a tall, thin, fretful man with steel-rimmed glasses and grey hair, felt awful. Looking for his cold medicine during the night, he'd picked up a bottle of linament instead, drunk some and burned his throat.

The worse things seemed to go for Luis, the better they went for Gene Keiffer.

"I got a wild turkey this morning," he said, casually. "Sorry, Vance. I'm afraid they've plucked it and cooked it already. We're having it for lunch."

Ray Baltzell and Bob Barry had sighted their tapir again, and launched more buckshot at it. Though the animal probably wasn't being injured seriously our group took the news a little glumly except for Mario who entertained at luncheon with an indignant-tapir dance.

"He's going to look for jaguar," Mario sang, waltzing and reeling towards the jungle. "He's going to say Mister Jaguar, if those guys don't stop shooting me all the time, you will eat me *por favor?*"

I couldn't laugh. I watched the Governor, and it seemed to me his smile was pained and polite; his only comment was that he thought he'd better stretch out for a while. His back was giving him a little trouble. We'd reached the point, I think, where each of us wondered how many of the others shared the same growing intolerance for our situation.

We must all have read or heard of other ways of hunting jaguars—they were stalked. Still-hunted. Trailed with dogs and driven. There must be particular techniques for going after each kind of jungle game—not just jaguar but ocelot, agouti, peccary, deer, turkey, even great curassows and chachalacas. On African safaris, unless the books and movies lied, each game species was approached in a special and appropriate way. Even hunting at home, after all, there were specialized dogs, loads, approaches, ways of using terrain and adapting to habitat—things of which we tried to learn to make use, changing as we went from quail to snipe to ducks to geese to doves to rabbits to squirrels to deer and bear.

What we were doing here was absurd: trying to jacklight whatever could be mesmerized at the edge of the road at night, or overtake it through mechanical speed in the daytime. It seemed to me it had about as much relationship to hunting as conducting a business might have to playing slot machines, and somewhat less to recommend it as sport.

I was only the reporter on the trip, not the prime customer, but I tried talking some of this over in Spanish with Luis and the guides, as tactfully as I could. They shrugged me off. It was the wrong season to try anything else. There was a chance what we were doing would work. Mostly they were puzzled by me, and seemed to doubt I represented general opinion; their past North American clients had been most pleased to hunt this way. I agreed that I was not a spokesman.

12

During the slack part of the afternoon, while the others dozed, I got at least a rudimentary idea of how things move in the jungle without tracks to follow. There was a dry watercourse, full of small stones and sand, leading from camp to a waterhole about a quarter mile away. We were staying too near for it to attract game, so I was doing nothing but experimenting, going along it, which was relatively easy. I could see that there were smaller, tributary watercourses branching out, and it seemed to me too that the vegetation wasn't nearly as dense once one was away from the edges of roads and clearings. Even where it was, a low-built jungle mammal, running flattened down, could use the watercourses effectively between dense places. I sat by the water-hole a while and watched a bird I have never been able to identify securely; it may have been one of the hermit humming-birds—big for a hummer, and brown rather than highly colored, with a long, curved bill.

13

When I got back to camp, Dick took me aside to point out that I'd been pretty well monopolizing the hunting-seat beside the Governor, excluding Bob Barry, the old friend who'd come along in the role of chief companion.

"Can't argue with that," I said. "Thought I ought to be there when the jaguar sprang . . ."

"You think we're going to see a jaguar?"

"Not unless there's a deaf one around," I said. "Those damn trucks all roar like mufflers were against the law."

So I went off with Ray Baltzell that afternoon, and as a result had my best moment of the trip, while Harold Hughes was having his worst.

What went right for the doctor and me was simply that we got quite far from camp by suppertime (wild turkey sandwiches and Black Crow licorice drops) and decided to keep going towards the airstrip, near where the guides said there was a different sort of terrain. About one A.M., after having done headlamp duty for forty miles, we asked the guide if we couldn't sleep where we were so as to wake there in the morning.

He agreed. We turned off onto a track which led away from the main lumber road, and not far down it found some abandoned lean-tos under which we spread our hunting jackets and slept.

We woke at dawn, stiff, the coffee cold in the thermos, no water, Black Crows for breakfast—and absolutely enchanted. The jungle was misty, still and beautiful. There was a haunting, melodic whistling, tinamou calling, rain-forest relatives of birds I'd hunted passionately for a season once in Uruguay.

"Look at these plants," Ray said. "Can they be philodendrons?" And they were, the same familiar, big-leafed houseplant, but growing the size of small trees, and with wild orchids hanging from the more conventional branches above them.

We walked off quietly, without waking our guide and driver, down the track and I saw them at last—just out of shotgun range, but close enough to be completely vivid, about a dozen of the ocellated wild turkeys of Yucatan.

There they went, taking wing before we reached them, sailing up and over the philodendrons and the orchids. They were smaller than North American wild turkeys and far more beautifully marked, with great, fanlike tails, the tips metallic bronze and carrying blue eye-spot markings like those on peacocks' tails. They were bright in the mist, then, in an instant, lost in it, so that they rose only to vanish, bird after bird, over the heavy, dripping leaves. It is a sight which does not leave me, and was, it seemed, exactly what I had come so far to see.

Then the truck horn blew.

"Do they think we're lost?" I asked.

"I wish we were," said Ray.

Later that morning they took us to the savannah, where the whole hunt would have taken place had weather permitted. I wished the Governor could at least have seen it, a vast, flat region of tall grass and marshland, rimmed by jungle-covered hills, extending for miles. It was a landscape of preconception: big game country. Jaguar country? I shall never know, but it was like an African movie, fit for zebra herds and stalking lions, and forty yards into it the truck went down to its axles in mud.

We took a walk there, got a chance to move our legs, while the guide and driver worked with jacks and winch to get their truck out. We got almost a mile away, at a guess, to the opposite edge, and naturally did exactly what we'd been warned not to do —went into some tall green, grassy stuff, twice my height, at the edge, to get to a mysterious-looking clearing where jungle and savannah met. We were still too close, I'm certain, to the noise and sight of the truck for there to have been anything wild in the clearing, but it was fun walking carefully into it, with Ray covering me a step behind.

We found it empty, steamy with evaporating fog, and we turned and went back to the truck.

But we loved the place, loved the whole morning away from camp. Driving back, Ray and I got into a fine, loud, silly argument: "I could graze five thousand head of cattle in that savannah," he yelled, starting it.

"Sure you could," I shouted back. "And you could build a highway through it, couldn't you? Four lanes with green and white goddamn signs, 'Jaguar Crossing'."

"Make it productive for these people, wouldn't it? Give them a better life. What's wrong with that?"

"I told you, I'm for it. Clear away that brush. Get rid of all the toucans and turkeys cluttering up the air around here."

"There's plenty of space. Why shouldn't it generate enough income to give the people elementary sanitation and clothing and school for their kids?"

"Sure. Then they could turn out to be doctors and professors, just like you and me. Where's the Holiday Inn go, Ray? How about the supermarket?"

My ironies were crude, and not too reasonable, but then of course, Ray hadn't heard how close the radio had brought those voices, just last night, from the power-boat set off Florida.

14

First Dick told me, then Bob Barry, and eventually Harold Hughes, what had happened while we were away.

They'd been hustled through the routine breakdown of one vehicle and change to another, and then gone off past the waterhole where we'd seen the jaguar track, feeling somewhat hopeful.

It was the roughest ride yet, with branches threatening to sweep them off the truck and raking them with thorns, grass sometimes up to roof level. And eventually, plodding and bumping through the darkness brought them to a clearing, where bright eyes reflected back from the Governor's head-lamp.

The eyes seemed big and green and wide-apart to the nerved up men, and Mario whispered ecstatically, *'Jaguar! Jaguar! SHOOT!'*

Accurately, and without hesitation, Governor Hughes shot once. Before he could shoot again, Mario leapt down from the truck, the driver cutting the headlights on, and flailed around in the brush, carbine in one hand, flashlight in the other, and then cried: "You missed."

"I did like hell," said the Governor, knowing how short the range was and how wide the buckshot pattern.

And then Mario, taking another step, cried, delighted: "Oh here. Look here, sir. You killed a deer."

There was a one-word reply to that, which I won't repeat. Harold Hughes was a truck driver once, and it's the word, for that matter, which most of us use by now to express total disgust.

"We didn't even need it for camp food," he told me later. "There's been wonderful venison around, but hell, we haven't often had time to eat it, the way they've been putting us on and off of trucks. All I saw was eyes. I was told it was a cat, so I shot. It was a doe, a little tiny jungle doe, with a fawn at her side. And I realized too late that if the boy'd really thought there was any chance it was a jaguar, he'd never have jumped off the truck so carelessly, towards where it might have been lying wounded."

But he'd said none of that at the time, only allowed himself to be driven back to camp in silence, the orphaned fawn captured and lying on its side in the truck bed beside him.

"Get Luis," he said, when they arrived. It was long after midnight.

"Oh no, sir," Mario had said. "Please. He have such a cold."

"Wake him up."

It would be nonsense for me to say that the Governor had come around to my way of thinking about hunting methods, for he was too much the more experienced hunter to have disagreed, even initially. But he was fairer-minded and more patient than I, and he was a guest. He had come to play, and been willing to have them teach him the game—until it turned out that the rules permitted things like jacklighting nursing does.

Luis appeared, Gene Keiffer was got up, and Harold Hughes

put it very plainly. We were to stop riding around in trucks, shooting off guns indiscriminately like idiot kids. If it was not possible for us to hunt like hunters, Luis was to get on the radio right now and order planes to take us out in the morning.

"I wonder how far away Ray and Vance are, if the planes are coming," Gene was reported to have said, his first fret in several days.

"Oh, you'll hunt, sir," Luis said. "Oh yes, sir. You'll hunt."

15

When Ray and I got in from our excursion about noon, they told us Luis had sent the boys out early to build tree stands.

"We're spending the night in one, Vance," the Governor said. "You'd better get some sleep."

They woke me about 4 P.M. A truck was ready to take us to the stake-out. What was proposed hadn't sounded like the sort of nightlife Gene Keiffer enjoyed. Bob Barry's physical state was such that he decided he'd have to limit his participation to lining us up and making certain each of us had a regulation supply of Black Crows for the mission.

Dick was discovered to have been secreting Black Crows unopened in a camera bag, and was just about drummed out of the corps for it.

We took off pretty cheerfully, talking for some reason about one of Iowa's Republican luminaries. Dick said the man was a real wizard at including himself in photographs, and I guess the way things work requires that I change his name in order to quote Senator Hughes's response directly: "Sam X. is the most superficial man I ever met. I doubt if he's ever had one honest emotion in his life."

We rode along, chatting and bumping for an hour or so; the way was not a road, but a particularly wide watercourse, dried out now in the afternoon, with some really remarkable bumps.

"I can't believe we're going so far," Dick said. "They're making it look good."

"I think we're circling camp," I suggested. "Around and around. It's really sixty yards over that way."

"That's so Luis won't have to lead the jaguar too far."

"Doesn't want to tire the poor old cat out," Ray said.

"Oh, I think they've probably got it tied up out here already."

"The cook's pouring milk in his dish, coaxing him to roar."

"If there's a jaguar tied up," Governor Hughes said, "I think we can assume Sam X. is with him, shaking his paw and waiting for Dick to arrive with his camera."

In the second hour we went downgrade, and the watercourse got rougher and rougher. We came to a log; the jeep had been able to go around it, apparently, but there wasn't room for the wider truck. It stopped, Mario got down to roll the log over, the driver cut the engine, and the truck started to boil. Mario called out in Spanish for the driver to idle it.

"What did he say?" Governor Hughes asked me.

"He said to start the motor so it would stop boiling. But instead, Vittorio has got out and is arguing the point . . ."

"God, Vance. Will you stop translating?" said Governor Hughes.

To our relief, the truck did start again, and we moved on for another hour, to a place where the watercourse widened at a curve.

A sack of bait, deer entrails, smelly already in the warm evening, hung low from a tree at one side. Across from the bait, up about thirty feet, the guides had made the first of our two stands; the other was about a hundred yards farther down.

Each was supported by three slim trees, three or four inches in diameter, with a pole about the same size for a fourth leg. There was a platform made of smaller branches, lashed together into a flat surface about six feet across by four feet wide. Rails were provided on three sides; the front, facing the bait, was open, except for a single lateral stick tied across to keep the whole thing in tension. Short logs had been tied to one of the trees to serve as ladder rungs; Governor Hughes climbed up, and I handed up our guns, blankets, head lamps and a box with sandwiches in it, and climbed after him, the trees and pole swaying with our weight.

We found places for the gear, I unrolled my sleeping bag for us to sit on, and we fitted ourselves into the space as well as we could. It would have been cramped even if both men had been my size. It was about 7 P.M.

"Hey, Doc and Dick," the Governor called when we had figured a way of getting settled, and as the other two went off towards the second stand. "Remember, once the truck leaves, no talking. And at least one of you stay awake."

"No smoking," Ray Baltzell called back. Governor Hughes grinned.

"I'm going to have to smoke I guess," he said, and the long night began.

For the first part of it the moon was out, and there were sounds to hear and wonder at though nothing much to see. The ribbed seating provided by a platform of sticks, unnoticeable at first, became rather painful after a while. I knew the Governor had back problems, and knew it was harder on him than me.

We began to take turns standing up, so that the other could stretch out. I fit the platform pretty well. Harold Hughes overflowed it. About eleven, it was his turn to stand, and we agreed in whispers that I might try to sleep.

I'd have said sleep was impossible, but hypnotic stars and a soft wind countered the discomfort and the growing chill, and off I went. When I woke an hour later though, I wasn't chilly any longer; the Governor had covered me up.

I stood, a man with a wide-wale corduroy bottom, and invited him to take the rear of the platform. I calculated that he'd be safe from rolling out that way, and that his weight, since I'd be forward where the thin front rail was, ought to tilt us back enough to keep me from sliding out. I didn't think I'd have any trouble staying awake. The thought of falling thirty feet into the path of a possible jaguar was not sedative.

The moon had gone down. It was really black now. I listened, hearing various indecipherable night sounds, and feeling a little as if I were back in the crow's nest, on our blacked-out troopship, standing submarine watch on the way to war.

To punctuate that melancholy thought, Governor Hughes began to snore. I wondered if I was supposed to wake him, to stop the sound, but it seemed to me our first good chance to lure a cat had been by moonlight, and our next would come at dawn. Let the man sleep.

But by 3 A.M. we were both wide awake. We conferred in whispers. We tried whispering into the walkie-talkie, to ask if anything was happening at the other stand. No answer.

"Those guys are both asleep," the Governor muttered. "Hey, shall I roar into the microphone?" The guides claimed they could call jaguars with a mewing sound, made between lips pressed tight together—and why weren't there guides in a third tree stand, trying it? We practiced, anyway, into the microphone, broadcasting mews into the night.

Then it was my turn to sleep again, and I don't know how long I managed to do it before Governor Hughes squeezed my arm to wake me. I knew from the pressure of his grip that I was to be still.

There were many slight sounds in the predawn—insect murmurs, toad shrills, creeping, rustling—and gradually, out in front of us, the sounds seemed to solidify into something more substantial. For only a few seconds I felt certain of it, before it faded again into the general low-level noise—the padding, breathing, muttering of a large animal. We inched into shooting position, ready to shine our lights at the bait sack, and the sound was gone.

Then, ten very tense minutes later, we heard it again behind us, and on the other side, heard it for half a minute; then it stopped, and the cheery squeaks and shrills began again.

Neither of us doubted that a jaguar had come quite close, circled us, smelled or heard something that disturbed him and gone away.

The tension gone, I realized there wasn't any place I didn't ache. My shoulders were stiff, my legs were cramped, my arms were tired, and I hadn't urinated for eleven hours.

Dawn came. Birds woke. Dick called up on the walkie-talkie. "I'm coming up the watercourse," he said. "The thing you see may not look human, but it will not be a jaguar. Don't shoot."

"Hell, Dick," the Governor said, trying to find room to stretch. "After a night like that, I've got to shoot something."

We tossed down the sleeping bag and blankets and musettes, and he had room to rise, stand up straight and start working out kinks. It had been thirteen hours by now since we'd climbed up here; I think we both felt, without saying so, that we were a little over-age for this kind of thing, and were pleased with ourselves for having done it.

"Governor," I said, full of respect and affection, remembering his bad back and wondering how much worse than I he felt. "You're the only person in the world with whom I ever spent a night sitting in a tree."

He swallowed a bite of turkey sandwich, threw a licorice drop across the watercourse at the bait sack, and said: "If you ever need a recommendation as a tree-sitting companion, I'll be glad to furnish it."

The truck came for us, and we rode back to camp comparing insect bites—something, a kind of mite perhaps, had been after us during the night, unfelt at the time. Dick, Ray and I had small eruptions on our wrists and arms; the Governor, clear winner of the mite-bite contest, had them on his legs, neck and chest as well. Bob Barry, who'd come along to pick us up, said he was sure they'd stop itching and disappear in a month or six weeks; turned out to be a pretty accurate prognosis.

That was all the climax our hunt had in Yucatan. We rode back to camp, slept a bit, and were all sitting down together for once for a meal in midafternoon. Ray Baltzell and I got into another of our loud, foolish arguments, this one about Medicare. Then, just for the hell of it I guess, the Governor and I got into it about Vietnam. That was 1965, you recall; he was still a friend and supporter of Lyndon Johnson's, and like many other public men who have worked passionately in the peace movement since— he has in fact risked his career for it—he'd at that time been sold the domino theory. In fact, he'd suggested and helped organize that Governors' tour of Southeast Asia during which his neighbor, George Romney of Michigan, later confessed to having been "brainwashed" by the military. I have searched my memory of that conversation many times; I remember myself as having sounded more emotional than well informed, but outside of my own feeling of ineffectuality in debate, can find no foreshadowing at all of the years of American change and bitterness and division which were about to start. The break between Hughes and Johnson which I've mentioned was still a year away, but what may be more significant is that I don't recall myself as feeling that depth of moral conviction yet which breeds intolerance and animosity. I just thought the big guy was wrong.

We were, as a matter of fact, so relaxed as a group in our disagreements that at one point Harold Hughes simply and spontaneously burst into song, singing something or other, an old hymn if I'm not mistaken, about halfway through in his deep, true voice.

"I've really missed this on the trip," he interrupted himself to say. "Just sitting around talking. We've all gone flying off so much, in so many directions."

"Anyway," I said, "I wouldn't have missed the trip for anything."

"Wouldn't you?" Governor Hughes smiled. "I can think of a few things I'd have missed it for."

It was our last day in camp, and toward the end of it we did quite a lot of shooting for a change—lined up across a hillside, we tried pass-shots at wild pigeons, swift, gray, almost impossible to hit, though Governor Hughes dropped a couple. And Gene Keiffer got one, too.

When we loaded up to go back there was a final, almost inevitable, truck failure. While we waited for one of the guides to walk in, and bring back a replacement, the Governor said, more in tones of wonder than complaint: "You know, they've got five of these things. And every one of them has broken down at least once, with me in it."

"I guess we know who the jinx is now, Gov," said Dick Swanson, taking his picture.

16

We all felt close on the trip back to Iowa. We hadn't hit the beaches together, or done a hard job of work, but it seemed we'd been through something or other. I noted having a sense of a real bond between me and Ray Baltzell, for example, though we are pretty much one another's opposites, and a real sympathy for Gene Keiffer for whom the failure of the expedition might have business consequences. The chief uneasiness I felt, though, was on my own behalf; I knew I didn't have a story.

In a muted way, Quintana Roo kept happening: a man met us on the runway at Chicago, to drive us to the next airline—went around and around the huge airport buildings, unable to find the place he was supposed to let us out.

"Your name isn't Luis by any chance?" Governor Hughes asked him, softly.

And our luggage was lost.

We sat in the V.I.P. lounge, and it was there, as the passenger agent phoned frantically around the continent trying to locate our stuff (it came a day or two later), that Harold Hughes, almost as an act of will, finally gave the trip memorable emotional impact for us all. It was as if he was compelled to give us something, some result, outcome, catharsis—it would trivialize it to say that it was my story; it was more and less than that. It was the redemption of what would otherwise have been a lost week of discomfort and small absurdities; he did it just by talking, and it took a while.

Dick Swanson, I'd guess, was on yet another plane as we sat there, near the end of the long, long flight over the Pacific, about to reach the rendezvous with war all young men wonder about. Gene Keiffer must simply have been relieved that the trip he'd arranged was over, good or bad; it could have been worse. The young doctor was perhaps counting calves or babies born in his absence, or treating laminitis in his horses or referring his human cases to surgeons. I was fretful about the difficult writing which faced me. Only Bob Barry was concerned, I think, that what had started as a dream of high adventure for his old friend Harold Hughes was ending in disappointment. But the Governor couldn't let the rest of us disperse like that.

First there had to be an atmosphere, the intimacy of men encamped together in an evening after a day of great deeds. The foam padded modern furniture of the lounge had to feel like logs turned up to sit on, or canvas chairs; the thick carpet had to become clay floor, under a tent. The Serengeti was around us; the tundra; and we were half-exhausted, still exhilarated, and the man hanging up the phone was not reporting luggage traced to Alabama, but that the lions were skinned out, the black-maned one is of record size, gentlemen, you've earned your gin. Dick, Gene and I drank it.

Bob Barry said to the Governor, using an old nickname: "Try some orange juice and seven-up mixed, Packy." We learned that came from high school football, when Harold Hughes and his older brother were both All State, and opponents said they were like a couple of pachyderms in the line. Jess was Big Packy, Harold was Little Packy; the brothers were very close. Not long after Harold was drafted out of his freshman year at the University of Iowa, all the formal education he ever had, Jess was killed in an automobile accident.

There is a tattoo on the Governor's arm in blue, of the archiepiscopal cross—the one that's used on Christmas seals—and his brother's name.

Nineteen and married, the younger all-stater was overseas and had been in combat when he tattooed himself. "Three of us helped each other do it in Oran," he said. "We had a needle stuck into the eraser on a pencil, and we dipped the point in carbon from a flashlight battery.

"I was just out of the hospital. In Sicily, I'd been in a hole with my B.A.R. when the Germans broke through with tanks. My ammo carrier wanted to get up and run. I told him to stay down, but he couldn't.

"They literally cut him in two with machine gun bullets when he stood up beside me. The Germans took most of the outfit prisoner. They would have me if I'd had anything white to wave.

"That time in Oran was a big drunk, and a lot of troops wound up in the stockade. I remember waking up inside the barbed wire, and later that day they marched us past a court-martial board. Whenever it was an infantryman, the officer in charge would say: 'You're going right back to active duty, soldier, at two thirds pay. You'll probably be killed. Next man.'

"In the invasion of Italy, we were supposed to cut the coastal highway above the invasion point, and be relieved after twenty-four hours. We cut it all right. But we weren't relieved till seventeen days later. I was posted out on the flank, just before the relief came, on the side of a little draw. Most of the outfit were down in the draw, and what rations we had left were handed out from underneath a little bridge down there.

"I was on my way for rations one day when German mortars found us and the world exploded. I went down flat and found myself staring into the inside of a man's head. The whole top had just been cut off. I started to throw up and rolled away. On the other side a man was blowing bubbles of blood. I crawled over to see what I could do for him, but he was gone, too. A piece of shrapnel had come in through his back, and the point was sticking out his chest.

"You know, I was raised to believe it was wrong to kill, and I never stopped feeling that way. I fought like an animal does, during the war. Just to survive.

"When I got home I felt that if I wanted to drink myself to death, I'd earned the right to do it. Not that I was the only one . . ."

He mentioned a name Bob Barry recognized, and smiled at.

"He was forty when they drafted him. Forty-two or forty-three, doing all those things in combat; just about the age we are now. When he got home he was another that didn't do anything but drink, and people in town would laugh at him and get disgusted. I had fights about that. I figured if he wanted to get drunk and lie in the streets, those people ought to get blankets and pillows and make him comfortable."

"He got straightened out didn't he?" Bob Barry asked.

"Yes. He's a school janitor now. He got his belief in God back and he's been doing all right."

Now that was an astonishing thing for him to say, even a little upsetting, "He got his belief in God back," as matter-of-factly as if reporting that the man had got straightened out through coming into an inheritance, or earning a diploma.

That was the opening, and from there it flowed like water from an unexpected well. He chatted about what belief had meant to and done for him. He discussed Christ as an example he'd taken in trying to live his own life. He remembered for us terrible dreams, which went on for years after he'd beat alcohol, of being drunk again and absolutely helpless, and then of praying away the cold sweats in which he woke. He talked about his family, of having failed his children as a young man, and how there was still some anguish in knowing it, and therefore a source of resolution—it was, I suppose, not altogether unlike what one might hear in a revival tent from a saved sinner, but it wasn't said that way. It was told us in the manner of serious, somewhat important conversation. I heard no self-righteousness in it, and certainly no intent to proselytize.

Finally he talked about his career: "Politics is my ministry," he said, and I was reminded of F. Scott Fitzgerald's phrase, which fit both the writer and his great, magnetic character Dick Diver: *a spoiled priest.*

No, that was not my story, any more than it was something Dick could photograph, but it was curiously exciting —I haven't, by the way, tried to recreate as dialogue the Governor's language that evening, because I shall be able, in another page or two, to offer an accurate sample of Harold Hughes on religion, transcribed from a taped interview we made in 1971.

And in any case, for my oblique, writer's mind, the excitement was less in the words than in what he was doing—an important man was exposing his core to a group of curious friends and acquaintances, and that was as remarkable as that the core, in a contemporary whom I admired, should be religious.

To realize how remarkable it was, I had to realize how impossible it would have been for me, even after our week together, to do the equivalent—to gather the car dealer, the photographer, the doctor, the ad man and the politician around me and try to make them comprehend the center of my own life in aspiration towards art, another of those mysteries whose reality has to be accepted as an act of faith.

So I guess I had my jaguar, whether or not I knew what to do with him; he delivered himself to me. And to the others, of course. That may seem an odd way to put it, but as things have worked out for Harold Hughes in this strange country, in these strange days, his fascination with religion has been turned into a political liability.

Nor is fascination too secular a word, for religion is sometimes a recreational matter for Senator Hughes; it's what he likes to talk about, meditate about, read and chat with his wife about. A couple of times a week he joins other Senators, most of them Southern Democrats and considerably older and less free-wheeling, at a prayer breakfast. And shortly after he announced for the presidency in 1971, newspaper reports began to appear of his interest in spiritualism and contacts with various Christian mediums. The reports were more or less true, and more or less damaging.

And the Senator was philosophical. More of those footprints.

Perhaps there is a service I can render Harold Hughes, after all, not in an attempt to explain anything away but rather a description of how his speculations about spiritualism and such matters have come to make sense to me, as they might, I would hope, to other reasonable people.

277

First, though, I must cite mysticism, an avenue of thought and feeling which seems perfectly respectable—even somewhat glamorous—intellectually to us when the mystic is a Catholic; or one who reads St. Teresa, or John of the Cross; or is someone involved in Zen, or some form of Yoga meditation; or who finds what seems to him the highest truth in the abstruse poetry of William Blake; or in the writings of the Protestant mystics of the Reformation (my encyclopedia mentions names like Böhme, and Arndt, and Tersteegen); the Hasidic Jews are in excellent repute, never better, and while I can't give you the current line on how Neoplatonism stands in the philosophy departments, I don't think we'd question a man's political qualifications because he was seen carrying a copy of Origon or Dionysius the Areopagite.

My point is simply that, given a religious temperament and a speculative or meditative mind (and perhaps a romantic nature), it may be expected that a man's thought will go beyond conventional theology. This happens not only at sophisticated levels in all faiths, but also at primitive levels, producing leaders like the shamans in some cultures, devotees like the dervishes in others.

But Senator Hughes is a Middle American Protestant whose formal education was stopped by the war far short of equipping him to read medieval or baroque theology. And for his combination of temperament, nature and mind (a mind developed to think subtly enough in terms of political issues), speculation about religious matters is indeed what I have already called it: a high form of recreation. The attraction of mysticism exists for him, as it must for any other adventurous amateur theologian, and his approach to informing himself has been eclectic. He has been interested in and shared the faith in meditation of the young, as well as in the far reaches of current discussion among his own kind of Protestant—which includes what goes on at serious seances, and the testing of prophets. And now it might be well, I think, to hear him in his own behalf:

278

for Ophelia

"I have an interest in mysticism," he said in our interview, in his Senate office. I have edited only for brevity, and have taken the liberty of filling in the ellipses instead of using the customary, somewhat irritating triple dots (. . .). "I have an interest in what's called Spiritualism. And that's a greatly misunderstood word, I might add, because most people want to look at that as hunting for Grandpa Jones in a cabinet somewhere or someone reading tea-leaves.

"But if you examine the Bible—the Old and New Testament —any man who has ever knelt to pray and says he doesn't believe in extra-sensory perception is kidding himself.

"You're communicating to an Unknown, expecting an answer from an Unknown.

"The Bible is filled with dreams that turned the points of history, for example, and the interpretation of dreams. It's filled with visions. What is a vision? Healing, which people choose to call 'miracle' if it takes place outside a hospital, is not unknown and not uncommon. I have an interest in these subjects.

"In fact, with me, if you were to take the mysticism out of the Scripture, you'd have a pretty hollow vestibule. You'd have a sense of morality that would be good to live by, but would lose, then, what it's contained for Christianity."

"Considerable excitement?" I suggested.

"That's right. What's the Communion of Saints, you know?" He'd been two years in Washington, and in the middle of some of the really hot liberal fights, the one against the ABM for example. But the deep voice still had a lot of relaxed, country music in it. "What's the Service for the Communion of Saints? What are we talking about? We're talking about communion with people that have long since died.

"What happened in the Transfiguration? What happened? If you want to talk about the birth of Jesus, or the Resurrection? Or anything in the Scripture that Christians choose to follow, and

279

live a life of hope? Leaving this out, you know, reduces a man's capability completely. To try to understand it shouldn't be odd; in fact, I think we should do more about trying to understand it and explore it. To know the recesses of the human brain, the mind, more about the subconscious, the so-called paranormal or supernormal. Maybe it isn't paranormal or supernormal at all. Maybe it's natural."

That's what he said, not at all solemnly; I have a note that as he went on speaking about the Apostles, he chuckled, as if accompanying the word he had an affectionate, comic image of raggedy, God-driven farmers and fishermen. But in any case, if what I've quoted is not demonstration enough that Senator Hughes is more an instinctive if undereducated mystic than a gullible devotee of table knockers, it seems to me that all the additional reassurance one deserves, under the Third Amendment to the Constitution of the United States, came at another point in the interview, when he said: "I've not really met many who maintain they're atheistic, and of those I've met I've been quite impressed that they lead well-disciplined, moral lives, and that their concept of atheism might be another man's concept of religion."

That's not precisely the view of atheism we associated with what were called Christers, down home on Godless Mountain.

17

There is a lost meaning of the word *genius:* the attendant spirit of a place. In that meaning, I expect all hundred of our United States Senators are geniuses.

"To know any one of those men is to know what the people are like where he comes from," a Senate functionary told me

for *Ophelia*

once. If it's true, it would be no less so for Eastland of Mississippi than for Brooke of Massachusetts. Nor does it seem to me inconsistent with this that many States are represented by quite contrasting men—it would take at least both Javits and Buckley, for example, to comprise the genius of New York.

The same case can be made for Iowa. At this writing, its senior Senator is Jack Miller, a canny, low-profile tax lawyer and former Notre Dame Professor, who can fairly be said to represent small-town Iowa, small-business Iowa, the Iowa of the settlers who brought New England caution with them cautiously across the Mississippi a century or so ago, to start the banks and feed companies, practice the professions, hold the mortgages and chair the greens committees.

But there is quite another spirit of the place, descended more from the men of the Southern border and the Western reaches, who came from Kentucky and Tennessee in the wagons to farm, build country churches, and take time off from loving their neighbors for the Saturday night dancehall fights. These were generous, hot-tempered men of colorful talk, who could outwork their horses, build barns together, inherit feuds and shelter orphans. If the bankers and lawyers took the best of their farmland in bad times, they dumped the milk till times got better, starved from pride and praised God on Sundays.

If Iowa produced Herbert Hoover, it also produced Henry Wallace. And Harold Hughes.

It has been instructive for me to try to fit this to the stock character of American myth, the new sheriff. He does not come to town to fight the bad guys—he'd rather forgive them, reform them, and often gives them more fair chances than makes sense. His mission is to help the weak, make the town safe for schools and churches, a decent place to raise children, one where women will be safe on the streets.

It is a mission of what used to be called "service," and if he must, in a showdown, become the toughest man in a brawl, the best gun, he is nevertheless a Christian soldier in the old, prairie hymn sense, and would be as much the logical man to lead the town in worship Sunday morning as the posse Monday afternoon.

Senator Hughes, if anyone needs one, is a Christian soldier— as much the good guy, busted back to private for carousing, who becomes acting company commander when the officers are killed, as the one who'd knock a few heads to get the shy chaplain a congregation on Christmas.

In the most often quoted lines from my profile of him for the *Times Sunday Magazine* I wrote: ". . . Governor Hughes is one of those men of balanced contradictions who sometimes occur in our political life. One thinks of the contradictions in figures as large and dissimilar as Roosevelt, who was both socialite and socialist; of Truman, the haberdasher who stood up to generals; even of Lincoln's improbable combination of country wit and melancholy profundity. . . . there is no intention here to claim, or to deny that Harold Hughes is likely to achieve some high place in national history . . . but it seems worth saying that we have seen these men of balanced contradictions before, as contrasted with those who, like Washington, Dwight Eisenhower and perhaps John Kennedy, are all of a piece; and it is as if, in the former, the checks and balances which our civics books speak of as being fundamental to the democratic structure were embodied in single human systems."

Christian soldier is a balanced contradiction perhaps, resolved by that particular decency of Christianity, that its soldiers, unlike Moslem soldiers or Old Testament Jewish soldiers, fight evil, not unbelievers.

This next is very tentative, and highly previous: I have a friend —another good old Godless Mountain boy, as a matter of fact, named Pete Neill—who argues seriously and persuasively that

for Ophelia

the man our country must find now will be not merely a leader but a saviour. I take this to mean not a religious saviour, but a man of equivalent strength of personality who can revive and restore our faith in the great, simple American political notions —ones with which we were, in fact, indoctrinated in our public schooling as if they were a kind of religion, so that we can never altogether lose our reverence for them. No potential saviour, particularly in the area of political faith, would ever have a sufficient share of the wandering American attention to be effective except in the office of our President. But I will not close the circle, and make this a nominating speech for Senator Hughes. My feelings on the point are clear, but what has been conviction may revert to hope without a loss of clarity. And I am still stalking my jaguar, frankly; he does not hold still. He escapes and changes. Instead of closing circles, I will try to say something of how the hunt goes on.

18

Among the circles I do not choose to close, for I do owe you acknowledgment that they exist, is the one describing the campaign of 1968. It was part of a rather extraordinary congeries of campaigns, it seems to me, which brought a great many previously indifferent people into politics, not for recreation but, quite simply, to try to save the country, as we saw it. Seen that way, the campaigns of 1968 are still going on, for the country is neither saved nor wholly lost yet, and though in sum we have lost ground, it will be some years before we really know the outcome. The thugs and bag men in both parties who feed on American decay (at this writing, as we see it) are in control of the country still, but we have challenged them, some of our champions are in office to oppose them, and we have not lost the will to fight.

I will not close another, lesser circle which might be done by writing what casual things I know about my subject's family life. It is no more and no less interesting than anybody else's domestic tale, and if it may become relevant eventually, the spotlights are off just now and no present purpose of mine would be served by writing as if they were on.

Perhaps I do, before I go on with what it is I want to discuss, owe you the same answer I made to the fine political writer Larry L. King, who phoned me when he was doing a piece on Senator Hughes and asked what I thought the man's faults were. We agreed that they were not in the area of honesty or sincerity; I suggested that, like any other politician, ours had a formidable amount of personal vanity, but neither Larry King nor I could think of a political figure without it—it would be as difficult as thinking of an actor or actress without it.

"He's a moody man," I said. "And a private one. People who respond to the warmth of his public presence are sometimes rebuffed or put off when they meet him personally. It isn't easy for him to relax or socialize. As Governor he sometimes spoke his mind with unnecessary fullness and frankness, and he was tagged as one of those whose loyalty in defending subordinates can get unreasonable—but those last two items. I don't know. I think there's been some growth. There are guys who just won't stop growing . . ."

That is what I want to write about, finally: that there are men who will not or cannot stop growing has preoccupied me for a long time. I remember when I first began to think about it— obviously because I was myself starting into my forties—I thought it was a matter of *will not*. I formulated it awkwardly in a conversation with a physician named George Bedell; I suspect it occurred to me to ask George's opinion because he has been

Harold Hughes's doctor, but the actual conversation had no reference to the Senator. I said: "George, let's say a man or woman reaches a position in a specialty—it could be medical, or literary, or I don't know. Making money."

"Okay."

"Anyway, you can tell yourself you've made a pretty good run at it. You're now among the first hundred, or five hundred, or fifty or whatever it is, people in the world at doing whatever it is you do. What is it that makes some able to keep going from that point, even harder, when it would be more pleasant to learn to be comfortable with what you've done? Until the uncomfortable ones know they are among the first half dozen in their fields, and then one of the five keeps on, and becomes the undisputed best of his times, or even manages to transcend his times. . . ."

"Are you talking about something like a second wind?" George asked, and I said I supposed I was, but that it seemed to me it would come, if it did, only after the act of will.

Later, and after I came to know Harold Hughes better, I changed my description so that it seemed less voluntary. The character to whom I gave these lines in a novel *(The Man Who Knew Kennedy)* was talking about John Kennedy, but I was wondering about Hughes, too. My character says: "We're never willing to acknowledge growth in this country after adolescence. I think he grew and grew and grew, like Roosevelt. I think that . . . persistent growing's what it takes to make a great man. There isn't time enough to grow up great in your teens, or your twenties, or your thirties even. You wouldn't be anything better than brilliant. You've got to keep growing, in your forties, your fifties . . . that's what's different about a great man. And I'll bet it hurts, all the way."

Five years after writing that, I find myself convinced of it as far as it goes, but I think it incomplete. It think it's *cannot stop* for a time, but ultimately *will not*. I think, that is, that there is finally a leap into greatness—a risky, agonizing effort—and that if continued growth is somewhat involuntary, the leap is probably willed.

If there is a leap into greatness, maybe Harold Hughes can make it, though I do not mean to claim that he is quite yet at the plateau of achievement from which it may be tried. I think, for that matter, that perhaps any man who reaches that plateau may try it—Richard Nixon, for example, or Leonid Brezhnev, though I do not have much hope for either. There is some deficiency, so far as I can tell, of vision—anyway, I have no way of knowing the real personal qualities of either one, and have been privileged to watch something of how they might come to exist for Harold Hughes. If the leap occurs, I hope I can stay close enough to know about it, and fantasize even that I might be able to be of some further service. . . .

But the risk is one a man takes by himself, and with respect for its gravity. I think that I have sensed, in their work, men nerving themselves for the leap into greatness toward the goal of writing great books; and I think a man who tries and falls may never stop falling.

I met a man just as that terrible fall began for him, General Efegui Ojukwu, of Biafra. And have been thinking of another who took it, not long after they started calling him Father of His Country, Marcus Tullius Cicero. After Cicero, that Republic disappeared; the first Caesar, J. Jumping Julius was making his leap at about the same time, leapt stronger, fell as far, but Agile Augustus leapt next, and made it, and bye-bye ballot box; adios democracy; arrivederci republic; you're nothing but a stupid empire now, Rome, nothing for your people to look forward to at all except for circuses and bread and franchise stands.

It is a Victorian view of history, I suppose, but one which by now I hold, that on the hope that sometimes the right man makes the leap into greatness at the right time rest all the chances that our flawed, flamboyant species will survive.

Nick in Iowa

Note, 1972: Lawrence Goldman died in 1968, after a brief illness.
He was in his middle twenties. He had nearly drafted a book about
his experience as a white radical, teaching at a black college. A
publisher was interested in publishing the incomplete work, and
asked me to write a preface for it. This was to have been the preface;
I have wanted to leave it as much unaltered as I could.

If you knew Nick Goldman and wrote fiction, you used him
as a character. I did, and Dave Godfrey, the fine Canadian
writer who was a student of mine when Nick was, used him,
and I even read a poem once with Nickie in it.

He was never called Lawrence around here, by which I
mean the University of Iowa's corrective program for

metaforgers, at which I teach shop. Nick did three years with us, and by the end of it he was teaching, too.

It was a dramatic poem, in which Nick was the abrasive character, who drove the sensitive principals into a state of helpless tenderness for one another.

In Dave Godfrey's story, Nick was a Peace Corps volunteer, just off the boat in Africa, getting into trouble through brashness, obdurate self-confidence, and a refusal to recognize mysteries.

In mine he was closer to his life role: a graduate student in a seminar on the works of F. Scott Fitzgerald. The character was rude, loud, brilliant, and did not suffer fools, especially the one who sat on the teacher's side of the desk.

This is how fiction works sometimes: it takes only what it can use from life, often leaving the best parts out. You cast a friend in a role as you might cast an actor, and modeling from a vivid and forceful man, if you ignore a few dimensions, it makes the writing easy.

So all three of the writers I've mentioned were lying by omission, but that was only the beginning of the distortion.

Nick was, as the poet knew, so completely sensitive we used to wonder if the vehemence with which he expressed those sensitivities wasn't something like a roar of pain. If so, it was absolutely pure of self-pity; Nick roared with the world's pain, not his own.

Dave Godfrey shared a house near mine with Nick, a trombone player and poet named Tony Whedon, and Ray Whearty who played piano and wrote. They had a boisterous, young male competition going: who could stand longest in the cold shower, do the most push-ups, slip down the street and make Vance believe the most absurd thing.

Dave's African story was an extension of the competition—which of us can present the other most comically and still keep the caricature recognizable? So Dave proceeded by ignoring what he knew better than anybody: that what he wrote of as brashness was a remarkable and entirely self-aware kind of social courage, that the appearance of self-confidence cost Nick as much as that appearance costs any one of us, and that far from rejecting mysteries, Nick invited them most reverently.

There was a high-spirited challenge implied to respond in kind, but the story was hardly done before the news reached Dave, just back from Africa, that Nick wouldn't be picking up any more gauntlets. And so of course the story has been put away, seen only by a friend or two who'd know how to read it.

Probably I can demonstrate best what it is I'm trying to say by speaking of my own use of the character: however it might seem to you on reading my piece, there was never a student I enjoyed having in class more than Nickie Goldman.

I always felt a wild, unacademic pleasure if, at the beginning of a semester, I saw him come into the room for the first class meeting, meaning he'd elected to register for this one, grin at me and take his seat. It meant the course was going to be a success, because he wouldn't let me—any more than he'd let himself or Dave, standing under an ice-cold shower—give it anything less than my best. It might be good or bad but it was going to be lively, and if there were days when my energy was low, Nick always had a surplus to put at our disposal, as well as a really nice sense of when to turn it on in class.

He pushed me through Proust and *Finnegans Wake,* two of the hardest things I ever tried to teach in what is frankly an amateur way, and could sometimes make me feel professional.

He was a phenomenal combination of energy, intelligence and love, and I am trying at last to write about him accurately, rather than just to use a minor charge from that vivid personality as a starter to get a story moving.

Nick was of medium height with a large head and a barrel chest. He wore his curly hair short, and I can't imagine that he wouldn't wear it that way even now, though kids with long hair would surely listen to and follow him. He was bespectacled, rough-skinned, and had the arms and shoulders of a brawler, though I never heard of Nick actually being in a fight.

Instead, he was always in joyful, high-velocity arguments—with me, with Dave, with Tony, with anybody who'd stand up and try him—but arguments of a very particular kind: Nick argued for the love of it, though never arbitrary or illogical in picking his side of a matter, and his magnetism was such that he made you love arguing back.

He'd concede a point, yelling at how dumb he himself was not to see that one, incorporate it and with a mighty leap be onto the next one using your own recent victory against you; or, winning the first one, give you a chance rhetorically to make the leap. You were both alive, intoxicated with words and reason, and I seem to remember times when I kept it going after I'd said all I really had to say for the sheer fun of it. As there are people whose flow of wit makes one in response wittier, so Nick made every opponent eloquent in debate.

Now I am not particularly disputatious by nature, and for me to enjoy that kind of argument requires something rare and particular in the other person which Nick had, more than anyone else I ever jousted verbally against: a complete absence of personal malice towards the man he argued with.

At the same time that he was impatient with stupidity, you felt in him no contempt for the man who was being stupid. He knew, I guess, the strength of his own intelligence, and must have regarded failure of intelligence in others as a weakness, not a fault—he may even have felt stupidity was instructable, a kind of optimism that makes great teachers.

His speaking voice was almost operatic, and I remember clearly the first time I heard it used. It was in class, in a session I was conducting jointly with, if I'm not mistaken, George Elliott and Phil Roth. I'd seen Nick around but he was working with one of the other two, so I hadn't heard from him. He sat quietly through half the discussion of whatever story we were trying, jointly, to criticize, and finally his hand went up.

In no way rude (as I'd represented the student character in my story), he waited quite patiently until George recognized him. Then he stood, which students don't ordinarily do, and looked across the shoulders of the others, taking our measure, waiting for our attention:

"All right," he said, starting quietly. "I disagree with everything that's been said in this class so far . . ."

And what he spoke then, in a voice which grew in resonance and volume, for he was emotional about literature, were four straight, well-organized, uninterrupted paragraphs: in the first he summed up the entire foregoing discussion, omitting nothing, fair to every point. In the second verbal paragraph, he returned to the beginning, criticizing and then discarding each of these points. Slate wiped clean, he began to construct his own reading of the story we were talking about, steady and persuasive, and in the fourth paragraph he defended his reading from all anticipated attacks.

I was astonished. In several years of listening to opinions delivered in language improvised as part of the occasion, the only man I'd ever heard come close to this in brilliance and thoroughness was C. P. Snow, who'd visited a year or two before—and Sir Charles had been speaking from notes.

I replied to Nick, but I felt like applauding first.

In Nick's final year in Iowa City we taught a course together. What I'd anticipated was a series of ebullient cavalry charges with him, riding after the undergraduates, trying good-naturedly to beat some work out of them with the flats of our swords. I was quite wrong.

Nick was no classroom cossack at all when he came over to the teacher's side. He was, rather, extraordinarily tender and concerned, willing to sit up late working at his corrections and comments, and to have long, sympathetic conferences over them with students who asked it of him. He was even, damn it, tender and concerned for me, as the senior colleague, wanting what I had to say to make sense (I hope it did), and looking for things he could do, as we worked together, which would make my part of it easier.

If all that sounds like a letter of recommendation for a man rarely gifted to teach, it still seems worth saying again—as I said it once in literal letters of recommendation—because it seems to me so unusual that a genuinely brilliant young man could have taken the pleasure he apparently did in putting his powerful analogic imagination and almost perfect articulateness at my service in so selfless a way. I'd have recommended Nick to anyone for anything.

I feel quite sure that my deep enthusiasm, shared as it was the year after Roth and Elliott left by John Clellon Holmes, who also taught jointly with Nick, along with Nick's unbroken string of A's in class work, the impressive early publications of critical writing, and the force of personality—all these things could have got Nick his first teaching job after Iowa at his choice of any number of prestige Universities. But I don't think any of us was the least surprised that his choice was to go South to a Negro college instead.

And that reminds me of something that happened between us in connection with a story Nick wrote.

I'm not sure that any of his fiction was published, though if I were an editor it would have been, particularly this long story which stays quite clear in my mind, even after five years and the reading of many, many manuscripts.

It was called "I Make My Manic Statement," and was both ferocious and funny, inventive in the way Celine is inventive, and finally, to me, very moving. I remember that after I'd read it for the first time I phoned Nick in some excitement to say that I wanted to hear no more of his writing criticism and political commentary; he was going to be too good at fiction to waste his time at those lesser things.

Nick was respectful, in the odd way he could be sometimes, and glad I liked his story, but I knew I was going to lose my case; writing politics and social comment would be the choice of idealism, like going to Morehouse. So the book at hand is not the draft of a first novel, which I, parochial about my genre, would have wanted Nick to write, but something else; perhaps something more valuable.

I am not going to try to comment on the draft. It speaks for itself, quite clearly, as far as it goes. I had, and wish I had saved, one letter from Nick at Morehouse. It started out to be a brief request for some sort of further recommendation, for a fellowship probably, the kind one gets routinely from former students who add a bit of family news and perhaps a graceful word of commendation for one's latest book.

Not Nick. Once he was started writing to me, he didn't stop till page five or six, single-spaced. He was too much of a teacher to have been able to. He had my attention, had started a letter, and now was going to share the experience he was having, and his conclusions from it, and teach me something. He did. That letter was like an outline for his book, and I don't think there was a sentence in it I didn't learn from.

To learn. In country vernacular it means to teach, as well; we say of a man, "he learned me how to read," and I think that well said. For at the best, most passionate level, the two are not separate functions but one beautiful reciprocal process, and I know of no one with whom my brief teacher-student/student-teacher relationship better illustrates this than Nick.

I can exemplify with jazz. Tony, Ray, Dave and I all tried to

play it, in about the same order of skill in which I've listed the
three names and the pronoun, and would meet in the cellar at
my house, around an upright piano, and work away at it. Nick
listened, probably no more than once, and more out of politeness
than interest. He was frank in saying that he had no idea of what
we were trying to do, and no comment on how our effort
sounded, but consented to borrow some records. I gathered the
matter seemed unimportant to him in a world full of books by
Orwell and Camus.

It wasn't until more than a year after Nick's death that I saw
Tony Whedon in New York, and heard from Tony, who had
gone down to Morehouse after Nick, that "Nickie had a tremendous record collection, and a really thorough knowledge of
jazz."

This from Tony, who plays really good trombone and owns
marvelous records himself, seemed uncontestable, no matter
how surprising. "But in Iowa," I said, "Nick wasn't interested
at all, was he?"

"Only because we were," Tony said. "But then he saw the
relevance . . ."

Nick learned it. And in the book, among other things, he
writes about jazz—he is teaching that relevance—along with a lot
of other things, of course, some of which may seem much more
important.

A book says something different, teaches something different,
to each of its readers. I think Nick's latest lesson for me is in that
music, about which I'd have thought I knew much and he nothing.

Not at all. It's the new surprise he has for me. "All right," says
Nick's voice as I read certain passages. "Listen to some music,
will you? There are things in the music that can't be said, aren't
there? Isn't that what you were trying to tell me? Come on now,
let me tell it to you . . ."

294

for Ophelia

He picked up and went past me, I expect in understanding jazz, certainly in knowing where it's gone the last few years, and now, since the book's unfinished, I find I want very much to know (maybe Tony can tell me) what Nick's records were. I'd like to get and listen to some of them.

You learned me plenty, man. There's no reason why that's got to stop, just because school let out so early for you.

4   "Fish sometimes . . ."

R ainwater collects in the farm ponds I have built. Strangers look for a stream and ask about springs, but rain, running through the grass in the pastures and the leaf mold on the forest floor, is the whole water supply. You can read about how the ponds were built to store this water—there are two, each covering about three acres—in the piece called "On My Place" in the next section.

In the ponds bass swim and so do we. The water has the soft, ozone smell of fresh mud puddles; ladies like to float their hair in it.

I am more caretaker than adversary of the bass. We fish for fun, and mostly put them back—but not always; and I sometimes harvest frogs along the banks on summer nights. I ought to trap the muskrats out. They make holes in the dams. But I don't like trapping.

One winter I failed as caretaker of my fish. There was an early freeze and early snow on the ice. I cleaned it once, for skating, and then again, but finally the snow got way ahead of me. We went abroad, and while we were away more than a foot of snow accumulated. There are plants underwater that ordinarily continue to grow all winter, but when the light is completely shut out, they die away. Growth uses carbon dioxide and makes oxygen; decay uses up oxygen and releases carbon dioxide down there, under the ice. The fish suffocate.

We were still in Europe when the thaw came, but my neighbor Earlis, who sometimes fishes here, reported that there were dead bass twenty inches and longer, that looked to be well over three pounds in weight, cast up for the coons and crows to carry off. I had started them four years earlier, and the biggest ever caught had been eighteen inches and exactly three pounds.

All gone.

So I have restocked, but it will be two more years before the bass are catchable, more before they are very large. I have bought an ice saw, and am thinking about a little garden tractor with a snow-blower on it.

I have not written as often about fishing as about hunting. Perhaps it was never quite so great a passion; more likely, though, the opportunities for it have not been so varied in Iowa, nor so interesting, as they are in other places. Nevertheless, what I'd prefer to think is that I was somehow a slightly more evolved specimen in my feeling for fish than I was in my feeling for birds —never much concerned with the big-fish sweepstakes, which is what fishing competition comes down to. Generally happy to eat a fresh fish now and then, but even happier to put one back and watch him recover, float for a moment, realize he was in his element once more, flip his tail and rush away.

Maybe the best way to say it is that, when I saw a field, I automatically estimated it as bird cover; but when I saw water, I thought with pleasure of what sort of water it was, not of the catchable creatures it might harbor.

This doesn't mean that I haven't been, and don't still become, excited about fishing. I do. And you may, if you like, read the particulars of fishing frenzy in the long piece about trout called "Rainbows Drowned in a Bucket." Much of it appeared in *Playboy,* and that version sometimes gets anthologized. The text as published here is quite a bit fuller, and I have added a note to it.

"Seawalking" was a later article, and I like the feeling I'd developed by then towards what lives underwater. "Seawalking" appeared in *Holiday* (and what a collection of headstones for dear, departed magazines the acknowledgment section of any writer's ten-year collection of essays becomes today, though it's the management of *Holiday* which departed; the magazine is still alive.)

What was a magazine, Grandpa?

Well, it was a collection of things to read, and pictures to look at, and advertising, that came out once a week or once a month. Groups of very bright, very able people were hired to put these periodical collections together, and they acquired a particular kind of staff spirit, and personality, and that became the spirit and personality of the magazine—with certain concessions to the theoretical taste of its readership. At their head was a man called an editor.

Like a television producer?

Like him in authority, but much freer than a television producer to try to exploit his personal vision of what was interesting, or exciting or funny.

Were editors nice men?

Probably. Writers like your grandfather didn't always like

them as a class, but usually liked some of them individually. I always wondered what happened to some of the nice, bright, able ones . . .   ·

What about the others? Why didn't you like them?

I'll tell you when you're older, dear. It's a little weird.

(Water. I guess I like clear, fresh water in a stream, running over a rocky bottom, forming small waterfalls and sudden pools, the way other men like rivers or oceans. I live very far from my kind of water. It's in my mind a lot, though, all flow and sparkle —I guess I like a clear stream the best of anything in nature, as if one were the place of my mythological birth. Womb yearning. My totem must be an anadromous fish, a salmon, shad or steel-head, that carries genetic knowledge of an environment different from the one he swims in, to which he must some day get back for some deep reason, like death or reproduction.)

I'm older now, Grandpa.

Well, then. There were editors, and many other people who conducted businesses, in a place we called New York.

I've heard of that.

And perhaps some of those people were stream-born, or ocean-born, or mountain-born, but it was hard to believe, be-cause their totem had become a device we called a telephone. This thing was a two-headed phallus. You talked into one head, and heard out of the other, but you couldn't see the person you were talking to, only see your own lap and knees while you talked. It tended to fix your groin as a point of vision while you used it. You smelled your breath coming back out of the mouth-head as you talked, while the other voice inserted buzzes and tickles in your ear through the earhead, and your hand squeezed the smooth in-between . . .

Let's talk about something else.

. . . so for the people who did business in New York the telephone was an instrument for transmitting and receiving pain and pleasure, and they used it all day long, and were exhausted by it so that they drank a lot in the evening. They bought nice things for their telephones, special knob things to dial with, and index deals full of painful and pleasurable numbers, and there was a Telephone Company that could supply instruments that were different shapes and colors. But of course it all broke down.

Why?

Well, you see, the telephone had to be connected to somebody else's telephone, who'd be transmitting and receiving all those thrills of information and stabs of reaction, and a lot of people outside of New York just didn't like to do it that way, I suppose. In any case, they finally felt a real revulsion towards this two-headed thing, and picked it up distastefully when it jangled to them, and finally wouldn't pick it up at all.

Sometimes I blank out the screen on the phonovision, Grandpa, and just listen to the voice.

Yes, I know. I guess everybody does when they're young, but you ought to try to control it. Let's not tell Grandma, shall we?

(A walk in the woods, a swim in rainwater.)

First published in Esquire
under the heading
"Outdoors," June, 1964.

The Catfish Column

My fantasy of success in fishing, as I contemplate this summer, is not what it has been in years past. Then it has been, variously, to travel east to catch an Atlantic salmon on a small dry fly; north, to learn if muskelunge are really fierce as barracudas; west to the steelhead run; or even south, where big bass lie among the lily pads. But this summer I could realize my private wish three miles from home, in eastern Iowa. You would know I had done it if you were to see me, some morning soon, strolling back along the bank of the Iowa River, with a respectable string of medium-sized channel catfish, say a pound and a half to two pounds each.

Perhaps the midwest, where I have lived for seven years now, off and on, is catching up with me. Back east I can't say I ever thought about catfish much, of any kind or weight, outside of supposing that they were what kept the Tom Saw-yer element out of school on sunny days. They would sit, barefoot and freckle-faced, on the stream banks, holding those somewhat crooked, knotty sticks with line tied at the ends with which boys fished in the funny papers. If the fun-nies were right, the thing they caught, nine times out of ten, would be a boot—in the State of Cartoonia there is a Conser-vation Commission which stocks likely streams with boots of catchable size; those provided by natural spurning could never stand the fishing pressure. The tenth time this small boy of my midwestern angling theory would catch something called a catfish, something so ugly and inedible that his mother would bribe him to throw it back.

When I learn I've been wrong, you may as well know, I am one of those pendulum guys, going from one extreme to the other without even a pause at the middle. It is my sincere opinion at the moment that the channel catfish is perfectly beautiful, a genuine delicacy, and as difficult to stalk, find, hook and hold as any game fish we have.

The channel cat is the lean, handsome, aggressive member of an otherwise ill-favored, sluggish family—a silvery gray, irides-cent catfish, sixteen to thirty inches long, with dark spots on its shimmering skin. It is wary, fast, strong and a desperate fighter. Omnivorous and voracious (according to the fishing books), indifferent to silt and heat, the channel catfish has even survived the introduction to our waters of the universally distributed and rather hateful carp—a fish which almost everyone agrees should have stayed in Asia, where it belongs. The carp, which have taken over our Iowa bass waters, were introduced by early Ger-man and Bohemian immigrants who liked carp as food, to the point, I'm told, of its being the traditional Christmas feast of the poor in Central Europe. It's a shame those nineteenth-century farmers couldn't have learned to catch channel catfish; carp (unless, according to my sources, kept in tanks and fed grain) are often coarse and ill-tasting.

Channel catfish, on the other hand, are so good to eat, just as they come from the rivers, that I frequently order them when we go out to eat in local restaurants, as I might red snapper in Mexico or bluefish in New York. Cynical diners tell me that sometimes restaurants will slip in flatheads when the menu says "catfish"; these, being fonder of mud than channels, don't taste as good. However, if the fish is served with the tail still attached, as it generally is, it's easy to tell the difference—the channel cat's tail is deeply forked; the flathead's tail is not.

Now admittedly, few channel cats are caught on artificial lures, and this might diminish my claim that they should be taken seriously as game fish were they at all easy to catch with more digestible baits. They aren't. Moreover those baits that do work, natural only in the sense that they can be eaten, must be selected and prepared with as much arcane knowledge as trout flies— "chicken entrails, hog melts, coagulated blood, live and dead chubs, sour clams," says my favorite of the fishing books I've been referring to. (This book is a remarkable volume called *Iowa Fish and Fishing,* published by our State Conservation Commission.)

But I have only begun to list the baits: worms, grasshoppers, frogs, bacon, slightly spoiled shrimp, and slices of other fish (including carp, by all means) are used at times—and like everything else I've mentioned so far are relatively sweet and pleasant to handle. Relative, that is, to the weird and revolting mixtures known as stink baits, for which each catfishing purist has his own, limburger-based secret formula. For dilettantes, and men whose wives won't let them use the kitchen, there are commercial approximations sold in jars at almost any Iowa crossroads store.

Now what catfish I have caught, and I fear I am still at the stage where I remember each of them, have all been hooked on shrimp

—but this is not to say that I consider shrimp the best bait, or hold the amateur opinion that anything on the list above may be considered interchangeable with anything else. As well claim that a trout fisherman can get along with one size and pattern of fly, at all times in all waters. Which catfish bait to use depends —and again I must refer you to the literature on the subject for accurate advice—on time of day, time of year, water condition, temperature and, for all I know, barometric pressure. There are times to float grasshopper, and times to reach for the hog melts, and given twenty years I may begin to know which they are.

There are also choices of method, and here I am surer of myself: as between fishing in general from boats, and fishing in general from banks and wadable water, I like to have my feet under me. One of the enormously attractive things about catfishing to me is that, at its best, it is stream fishing—downstream, generally, wading, with a lot of line out and bait that moves lightly with a current through a channel at feeding hours. At other times one must weigh down the line and fish the bottom, around snags and other hiding places, and to be truthful, that is the way my shrimp offerings have been most effective—to do the wading and floating properly I am, apparently, going to have to coagulate some blood. Somehow this has always sounded so recondite to me that even when I read a perfectly clear description of how it's done I resist understanding it; what I shall have to do is find a catfisherman this summer and watch him at it.

Meanwhile, there is one claim left for me to make in detail, and that has to do with the channel catfish as a fighter. Let me say, quite incidentally, that the use of the word *fight* for a man's part in the contest always makes me uncomfortable—it seems to me correct enough to say that a man plays a fish. It is only the fish that does the fighting, and I suspect that it is often the role of pagan god—my clever whim against your life—that we enjoy in our unequal combat with the creatures for which we hunt and fish.

In any case, here is what a catfish does, or so it has been with those I've caught: he runs, with great power and violent twisting, for the bottom. One does not see him go, because the water is almost always murky; one does not know what is down there, in the way of snags and rocks to try to guide the fish away from. He must be given play, unless one is fishing with rope, yet kept away from those unseen things, which can catch and break the line, by a kind of intuition.

I have found, and don't seem to feel too abashed at saying it, a good deal of excitement in these passages. I have found, too, a good deal of pleasure and interest in some of the country ways of catfishing, with set lines and pole lines. And I remember some magic times, whatever my usual feeling about fishing from boats, when a friend and I would set out to drift all night, covering eight or ten starlit miles of river, stopping here and there to let our bait work down in front of us. If you choose the right stretch of river, there are no sounds to be heard after ten o'clock except natural sounds, and no light to be seen but natural light. A bottle of decent whiskey is permissible cargo, as we do it, and a jug of water and something to eat for after midnight; even familiar water looks strange, and it is exhilarating to know that out around you anywhere, as you go, the channel catfish may be feeding.

If fishing is to be called an art, then catfishing may be only folk art. But I shall study it this summer, for it seems as valid to me, being indigenous to where I live, as some of the more elegant fishing arts imported from Europe.

First published in
Playboy, *necessarily in a
somewhat briefer form,*
October, 1964.

Rainbows Drowned in a Bucket

Yes, masters, I have caught trout on worms and even
salmon eggs, and may, I fear, do it again tomorrow if the
weather's nice (and if no one's looking, of course, and the
fish won't take my sporting, artificial flies). If the weather's
threatening, so that it doesn't seem wise to drive ninety miles
north to the nearest trout stream, I may just snag a few carp
from the Iowa River near home instead.

That I, who am relatively pure—or anyway self-righteous—
as a hunter of birds, should be so infinitely corrupt when I
approach a trout stream causes me more concern than it
might seem worth. My defects of character tend more
towards weakness than towards shamelessness. Anyway, just
to show that there's good stuff here, if one can get to it, I
might tell you that I've about given up carp snagging—

snatching them illegally out of the water with an unbaited treble hook, that is—since I learned that one's permitted to shoot them with a bow and arrow. The arrow is barbed, the bow has a simple reel to it, aiming becomes no more than a matter of general direction if enough carp are congregated close to the surface. Once I impaled three indignant fish on a single chance arrow; as my friend Con Carter says, it seems like too much fun not to be against the law.

So, you see, I'm very nearly a redeemed man on carp. Further, I fish correctly for crappie with weighted streamers; for bluegills with feathered popping bugs; for bass, pike and walleye with plugs and casting rod; and if I catch (or fail to catch) channel catfish with anything I can think of, that is entirely within the bounds of fisherman's ethics, too. It's with trout that I break down, the fish towards which ethical behavior is so rigorously and traditionally codified that the approved way of catching them seems more a ceremony than a method, a ceremony with which, at home in winter when the streams are frozen, I wistfully identify.

The pricks under which my trout-fishing conduct becomes so deplorable are those inflicted by the old barbed arrows shot into carp snaggers from the bowstring stretched between illusion and reality. Around the next bend of the trout stream, up past the rapids at the pool, I had always expected (if I saw a fellow fisherman at all; I hoped not to), a knight, parfit and gentil, let alone compleat. He was to be a lean and stream-wise intellectual of fishing, gracious, something of an aristocrat in his quiet way, with bamboo fly rod, battered hat and heirloom creel. The hat would be stuck with dry flies and I would pause, hushed, to watch his style as he stood there in waders, calculated the current, selected a fly and, having tied it on, made his studied and impeccable cast.

I have never seen him. At long intervals, I see a man something like him; a little more often I see a man like me, trying to be like him, though actually we might better be trying to emulate Con Carter. Con is one of a new sort of expert, trained to compete for today's trout in today's streams, against the currently prevalent kind of competition. This competition is represented by what I more generally see at that pool above the rapids than a knight, a Quixote, or a brilliant young technician: she is a cheerfully aging rural housewife, stout and red-faced very likely in her print dress, sitting on a canvas stool about four feet away from a two-tone sedan which came through the woods by a road I did not know was there. She is waiting, perhaps, as her husband solicitously puts a cheese-flavored marshmallow on the rather large hook at the end of the line on her spin-casting rod. There are three or four fair-sized rainbow trout floating belly-up in a bucket of water between them.

My lean, aristocratic trout fisherman who seldom is—perhaps he seldom was; I do not know—with his meticulously chosen British-style equipment, was a product of discipline. It was his lean, aristocratic father who took the boy's worm can and, hardly even feeling the impulse to hurl it away, dug a little hole in which to bury it so as not to clutter the woods. Then he undertook, as his own father had, of course, to teach the boy: to tie short lengths of gut of diminishing diameters in sequence to produce the proper tapered leaders for different weights of fly, using something called blood knots. To air and dry silk lines, after each use, to protect against mildew, wiping and casing the delicate split-bamboo rod, cleaning and oiling the reel. To cast, not merely the basic fly cast but the roll, the whip and the double-haul. To choose a well-tied fly from hundreds like it on display and even to know what thread, which birds' feathers, to carry along so that, deep in the still woods by a beaver dam, he might observe the particular insects trout were feeding on and tie his own flies on the spot in order, so the phrase goes, to match the hatch. Once initiated into these and other mysteries the boy was ready for twenty years or so apprenticeship, learning the ways of running water, the life and feeding patterns of the fish, after which he could regularly produce trout, wading to find them through the cool solitudes of New England and Canada, the mountain areas of the middle Atlantic states or the wild rivers of the West. And by now he could match any other pilgrim in effortless adherence to ceremony when, making the journeys he had dreamed of, he approached the fabled waters of the Beaverkill, the Flathead, the Gunnison or Neversink.

I had no such discipline. There were trout in the Virginia hill streams in which my brothers and I swam summers, down from New York, but I don't recall that we ever caught many of them; when we did, we must simply have thought of them as fish, making no special distinction between trout, chubs and suckers when they swallowed our worms. But save your sighs, masters; as things go today, who needs a father? We have wise, corporate uncles who take care of many things. Uncle DuPont, for one, who sees to it that my leaders come in nylon, not gut, tapered by machine without a knot. Other uncles make fly lines in dacron with built-in air bubbles which, unlike silk, will float without dressing and will never rot. Rods, if one insists, may still be bought in bamboo—often impregnated with something to reduce maintenance problems—but most fly fishermen use fiberglass rods which, in my experience, can be thrown in a corner of the garage without thought and regardless of weather between fishing trips. You might still fly-cast as, after six years, I am still trying to learn to do adequately, but there is light spinning tackle now with which you could duplicate all I can do with a fly rod after ten minutes' practice. There are still fine, hand-tied flies for sale, but they are rather expensive—the alternative formerly would have been to learn to tie one's own. Nowadays we have Japanese uncles who make them for import at a few cents

each, machine-tied and inferior but a good deal better than anything I could produce. Matching the hatch? The trout I fish for
take artificials all right—take them from Con Carter anyway, but
far from imitating natural foods the artificials that Con favors are
so outlandish that one could imagine them hatching only from
a clutch of Easter eggs; I will detail them—they can be matched
at the counter of any sports store. One may, as things have been
worked out for us in our version of the good life, become self-
taught if second rate at almost anything, even, as in fly-fishing for
trout, a self-taught anachronism.

I use the word anachronism with care and with regret. The fact
is that while the old-style fly-fisherman would still, of course,
outfish me with the old-style methods, we might both stand to
be shown up, on a given day, in number of fish caught per hour,
by the lady with the cheese mallows. And then Con Carter would
outfish us all three, any day. I have watched Con closely; I will
herein and without hesitation reveal such of his secrets as I
understand, hoping that knowing them will do you more good
than it has me.

I will also reveal, at some additional cost to you in reading
explanations, a fishing secret of my own. It is guaranteed to
enable you to do as I have done just once: pay close attention to
the account of how I managed it, follow my example scrupu-
lously, and you will positively catch a limit of trout on dry flies
in less than half an hour. There is nothing to add to or qualify
this guarantee except to forewarn you that, having so triumphed,
I felt a good deal less pride in that creel full of fish than I do about
trout caught on worms. Or even salmon eggs.

Let me begin the explanations. To go back for a moment to
the dry-fly purist, it should be understood that his present relative inefficiency implies no loss of skill. It is rather that the fish
to which that skill applied have, in most places, pretty well disappeared. They swam, half a century or more ago, in clear, cold-

for Ophelia

water streams which ran swiftly over sand and pebbles, through shady woods, over logs and boulders, with rapids, falls, small pools and no pollution. They were native fish—brook trout in the East, cutthroat and rainbows in the West—native as the bison and the Carolina parakeet. Immemorially established in their lightly fished, unsilted habitat, the trout reproduced naturally and grew up wild. There are such streams left, hundreds perhaps, if no longer thousands, and among the trout which swim in them may be some few naturals, for which you might fish as ceremonially as you like. In fact, to follow at least the rough outlines of the ceremony would be quite necessary: move upstream, so as to come along behind the fish which face upstream to feed, stalking, wading, taking advantage of concealment, keeping your shadow off the water. Recognize the sort of place ahead at which a trout should be; cast to it from as far away as possible, landing the fly lightly and naturally (this is the tough part—I want to keep inching closer and I have more than once landed the fly heavily and unnaturally in the lobe of my right ear). Somehow you have chosen the right fly, the one which represents the precise kind of insect which is being eaten in this stream today, for trout are selective feeders, and as the current begins to float the fly back towards you, there is a swirl, you twitch the rod backwards pulling the line abruptly taut . . . a fish like that might have ignored, might even have darted away in fright from, a worm, let alone some sort of mallow.

But remove any single characteristic of the habitat—the trees which shade the stream, for example—and the fish will not reproduce. Or simply fish it heavily, by whatever means (there are something over twenty million people licensed to go fishing in this country), and there will shortly be no breeding stock, whatever the conditions. This is not to say that trout are scarce; actually, they are very plentiful indeed, some popular streams carrying far more fish at certain seasons than they conceivably

311

could have before the first Indian discovered them; trout are, as
you very likely know, distributed among our streams in the
hundreds of thousands every year, trucked there from the state
and federal fish hatcheries at which they are born and reared.

(I shall not, by the way, try to deal with lakes and ponds and
large rivers, which are stocked, too, and which often have large
natural trout populations as well, though it is from such places
that most fish of trophy size are caught. But these trout must be
caught from docks, piers, beaches and, least interesting of all,
boats. I am easily bored in a boat unless the fishing is fast, perhaps
because I do not know how to read the water and what procedures to try, in large bodies; I am never bored in the woods.
Pottering along a stream bank, wading in clear water, working
out fisherman's problems I have begun to understand, checking
the birds and wild flowers and mushrooms, I don't need fish to
keep me interested, disappointed though I shall be if I catch none
at all. So I regard the trout in lakes and so on as outside this
discussion, if only because it is I who am doing the discussing.
Masters, leave me one clear brook and you may have the oceans.)

Now there are, as I understand it, two chief kinds of stocking,
for streams and lakes alike. One consists in putting immature fish
into places in which they can grow up, through several seasons,
to catching size, in order to supplement what natural reproduction may still go on. The other, and the kind which must account
for most of the trout I personally have caught, is called put and
take stocking. For this the fish are of catchable size when they
reach the water, and the habitats generally spoiled to a point
where the fish have little chance to survive in them, uncaught,
for more than a few months. Moreover, if I am not mistaken,
there is a great deal more put and take stocking than fishermen
like to think in the remaining good trout areas, in response to
simple fishing pressure.

The catchables—the term is one I have heard used by hatchery men—are anywhere from eight to sixteen inches long. They are produced by milking breeder females of eggs, inseminating the eggs artificially, incubating them, and then raising the resultant fish in outdoor tanks for two to four years. Their responses, even when they have been in the stream for some time, so I contend, are not like those of trout born wild. Nor do I mean by this that they are always and necessarily easier to catch; sometimes they are quite impossible. But they are certainly a different fish, and the rest of my contention is that the man whose trout-fishing intuitions are acquired from experience with wild trout, not to mention the one whose misintuitions are acquired from bookish fantasies of wild trout, will be less successful with the hatchery catchables than a man like Con Carter at twenty-five, whose fishing life has been spent learning their somewhat different ways.

Who am I to assert the distinction? What wild, native fish have I caught in order to perceive the difference? Few, very few, and in far places: in California, early one spring, there were several people who advised me not to bother fishing a particular stream, saying that the year's first hatchery truck hadn't been by yet. I went anyway, and they seemed right, for I tried place after likely-looking place without results. Then I came to a little waterfall, dropping twenty feet or to where a rocky pool received it; I could see sunfish there. I thought to amuse myself by dragging a tiny spinner through the bubbles for them to chase, and something caught the lure, there in the swirl, something small, flashing, and ferocious, which danced on its tail as I drew the line towards me and turned out to be a native rainbow, five inches long—no catchable ever moved, in my experience, with such speed as to outrace the darting of a cold-water sunfish.

In Idaho, in summer, when one could see big rainbows hanging together like suckers at the bottoms of clear stretches, a fisherman native to the region told me as he watched in disgust the way the fish ignored his worms: "They're hatchery fish. Don't seem to be feeding time yet. It'll come." And I discarded my own worms, crawled through the brush above the clear stretch, made my way around a ledge partly covered by running water until it widened and I could stand above the point where the current entered the pool. Tied on a royal coachman, lowered it into the swirl so that it would float a few feet before pulling under, and felt a strike like those I'd dreamed of. I walked back past the worm fisherman an hour later with four eight-inch cutthroat trout, stopped to compare them with the twelve-inch rainbow he had caught. The color of my fish was so bright, the flesh so firm, the tails and fins so sharply edged—undamaged by the fighting and abrasion against concrete which goes on in close packed tanks—that I'd not have traded one of mine for the pale, flabby fish he had, had it been twice its size. No catchable, I thought, smug for the only time in my trout-fishing life and with a smug man's affinity perhaps for generalizing luck into law, ever gets over feeding on the bottom in slow water, or becomes really selective as these cutthroats were, selective not only in that my royal coachman was the only fly they took but also in that they took it only when presented in the particular way I'd happen to present it on the first cast. Oh, all right; it *was* a mistake. I'd meant the fly to float a long way, not to drag it under.

In Chile, there was an Andean stream. I was fishing with bait, a white grub called *gusano de tepo,* up past the foothills where all the water that runs is newly melted from snow. The place I was in was a deep cleft with rocky sides and the descent of the stream was so steep it seemed a continuous fall, interrupted every six or eight feet by a ledge in which a basin had been worn. I cast a *gusano* into a basin at shoulder level, saw a trout leap for it, miss, flash around and slide after it with the current, hurtling into the next basin at the level of my feet, and then the next, six feet below as I stripped out line, and there the fish had the grub and

I the fish though I didn't have him long. I had to invent a technique for landing them, for that pattern would repeat itself, and I found that if I slowed the worm a little, trying to make the trout take it in a convenient place, it wouldn't work. Finally I found I could time it, allowing just so much line as would extend through two small basins and jerking the fish instantly out of the water, onto the rocks, as soon as I felt the pull. It was tremendously exciting, though again the trout were not large ones nor, to be factual, are they native to Chile. They were, I was told, introduced from California during the last century, along with the lovely, crested California quail. The birds, it seemed to me, while still around have thrived indifferently, but the trout are surely a fish for the Andes, and I cannot imagine an underexercised catchable, fresh from the hatchery, without those generations of acclimatization, able to withstand the pressure of that current. I think he'd wash right out of the stream.

There was only one other time I caught what seemed to me to be fish born wild, and that was in New Hampshire, at a friend's place in the woods. He has a stream so narrow one can step across it in most places, and with its banks so thick with alders one often cannot see the stream. In it we caught brook trout, hardly more than minnow size, on black ant flies my friend had tied himself, caught them at will really, but on our hands and knees and from behind rocks or tree trunks. Where there was no concealment, or where we were clumsy, casting shadows or making sounds, the little fish would disappear with incredible speed and thoroughness, incredible because I could never make out places between the narrow banks in which they might have hidden. Catchables—of this I am sure—are not like that; there are times when I have caught them after staring them in the eye.

Still, how can I say those little brook trout, rainbows, cutthroat, were native to the streams I found them in? I can't, of course; it seemed they must be—how is one to tell the robots from the naturals when they have succeeded in synthesizing human beings? Size is a factor, species a factor—but all right. Maybe I have never caught a wild trout in all my natural-born life; but I think I have, and shall proceed, now, to write about the other kind as if it were so, as if I knew what I was talking about.

The trip which was to make a successful if phlegmatic fly-fisherman out of me began on a very hot day, like most summer days in Iowa. I had decided to drive up to the northeast corner of the state, near the Minnesota border, to a place I had never been before called Westerly Creek where I would fish, sleep on the bank, and fish again in the morning. Westerly Creek is the longest stretch of trout water in the small part of this state to which the original range of the brook trout extended, an area in which natural reproduction may still, if very rarely, occur. It was not that I thought I would catch a native fish, but it did increase my anticipation of the stream to know that a hundred years ago, when the land lying west of it was prairie, and the upper Mississippi River into which it drains an insufficient barrier to the men who were coming to plow the plains, strip the timber, erode the land and silt the streams—in a time the oldest farmers around there might still remember as their boyhoods—wild trout swam in Westerly Creek, Waterloo, French, South Bear, Little Paint, Buck, Joy Springs, and Ensign Hollow. The oldest farmers must have caught them, playing hooky from the one-room schools, as Indian kids must have, before them. Caveman kids, for all I know.

The brookies were there through all the world's life until the instant of it which is the past hundred years in which we wiped them out and, seeing our mistake early, began replacing them with production models. For putting fish in those streams started as early as 1872, and by now the manufacturers stock a more complete line than was ever offered here by nature—in addition to the brookies there are brown trout, whose native range is Scotland and Germany, rainbows which began in the Rocky Mountains, and a hybrid brook-brown whose native range is the cross-fertilization tank.

Much of what I am saying may sound like false nostalgia. Much of it is. Nothing could have been better arranged to expose it than the drive I made to reach Westerly Creek from my home, four hours north through the Mississippi River valley. Choosing secondary roads, passing through little towns which not so long ago had steamboat docks, I hugged the big river as closely as one can by car, for I have a bookish Easterner's craving to watch the Mississippi which is never sated. And I was perfectly aware that, history or no history, the brook-trout range in the northeast corner of this state was marginal, the bottom edge of a range happening across the Minnesota border.

I reached Westerly Creek about two in the afternoon. The first I saw of the creek, turning off a secondary road onto an unpaved one, was disappointing. We were still below the point, a town called Brinkley, where the map indicated that trout fishing started, and that was hopeful; the water looked clear, and that was hopeful, too. But the creek moved slowly, spread out flat and shallow between level meadows, and not even turning often. By the time I reached Brinkley, though, things looked a little better. The banks were cut deeper, twists came more often, and the bed of the stream was two or three feet beneath the surface. Just at Brinkley the creek and the road crossed, and under the bridge it looked quite deep—six or eight feet, perhaps—but murky and not very fast, a good place for turtles. But on the bank, near the bridge, was the closest thing we have to an infallible sign that trout are present, a small green sign put up by the Conservation Commission reminding anglers that a special, two-dollar trout stamp must be purchased and fixed to one's license before fishing any area so posted. I cheered up. Between this sign and the

Minnesota border were eight and a half miles of stocked stream; there should quite a few fish in it.

Resolutely, I drove on into Brinkley—one church, one store, one filling station, and one tavern—and took the customary first step in fishing unfamiliar territory; I stopped my car and went into the tavern. It was a dark, damp little place with wooden bar, soda fountain stools and a winy smell; the smell was misleading since Iowa taverns served nothing but beer.

There was a thin, red-headed woman who looked to be in her fifties behind the bar, and a man who, from his overalls and ankle-high shoes, must be a farmer. I ordered a beer, not because I wanted one especially since I never much cared for following beer with exercise, but because it's hard for me to imagine bar customers talking fishing with a man drinking Coca-Cola.

The bar-mistress and her customer were holding no conversation at all; I was free to ask my question as she handed me the glass:

"People getting some fish around here?"

This question is asked with false casualness, which sometimes leads to its being dismissed, but I don't think I'd ever had it totally misunderstood before.

"My husband used to go every morning of the week in summer, when he was alive," the woman said. "Get up at four o'clock, drive over to the Mississippi forty miles, and be back at noon to open up, and he always had fish."

"You're off your road if that's where you're going," the farmer said.

"No sir. I thought I might try to catch some trout," I said.

"He'd get walleyes mostly," said the red-haired woman. "Once in a while a Northern, but they're so bony."

"I don't like any of them," said the farmer. "I never did."

I reminded them that there was a trout stream running through town, a fact they knew, of course, but to which they

for Ophelia

attached no interest. Still, they had no apparent wish to be disobliging; they recalled a timeless local topic or two for me about Westerly Creek and its trout: the big one which a schoolboy caught right under the bridge in town a few years back, an old man who used to smoke them (or was it sturgeon he smoked? Well, where would he have got them?); nobody smoked fish now, with freezers.

The farmer cited a family with a freezer full of trout, allegedly replenished by forty or fifty fish every time the hatchery truck came through: "It goes by my place," he said, as if it were a kind of intermittent wagon, delivering food. "But I haven't seen it this month."

In the next half hour I drove slowly, up to the border and back, observing what I could of the water. Perhaps six of the eight miles had pasture on one or both sides, but there were two stretches of about a mile each which were wooded. The bed seemed to be cut through limestone, there were some pretty pools and rapids if no falls, and in several places I saw, from a distance, fish rising though it was impossible to say whether they were trout or creek chubs. A little more than halfway back on my return trip, I saw a man fishing, a portly man of middle age in waders who used his fly rod quite adeptly, working a nice-looking pool which, though it was in pasture land, was shaded by a big willow tree. I stopped the car, watched him fish for a moment, got out, told the dog—it was Moon, the Weimaraner —to stay and walked over.

"Doing any good?" I asked, that being the midwestern translation of the Eastern phrase, *any luck?*

"Not much," he said, a correct answer regardless of how well or badly things are going.

"Catch any at all?"

The correct answer to that, as I could tell by glancing at the bulges in his fabric creel would be *a couple of little ones,* followed,

319

if one warms towards the stranger, by whatever additional information is accurate *(I did get one nice rainbow,* or *they're feeding in the current).* He chose, to my mild surprise, the lie direct: "Haven't caught a one."

It seemed pretty bad form to me, but at least I knew now what information to ask for and how to use it. "Where do you generally catch them in this creek?"

"Downstream," he said. "Towards Brinkley."

I thanked him, went back to my car, turned, and headed upstream away from Brinkley.

About a mile up from where I'd talked to him, the creek swung close to the road. There was a gate there, opening into pasture, with a little sign on it saying, "Please close," which seemed to imply that it was expected people would open it. There was a long, deep, rather slow pool there, and a hundred yards above it the woods started. I drove in, closed the gate, and drove down through the pasture to a little clump of trees where I stopped the car and set my tent up, forty feet or so from the water. Cows were grazing across from me; the dog needed water. I gave it to him in a bowl, to keep him away from what I hoped were carefree, unsuspicious trout, put my two-piece rod together, and strung it up. At the tip of the new leader, I tied on a royal coachman—I always tie on a royal coachman, possibly because its the only dry fly whose name I knew before I started trout fishing. It's a pretty little thing, with a red body and white wings, but if I've caught more fish on royal coachmen than on any other pattern, it could be only because I fish so often with it.

I walked to the nearest part of the stream, keeping the dog behind me, and found myself standing on a spit of sand and pebbles. The stream was about twenty feet across here, running very shallow at my feet but with a strong enough current opposite to have undercut the bank; a few tree roots were exposed through the undercutting, and among them a trout might well be hidden. I made my first cast, if tossing a trout fly that brief a distance may be called a cast, and landed four feet out from the bank against which I'd meant to land for an error of about twenty per cent. Still, the fly was floating nicely, so I let it go. I got the range a little better on subsequent casts, which comforted me a little though I theorize that it's the first which counts—the one which lands before the fish has any reason to suppose he's being fished for. I suppose I cast five times, covering most of the water which looked good to me, before the dog decided to jump into the stream and cool off. I said cross things to him, but not very vehemently—I was already pretty well convinced there'd be no action from the undercut bank and I started upstream. There was some shallow, fast water next which hardly looked as if it would harbor a trout, but since such places sometimes do, I tossed up into it. It would be splendid to report that a twenty-inch brown trout swirled from behind a rock, leapt three feet into the air hooking himself on my coachman, and that, as it is put in the sporting magazines, the fight was on, but no such thing happened. The fly bobbed back towards me, got wet, submerged and snagged on a rock; there being virtually no fight in rocks, I waded in and detached the hook by hand. My purpose, by the way, in citing such examples of my misadventurous ineptness with fishing tackle is not to produce moments of traditional sporting farce to decorate my explanations; you are welcome to smile, of course, if it's your kind of comedy, but my purpose is to establish how low in caliber a trout fisherman might be and still expect to land them at will on dry flies by learning my secret.

Above the little stretch of rapids, and feeding current to it, was a marvelous-looking place. The stream narrowed to ten feet, and deepened enough so that the water looked green, in the deepest part. The green water flowed on both sides of a forty-five-degree angle in the stream course and at the point of the angle was a big old tree stump. There had to be a trout down there; I watched for a moment or two to see if one might be rising. When none did, I caught myself looking around on the ground for likely stones or rocks to be overturned in a hunt for worms, reminded myself that I'd been fishing only ten minutes. Wet fly! Hell, I never catch anything on a wet fly. Nymph! Well, yeah, but, see, the current's pretty fast and it wouldn't really look natural to see a nymph moving against it. I opened my tackle box, passing up six or eight dollars' worth of wet flies and nymph flies, and dubiously took out Con Carter's favorite lure, a thing on which he has caught so many trout, he says, that he feels the same reluctance towards it that I feel towards worms.

No fishing book would ever endorse this thing, for it is an object so gaudy, so artificial, that it makes the longest, brightest peacock-feather streamer fly look natural; nor can I imagine what trout take it to be. It is something called a Flatfish, a miniature version of a plug used quite extensively on casting rods for bass fishing. Con is extremely particular about his Flatfish; the only model which will do is the F-4 size (not even the smallest available), and it must be in yellow with red spots, though there are one or two streams, he says, in North Carolina where black with red spots will do. The F-4 is a little under two inches long, slightly curved, and flattened at the front so that when it is in tension against the pressure of water at the end of a line it wobbles busily, as no minnow, frog or salamander ever could. In shallow water, Con fishes a Flatfish just as it comes from the box, on about eight feet of level leader; in deeper water, he weights the leader about four inches above the Flatfish with a single split shot. It was thus I now rigged mine, shaking my head and muttering at it—a foolish indulgence since one seldom catches a fish in a particular place with a particular bait unless one genuinely expects to; but only a worm would have enabled me to fish just there with real conviction.

for Ophelia

Con can land a Flatfish in the birdbath in my yard from thirty yards away; I doubt that I could rely on making it first try into a bathtub from ten, though I comfort myself that a fly line is designed to float bits of feather through the air, not to handle things which exceed its own weight. I walked above the stump and did what I always do, dropped it into the water and let the current carry it down to where I wanted it. Then I took up the slack and started to inch the Flatfish back towards me, and I have no idea what I may have been thinking of when something slapped it, knocking it nearly to the surface. There was a brief gleam, about four feet down, and that was all. Apparently my agitation, which was partly annoyance with myself for inattention and partly excitement that there was a trout down there, was communicable because the dog began to bark. I got him quieted and repeated my Flatfish maneuver. I did it, in fact, again and again. I told myself finally that I would try five more times, and tried fifteen. Then I snatched the lure off, turned over twenty rocks, finally found a worm, tied hook and worm to leader and drifted that through, tensed for a strike. It didn't come. When I had done it often enough to drown the worm, I looked through my tackle box, sighed, decided there was nothing there which could tempt the fish out again—Con says he thinks trout strike a Flatfish out of anger, and I saw nothing there which looked like it would produce a temper fit. Okay. He saw me. I just happen to know the way to get him when he calms down; let's go on.

Moon got up and trotted out in front of me; I called him back. He has an excellent eye for trouty-looking places, and a strong liking for swimming in them just before I get there. Not that the next place should have been one—it was the deep pool by the gate, possibly forty yards long altogether, through which the water moved quite slowly. According to the trout books, it ought to have two fish, one feeding near the tail, where the current picks up, the other feeding at the head where the current enters,

323

before it slows down. The beaten-down grass on the banks, and the fact that the pool swung in near the road, read differently: this was a most popular and productive fishing place, being a natural one for the hatchery truck to discharge fish at since the driver would be spared from walking. In Iowa today there may be fifty trout or more in pools like that, schooled up, bottom feeding together as in a tank.

I found another worm, hooked it on and let it drift in, sink and settle—worms found at a stream are best; look like what the fish see daily; should be presented as if they had fallen naturally into the water, and are carried along without drag by the current. I watched my fly line. A fly line floats. Only the long leader goes under, making the line itself serve as that piece of equipment no trout fisherman would sanction, a bobber.

I waited about five minutes; then the line jerked, but I knew from the way it moved that it was the wrong fish down there. There are three sorts of indication one's line may make in our streams: if it has been stopped, but makes no further movement, it is a sucker (unless it is a snag). If it dances rapidly, in a series of short, nervous movements, travels around in random directions, it is a creek chub. If it moves slowly, stops, moves out again determinedly, then a trout has taken the worm in his mouth and is swimming into the current in order to swallow it. When one has this last, surprisingly deliberate kind of movement, it is crucial not to strike too soon—how very different from the fierce little Andean rainbows who took my *gusanos* down in Chile.

In the big pool at Westerly Creek it was the second kind of movement, the chub kind. Still I was careful, first because what I take to be the beginning of fulfillment of fisherman's passion is in that instant when one knows that something, something alive and unknown, is lured; and next because there is, now and then, a trout which hits like a chub. So not until the line pulled tight did I strike, but it was neither trout nor chub. As a matter of fact, it was a crayfish this time, and so was the next thing I caught before, working the worm into the current at the head of the pool, I hooked a considerable fish—a big chub, twelve or thirteen inches long with horns growing out of his nose, a kind which is called a horny-head. Some remarkable things come out of trout streams: suckers, with their white, human-lipped mouths, set down under their chins so that the fish may scour the bottom. A kind of salamander called a water dog. Mud-minnows, which seem to live as much on the bank as in the water. And, most remarkable of all—I caught one just once to the amusement of the friend who was fishing with me—a creature called the Eastern Slimy Sculpin, for a brief description of which I can do no better than to refer you to its name.

I had decided to give up the big pool and get on upstream, into the woods, when I noticed that the dog was gone. I looked anxiously towards the cattle, though he's pretty good about not chasing them, saw the dog lying in the shade of a bush with his tongue out, and saw that someone was fishing behind me, casting now towards the undercut bank where I had started.

My first impulse was to slip on up the creek, calling quietly to the dog to follow so the stranger wouldn't get ahead of me; my next impulse was to call the dog very loudly and angrily, for just at the place he had jumped into the water when we started fishing, I saw the distant man lifting out a fish; my third impulse I followed—it was to walk back down the creek for, though the fisherman was too far away for me to recognize, there was a familiar car drawn up beside mine. It was Con Carter. He had said he might come up, after some early-afternoon duties, and since he drives fast and had used main roads instead of following the Mississippi, he'd arrived very shortly after me.

We met by the stump where I had had my strike, and I said: "What'd you get down there by the bank? Nice big chub?"

"Trout," Con said. "Or he'd have gotten to be one if I'd left him in there to grow." And he showed me, in his creel, a ten-inch rainbow.

"What'd you take him on?" I asked, forseeing the answer.

"Yellow Flatfish," said Con apologetically.

I pointed to the stump and said a trout—or probable trout—had brushed my Flatfish once but wouldn't come out again.

"What else did you try?"

"About everything," I lied. Trout fishing really is bad for my character.

"Super-duper?"

"Don't have one."

A Super-duper is a flat, shiny piece of metal bent almost double, with its outer surface lacquered gold and its inner surface red. Con offered me one, which I declined.

"I'd like to see you use it," I said.

Con flipped the thing in, landing it exactly above where I'd seen the trout flash; whether he chose the spot by intuition, calculation or accident I don't know. The Super-duper danced and glittered in a tantalizing way, but nothing showed.

"It's a good lure for big trout," Con said. "It may scare off the little ones."

"I don't know what size he is," I said, sneakily pleased that my trout wasn't being caught.

"Think I'll go to a spinner and fly." He removed the Super-duper, and attached in its place a tiny gold spinner on a flexible shaft. To the spinner he coupled a brown and green, iridescent, heavy-bodied wet fly, somewhat larger than anything I had; it was on about a number six hook. Con guessed it might look like a caterpillar, and that the spinner might be taken for a minnow trying to make off with it. He drifted this contrivance in under the stump, and began to twitch it back upstream towards us.

"There he is," he said suddenly.

"He hit it?"

"No, looked at it. Didn't you see him?"

I hadn't.

"We'll get him now," Con said, casting again and teasing his lure around the stump. It took three more casts, and a change of flies (brown and tan, longer and lighter-bodied than the first, with a small red tail feather); the fish struck the new fly first time past. Con hooked it, played it, and was moving it towards where we stood when the dog hit the water, taking the flopping object for something to retrieve. The trout was gone, off the line and back under his stump by the time I got the dog called out, and while I was furious, Con took it pretty calmly.

"Another ten-inch rainbow," he said. "There anything up in that big-looking pool?"

"I don't know," I said. "Nothing I can catch, anyway. There's some pretty water up above it."

"I drove across French Creek about twenty miles before I got here," Con said. "It's faster and clearer and has more cover, and a man told me it was stocked day before yesterday—might be some good fish there."

"I'll take the ten-inchers if I can get them," I said, for there is one respect in which I am an atypical fisherman: I have no exclusive yearning to catch large fish. The smaller ones are, by common consent, the best to eat. Con, who has a six-pound brook trout mounted on his wall at home, was persuaded there might be something like it back at French Creek, and decided to return there. I said, having seen two acceptable trout come out of Westerly (or one come out, and one snagged on a dog), that I thought I'd stay. With that we parted; I checked with him the following day, though, and found he'd caught a limit and among them a splendid brown, eighteen inches long, which he judged from its condition must have been in the creek for several years. I wished I'd gone down there with him.

Not that I failed to catch trout. By the time Con left, there were two ladies sitting on the bank of the big pool, still-fishing with night crawlers, bobbers and weighted lines. I called the dog, went past them and on up Westerly. I fished hard that afternoon. Tried Con's fly-and-spinner method for a time, but I didn't seem able to control it as he had and nothing struck. I came, up in the woods, to a place where I saw trout—two at least—rising and splashing in the current at the head of a small pool, feeding on insects, and I threw five or six different dry fly patterns up their way without doing anything but alarming them, for after the first few casts they began reacting to the sight of the line in the air. Come on, come on, catch one. They're feeding on flies, right? You don't know what kind, right? Okay, get one on a worm, open his stomach, and see what color insects are in it. Right.

The first stone I turned over had three worms under it. I put one on a very small hook, moved up above where the fish had been feeding and lowered the worm into the current, and as it reached the place where water spilled into the pool, saw one of the fish coming up fast to meet it; the sleek spotted shape, the bullet head, the cruel intention of a predator—in the instant when a trout strikes, I sometimes think of tigers. I had him, joyfully, even with some skill as I set the hook, gave him a little line to dash away with, turned him towards me then so that he swam almost into my boot, a nice brown. I cleaned him, put him happily into my creel, and laid out his stomach on a rock. There was nothing in it except some decomposed blackish material, and one undecipherable insect leg; I had already tried my black flies, but I'm not sure I'd have gone back to flies, really. I was quite happy with the way I'd caught him; I got his companion on the same worm.

The dog and I went on through the woods, cool and pleased; when I have the first fish or two, I become calmer and I fish more skillfully. I missed a trout, back on the fly and spinner again. I found more worms and caught a rainbow so small that I was certain he'd been spawned in Westerly—no more than four inches; he hadn't been hooked badly and I returned him to the creek. Far from the road, we came out of the woods in an overgrown pasture where the stream divided. In the smaller of the branches, watercress was growing and I picked some to put in the creel with the fish, to keep them moist. To the stems of the cress were clinging little black fresh-water snails, a favorite food of brook trout; the arm of the stream in which it grew was six or eight feet wide, and ran straight, about two feet deep for forty yards or so. The cress grew on both sides, leaving about a three foot channel in the center. It seemed to me I knew how to fish it. I shortened the line until there was no more than three feet of leader dangling from the end of my rod, put about a third of a worm on the hook, and went quietly up the stream a little. Then I lowered the bait into the rapid water, and followed it along, walking, and five steps from where I started a brookie dashed out, hooked himself, and I used the impetus of his rush to flip him out of the water. If he'd got back into cress, it would have made a hopeless tangle. It was splendid there; I lost two or three, hooked another; its stomach was full of snails.

Evening was coming, and I had four trout. I'd caught them all on worms, but I felt I'd done it properly; I started back down the creek, pretty satisfied. When I reached the big pool, the two ladies were picking up their stool and cleaning the night crawlers off their hooks. I watched indulgently; a night crawler is a huge worm, seven or eight inches long and as big around as your little finger. They are fine for carp and catfish, but I was amused at the idea of anyone's fishing for trout with them. I asked the ladies how they'd done.

"I don't believe they've stocked this creek lately," one said.

"We just got four," said the other, and showed them to me on a stringer, three rainbows and a brown and all bigger than the largest fish I had.

329

"We got eleven last Saturday morning," the first lady said.

I was back again at the stump, as the ladies drove away, thinking about the trout I knew was under there. He might have recovered by now from his fright, and his sore mouth. Since he was away from the pool, it argued that he'd been in the stream for a while, though, and ought by now to be wise. I considered worms, fly and spinner, Flatfish, but I had known all afternoon how I was going to catch him; now that I knew the night-crawler ladies had as many trout as I, there was no chance I'd reconsider.

If you have eaten red caviar, you know what salmon eggs look like. Prepared as trout bait, they are firmer and less cohesive than what may be bought at the grocer's; they are also illegal as bait in some western states and unheard of in most eastern ones. Actually, they are useless, at least in my experience, in eastern states; I took a bottle with me to Connecticut one summer and tried them pretty thoroughly—not a nibble. In the far West, where salmon eggs are part of what a river normally contains, they are, I suppose, something trout feed on naturally. In Iowa, dyed white, or pink or fluorescent red, they are part of what trout are trained to eat (or so I am convinced) by the hundreds of salmon eggs thrown in by fishermen in the course of a season. Now I cannot disapprove of the notion of baiting a salmon egg on a very small hook and fishing with it in a place where a trout may be, cannot disapprove and don't. But I do disapprove of what I proceeded to do next, for it is a form of chumming. I took half a dozen eggs out of the bottle and tossed them into the creek above the stump. Then I sat and smoked a cigarette, waiting for the trout to find and sample them. When the cigarette was finished, I tossed in four or five more, baited my hook with yet another and threw that in, too. I waited about a minute. The fly line moved, pulled out straight; I flexed the rod and felt, for a moment, the pressure of the fish at the other end. I failed to hook him, but once a trout has started feeding on salmon eggs he's not likely to get discouraged. Two more free ones, and one with a hook in it took him. He actually came up off the bottom to meet the descending egg, and I could watch him all the way, running with it in his mouth upstream until I hooked him. He was a pretty greedy trout.

Nor could I really feel apologetic about the way I'd caught him, though I'm not sure why. I suppose merely that I'd been fishing hard, tried a lot of things, and wanted that particular fish.

It was still daylight. I started gathering wood to make a little fire to cook my fish on and it was while I was tearing a dry limb off a fallen tree that I saw the truck drive up, stop at the same gate near the big pool that I'd come in by, and the driver get out to open the gate. It was a small, green pick-up with a barrel in the body, and though I'd never seen one before, I was pretty sure it came from a fish hatchery. The driver brought it on into the pasture and stopped beside the creek, and I walked up to watch him. He filled a bucket with creek water, carried it behind the truck, and then reached into the big barrel with a dip net; he filled his bucket with fish, carried it to the creek and emptied them gently into the water. He went back to the truck for a second load and, as I came up, a third.

"How many are you putting in?" I asked.

"Fifty or so."

We stood and watched. At first the fish swam around quite frantically. Then they began to congregate in the shallowest part of the pool and to turn, facing the current.

"Tomorrow's Saturday," he said. "I expect most of them will be in the frying pan by tomorrow night."

"There were some ladies here said they caught eleven last Saturday."

"Some of those old women really can swish a worm," he said. "Better get your rod. They might start coming any time, if they saw me drive by."

"Isn't it better to let them get used to the water?" I asked, meaning the fish. The hatchery man smiled and shrugged, wished me luck, got in his truck and drove away.

Chiefly, I was irritated. It destroyed my sense of having accomplished something to see all those new fish, easy fish I thought, lying in the same creek in which, with what skill and knowledge I had, I'd fished successfully before they came. But finally I began to feel as children do, when they see fish thick in a hatchery. "Couldn't we catch a couple?" the children say, and I trotted down to the campsite for my rod.

But it was curious. The fish, so newly in the creek, struck at first at almost anything, but half-heartedly and, it seemed, in annoyance. The Flatfish and the spinners would be followed, slapped perhaps, but not bitten at. Eventually one did take a spinner, but he was so listless as I hauled him out that I put him back in again. He swam back only far enough to join the others. When they had been in the creek twenty minutes, they stopped following the things I fished with. They simply lay there, twitching their tails occasionally, distrustful of me but without having formed the idea of hiding.

It was the following morning that I made my record. I knew where fifty fish were; it barely occurred to me that I might ignore them, go off along the stream fishing as I had the day before for the resident trout . . . through the woods, thinking out the problems, using what skill and knowledge I had. There were fifty trout in the pool! The ladies might be on their way this very minute! Would Con have ignored them? What about a fisherman-knight? I gulped coffee, jammed my rod together, tied on my last royal coachman, told the dog to stay in the car and trotted to the pool.

It was swirling with trout. They had waked up hungry, and were dashing about, free for the first time in their lives, missing breakfast perhaps for the first time, too. They were leaping,

for Ophelia

pushing one another out of the way, at whatever may have been in the pool or on its surface—bits of leaf, sticks, possibly even an authentic bug or two. There I stood, a tyrant with a fly rod, smiling at the disorder and gullibility of liberation, and cast my fly at random onto the center of the pool. Three of the mob were after it instantly, and the one who won swallowed it so firmly there was no need to hook him. Out he came, a twelve-inch rainbow, and instead of dashing off in terror at his thrashing there were fish who followed him across the pool.

The coachman took a second on the second cast. On the third, a fish struck but I was slow to strike back and lost him. On the fourth I snagged a tree behind me on the back-cast and lost the coachman. I tied on a gray Wulff fly, which floats very high in the water; it took a fish. I deliberately changed to yet another pattern—I cannot now remember which—and it worked, too. There was a lull, then, during which I cast without answers three or four times; then they began to feed once more, even more violently than at first, and a tiny black gnat fly on a number-twenty hook caught a big limp brown, the biggest fish of the day. The final fly I do not know the name of—it was a gaudy, machine-tied thing in yellow, blue and red which I kept in my fly-box only because one of my children bought it for me once with allowance money, getting it off a card of fifteen-cent crappie flies in a country grocery store. It was sensational. A rainbow met it at the surface and leapt clear out of the water, winning it from the others.

There were my six fish; they had been caught in less than half an hour, I had moved less than twenty feet. And you have the secret: take your dry flies to the hole where the green truck stops, give the fish one night to grow confused and hungry, and you can make your trout-fishing grandfather look as slow as the buggy he drove to the unstocked brook in the woods, six miles from home.

333

I think of two people when I remember how gracelessly I caught those fish. One was an Englishman, a very pleasant man who visited the university at which I teach and who, when I met him, said he'd like to see the countryside. I took him walking along the bank of the Iowa river, our carp and catfish water, and found he was quite excited that we were free to carry along a fishing rod. He was one of those brilliant, profoundly educated men of a recent sort in England, as I understand it, who have managed to come up from working-class origins through sheer intellectual power, taking advantage of the scholarships and the entree which the postwar labor government opened up in that stratified country. It was a wonder to him that we were allowed, any of us, to angle freely almost anywhere we liked. He took the rod I offered in his hand, and it was the first time he had ever held one; something nibbled, down in the muddy water—a bullhead, I imagine, which is a small and not very desirable sort of catfish. His pleasure at having had a bite seemed so great that, though I couldn't tell him quickly enough when to set the hook to catch whatever it was, he was still strongly gratified. And when I said it was a shame we didn't have more time, we might have gone trout fishing, he could barely believe it.

"But those rights are terribly exclusive in England," he said. "Of course, if you're very rich, you can rent them sometimes."

We've democratized fishing pretty well. ("Some of those old women can really swish a worm," the hatchery man had said.) The second person whom I think of was a hip young man who worked in advertising in New York. He and his wife were visiting mutual friends near where we summered in Connecticut, and I was surprised to have him ask to go trout fishing with me. His equipment explained it; it was good equipment and had been given him by his wife's father. It was important enough for him to show his wife that he could bring home trout, just as her father had, so that he got up at the very unhip hour of five thirty to do the dry-fly bit with me.

He was tense, full of self-doubt and overeagerness, and when we caught the first trout of the morning, using a little device called a Colorado spoon, his relief was rather touching. We caught six more that morning, a couple on dry flies, and I recall what he said when we had cleaned them and laid them out on the bank:

"Like, Dad, they've really cooled the trouting scene, haven't they?"

Yes, masters, they truly have.

That is, or ought to be, the last word; it's last word enough for me. But another summer has come and is nearly gone. The cheerful underhandedness with which, in my trout-fishing boyhood at last year's age of thirty-eight, I could use any method that brought fish out of the water, is under continuous attack.

A most effective member of the puritan guerrillas is my daughter, who has just turned nine. We were camping on a little creek called Elk, ten days ago, and there was a pretty limestone pool close by where we pitched the tent. I rigged a rod for her shortly after we settled in, with a small hook and a lively worm, and offered it to her to drop into the pool. This she agreed to do, not with any great enthusiasm but with the tolerance for adult enthusiasms which agreeable children have.

She stayed with it no more than five minutes, and I swear she was getting a bite when she laid the rod down carefully and walked away to where her mother was building a fire.

"I guess I'm not very interested in fishing, Daddy," she said as she passed me. I grabbed the rod from the ground, but was too late. The worm was gone. Then it wasn't long afterwards that she came running to find me along the stream not far from camp, and cried: "Daddy, Daddy. You know that deer-hair fly? Are you going to use it?"

It was a fly called an Irresistible which I had been showing her when it arrived by mail the day before.

"We saw a trout jump in the pool," she said excitedly, hurrying me back to tie it on for her. Well. I must say. She casts very badly. Didn't raise a fish, either. But there she stood trying, requesting a change of patterns when the first didn't work, for half an hour. She went back to it again, still unsuccessfully, first thing the next morning.

Then there's her brother, who is four, and on whom her ideas of what's fun have an inordinate influence. He wouldn't have a worm either, or even a salmon egg, when I strung a rod for him. Fine trout fisherman he is—wouldn't even let me give him a proper fly when I opened the tackle box. He insisted on taking a bright yellow popping bug, suitable only for bass and bluegill, and if you think his sister's an awkward caster, you ought to see him. They stood together fishing and laughing and flailing the water so hard that it must have scared the trout to a point where his judgment was affected, for later their mother caught him on a blue-gray nymph called a Muskrat's Revenge ("Con Carter said it might work," she told me). It was exactly the third fish she ever caught in her life, and when she hooked him there was one child running for the landing net and the other jumping up and down beside her on the bank hollering, though they've seen me haul out dozens of trout with various devices without displaying more than passing interest.

Women and children. Players at a game. What can you expect? But I am also losing Con Carter.

Back when I had written the first draft of these recollections, I asked him to read it through, thinking he might offer corrections on points of technique. But what interested him more was my discussion, in the early paragraphs, of the ideal trout fisherman as I conceived him, the purist, of whom Con said:

"I guess I'm like you. I've been looking for that man, too."

"Maybe you'll find him in the East," I said. For Con, who comes from Tennessee originally, has found a job in northern New England, and will be leaving soon.

"I hope so," he said, and very likely he will. Or if not, then there's a chance that he may very well look into the water one day and see that man in his own reflection.

For consider this: Just a day or two ago we fished Westerly Creek again together, and came to the same stump where his second fish was caught and lost last year. We were fishing companionably rather than efficiently, taking turns from one spot to the next so that each could watch the other fish, and it was Con's turn.

He made a beautiful cast to the stump, using a little dry fly called a Red Variant, floated it past two or three times, then tried another pattern. He took the second dry fly off, moved up opposite the stump and worked a wet Queen of the Waters past it. He said he thought he'd seen the fish, but it didn't take.

"How about your Flatfish?" I said.

"I don't actually have it with me," Con confessed.

"Here. Use mine."

He smiled and shook his head. He was busy changing to another wet fly, a brown and yellow nymph.

"Need a spinner for that?" I asked him. I've been scoring very heavily this summer on wet fly and spinner, and had already on Westerly Creek, not long before.

"I'd like to see if I can get him without," Con said, and indeed the fish did strike once at the nymph, struck short and went down under his stump for good.

I still think the spinner would have brought him out, but Con felt we should press on, working our way upstream.

Note, April 1972. In the ten years since this was written Con Carter and I have both become purists. "Con" is based on two

337

friends, both of whom live in New Hampshire, John Yount and Tom Williams. Living there, they are hundreds of trout ahead of me, but I still have the pleasure of visiting them sometimes and fishing with them, and it's a long while since any of us floated a worm. But, speaking for myself, the purism is pragmatic rather than idealistic; fly fishing works, now that I understand it a little better.

The four-year-old in the article is now fourteen, and more the idealistic purist; he does not always fish successfully, but flies are all he will use and he prefers them, generally, with barbless hooks, so that the trout may be released as harmlessly as possible.

His older sister would be nineteen now, and I often think of her when I am by a stream.

*First published with a
number of cuts in
Holiday, June, 1968,
under the title "Scuba."
Dr. Webb, who appears
in this piece, is my brother
Paul.*

Seawalking

"You'll have to change that shirt before you can go to
school," I heard my wife say, and I knew exactly what
our nine-year-old son's reply would be.

"Mom." On his way to comply. "You think you're so big
just because you saw a moray eel."

He said this in our Iowa farmhouse in the late fall of the
year, as the morning log picked up flame in the fireplace and
snow fell outside. It had been his formula, whenever family
tone permitted a comic answer to mothering, for about ten
months.

True, too. The winter before, when the three of us came
in from floating along a coral reef off Ocho Rios, Jamaica,
our wife and mother had been just a touch overweening
about being the first in the family to see a moray. This eel is

339

an ill-favored, spotted creature which hides in coral pockets by day, sticking its head out of the hole to look around from time to time.

Skin divers, which is what we were equipped as, fear the moray mildly. It is rather slimy, it bites, and the bite usually infects. It is not aggressive, though, and the people who get bitten are almost always ones who have reached into the wrong crevice to pull out a rock lobster.

I have read that morays come out hunting at night, and can be more of a problem, but I don't know. As is true in any new territory, people who are learning the land below the sea exchange a lot of scare stories about the wildlife.

"There's catamounts out there, sidewinder rattlesnakes big around as your arm, and cactus that can cripple you for a week," could be translated: sharks, stingrays and spiny urchins. There'd be the same low probability of having a bad experience with the latter group, while seawalking, as with the former, taking a walk in the desert. Distribution within the region, frequency of use by humans, and behavior patterns of the animals are pretty much in your favor.

This is not to say that sharks, in particular, don't scare me. I would not knowingly swim where sharks were plentiful, any more than I would stroll around calmly in country known to be infested with grizzly bears. You find that almost anywhere you might go seawalking, though, there is someone who knows the area and can tell you which the safe reefs are. Consequently, I have never seen a shark, outside of an aquarium. As for barracuda, which also seem alarming, I see them frequently; they are, as far as I can tell, quite indifferent to my presence, and so I have grown more or less indifferent to theirs.

My wife, once more, gets credit for the word, *seawalking*. As noted, we go out equipped like skin divers, but it is neither exercise nor the simple adventure of breathing underwater which takes us out to the reefs, wherever we find ourselves on the coasts of the world.

"We go seawalking," she says, meaning that the pleasure is much more like that of birdwalking than it is a sport or a perfection of skill.

But it is a crazy dream of birdwalking, because the things you see and name are so profuse, so strange and so bright; and because you are there, gliding, silent and weightless, alien, in an environment into which you have intruded by something not unlike magic. It is a birdwalk, then, aided by sorcery, in a secret garden populated from the bestiary of a color-mad monk, things swarming past so thickly at times that even keeping track of species is impossible, let alone counting numbers.

Have you taken those three-mile hikes through briars and weeds, to find a now-deserted puddle where someone sighted upland plovers yesterday? Looked for the berries where the cedar waxwings feed? Sat in the cold wind on a Mississippi bluff, hoping a bald eagle will soar by close enough so that you may, for once, be sure of him?

Seawalking will always be dreamlike if you have, not just for the splendid traffic but because it is all sight and no sound; only by a change of light do you know the weather above, and communication is a silent hand moving slowly through clear water.

Dreamlike because it is movement through fluid at an even temperature, so that the body sensation is uniform, face, ears, neck, chest, knees and toes all registering the same, and with hardly any awareness of effort; feeling cold comes as gradually as it does in sleep, and tiring is something you will not realize until afterwards.

Dreamlike, finally, because the level of interest is so unremittingly high, and of involvement total—with always, for me, an undercurrent of fear at being where I do not really belong, never any of the reassurance of boredom or routine.

It may, perhaps become routine for my son, starting so young. If the environment, and being in it, should become that familiar to him, he can go on if he likes to equipment more sophisticated than air tanks and snorkels, to deeper dives, faster movement, longer times below, and the research projects of the professional and the scientist.

For me, what I know and can do now is almost too much. On the day of the first moray, for example, I was thinking of something called fire coral. It is described as mustard-colored, and the only photograph I'd seen was an underwater blur, which showed very little more than color. If one brushes against it, so goes the appropriate scare story, it causes stinging and a rash—like poison ivy? There was some yellow stuff growing on a coral head, a big one, six feet or so in diameter, over which my wife was swimming. I couldn't even decide if it was a coral or a plant.

She was pointing. We were using only snorkels that day, staying mostly on the surface. I made a shallow dive, assumed it was the yellow stuff she wanted me to notice, and signaled back that I saw it. She shook off my signal, turned, went around the coral head and pointed again. I followed her course, looked down: fifty blue-headed wrasses, a dozen sergeant majors, ten parrot fish, three squirrel fish, anemones, spiny urchins . . .

We surfaced, she raised her mask and said,

"Did you see him?"

I raised my mask and asked what. The boy was swimming about ten feet away, face down, unaware that we were having a discussion.

"The moray." We refixed our masks, and I followed her around the same circle: a hundred surf silversides, a trumpet fish, four small barracudas off to one side (the boy was following them), houndfish, a different kind of urchin . . .

I never did see the eel. But then, neither my wife nor I saw the cow ray to which our son tried to attract our attention, and in the same afternoon I tried unsuccessfully to show both my collaborators one of the most beautiful sights in the sea, a school of squid, iridescent and unbelievably fast, moving away like jet-propelled balloons.

It was an afternoon of excitement and delight, from which we all came in exhausted, with a dozen things to tell one another, and the boy said what we all felt:

"I can't wait for it to be tomorrow, so that we can go out again."

I would have said, up to a year ago, that when it came to winter vacations I was more of a skier myself. On the other hand, it had been several years since I'd laced on boots, for we do not live in ski country and my family hasn't learned. But as for going south—beaches are boring, hotels expensive, swimming around rather pointless, the whole thing a remarkable waste of money. I'd have said.

Through the years when I was binding my hide in this stuffy position, our inland boy, coming to it as mysteriously as those Kansas and Nebraska kids who join the Navy, was patiently requesting swim fins and a mask in exchange for learning to swim without them. The visibility in our farm ponds, where we swim, being about two feet, I couldn't understand what he wanted such things for. I realize now that, having seen Cousteau movies and read books, he was preparing himself.

There came a day when we were traveling east, and stopped off in Ohio to visit the laboratory of Dr. Paul Webb, an ecologist whose physiological research involves him in the problems of all the frontier environments, from underwater to outer space. Dr. Webb had had a tank built for experiments with SCUBA gear. It was a cypress tank, with observation windows, made for him, as a matter of curious fact, by a firm whose regular product is pickle vats.

His experiment was finished by then, but there was a pretty

wide selection of regulators, back packs, masks and air tanks around. He asked if we'd like to try them out, and before I could think of a calm way to say no, my boy said yes.

So in we went, all three, and while there was nothing much to see besides Doctor Webb's rather hairy legs and my own tufted toes, it was an extraordinary experience. I thought, sitting there underwater, breathing in and out through the mouthpiece with no alarm or discomfort, of a game we played as boys at camp. It was called tea party, damned if I know why, and the idea was to teach us to stay underwater with our eyes open. Boys were paired off to sink together, facing one another, to sit on the bottom in three or four feet of cold lake water; there you watched your partner and he you, emitting streams of bubbles, and the pair that stayed down longest won.

Here I went, forty years later, playing tea party in a pickle vat with an ecologist and a nine-year-old, but the situation was a triumphant cheat: we could sit there and watch bubbles as long as we liked.

We had the power to live and lounge about in an environment not merely alien but, beyond a minute or two, deadly.

The best way I can tell you how much anticipatory pleasure this gave me is to say that my son had won: when winter vacation time came and a friend wrote suggesting the Laurentians, I wrote back and said no, indeed. Jamaica.

I feel quite sure that more and more of those restless people like me, who feel that a vacation isn't worth taking if it can't be focused on a particular and intense activity, will make the sea-walking choice in the years now starting. A good many already have.

Since my own first dives in Ocho Rios I have tried the waters off Sardinia, at Villefranche, in Provincetown, Cozumel, and in the kelp beds off Newport Beach, California. I have learned a little, and have much to learn.

344

The most important thing I've learned, I guess, is also the simplest; like most simple lessons, it is not at all self-evident. I learned it at Newport Beach, where a friend had arranged for me to dive with a very experienced man who teaches at the University of California campus at Irvine, and lives in a house near the beach. This athletic young professor and his family and friends go seawalking nearly every day.

What impressed me first was how his gear was stored and maintained. I'd seen such equipment, of course, on display in stores and in commercial dive shops, but this was a man's personally chosen and personally loved selection. I remember thinking of tack rooms, gun cabinets, and the onshore lockers of small-boat sailors in the winter time. Good sports equipment has a real beauty to it; it is expensive stuff, and the owner's pride and pleasure in it is a pleasant thing to see.

Here, instead of Kieffer saddles or Purdey doubles, were brightly painted metal SCUBA tanks, made by Captain Cousteau's American affiliate, U.S. Divers Company, carefully racked. There were black, hard-plastic back packs; strong, somewhat faded webbing for straps and belts; bright chrome regulators. A shelf of underwater instruments, cameras and watches and depth gauges. Fins ranged in pairs, wet suits hanging, spear guns cleaned and racked, each item reflecting careful choice in a room whose interior was particularly modified to store them.

"What do you need?" my host asked, showing me in there.

"Wow," I said. Then, "I've brought a mask and fins." The fit of these items is fairly critical, and, along with a snorkel and an inflatable belt, not burdensome to travel with.

"Good. What sort of regulator do you like?"

"I haven't used the stuff often enough to have a preference," I said.

"I've got a new Conshelf Mark V," he said. "Want to try it?"

I protested, of course. What would he use himself?

My host smiled. "There are plenty of extras," he said. "But it's only twenty feet where we're going. I don't think I'll want a tank today."

The same, it turned out, went for the wet suit. It would be a little chilly, admittedly, and the third man who was going with us preferred to use a jacket. My host said he'd rather swim without.

I thought once more of riding, shooting, sailing—when you go out with a man for the first time in a place he knows, it's best to do as he does and use the equipment his example recommends.

"Let's not take tanks at all, then," I said.

Off we went, swimming out to where the kelp grows. This is where marine life is, off California, rather than in coral. That day we saw hundreds of Garibaldis, which are like goldfish two feet long, and are protected. And abalones, which are protected, too, if they are less than five inches across the shell.

("You'll see a world of four-and-seven-eighths-inch abalones today," my host said.)

Most exciting was the kelp itself, growing from the bottom almost up to the surface, some of the stems as big around as a big man's leg and the branches waving forest-like, echoing wave motion, back and forth. Among it swim the fish, and after them we went, in and out among the plants with light sifting through from the surface—it was a lovely seawalk. I realized, when we came in from it, that there was nothing out there, at that depth, in that light, that I'd have got a better look at using an air tank. And that, of course, was the lesson: men with hundreds of dollars' worth of equipment and hundreds of hours of diving time, more often than not prefer the simplicity of leaving everything home but the mask, the fins, the snorkel and the safety belt.

What this means is that with one minute of instruction, and gear costing less than twenty-five dollars, you can go seawalking safely and with full pleasure in all but one of the places I have been, some of them among the world's most celebrated. In such places, where the things you want to see are at twenty feet or less in clear, well-lighted water, everything is visible, even somewhat magnified from the optics of mask and water, simply floating on the surface. For close inspection, or for seeing underneath things, a fin-propelled surface dive will take you down deep very quickly.

The fins, by the way, move you along so quickly that it's a little ridiculous—swimmers so poor that they have trouble thrashing the length of a country-club pool can go for miles, with ease and grace, using swim fins.

I shan't try to offer the one minute of instruction here. The old gentleman on the beach, just coming in from a half-hour sea-stroll, can give it to you, and will be very pleased to be asked. Every diver I've ever known was a proselytizer. Or if you'd like to get it from a book, we've enjoyed one called *The Complete Illustrated Guide to Snorkel and Deep Diving,* by a man named Owen Lee who has a nice, clear, low-pressure and good-humored expository style, and clearly knows what he's talking about.

As for the equipment bill, ten to twelve dollars buys a good pair of flippers, seven or eight dollars for a mask, a couple for the snorkel and a couple more for an inflatable belt.

To use underwater breathing equipment, which enables you to go deeper and stay down for about forty-five minutes per tank of air, Owen Lee will tell you that you'd better take a regular SCUBA course, and I'm not going to contradict him.

What you would learn in such a course, to summarize, is that a tank of compressed air allows you to stay underwater for about forty-five minutes, with a reserve air supply, available by opening an extra valve, of three minutes more. This is to give you time to get back up to the surface if you run out below. Though the SCUBA tank (its stands for Self Contained Underwater Breathing Apparatus) seems very heavy, it is virtually weightless in the water. In fact, you will need to wear about a pound of lead for each twenty pounds of body weight to keep yourself down. This may seem a little scary at first, but the fact is that unless you create a slight negative buoyancy, you'll spend your forty-five minutes bobbing up towards the surface and having to dive back down again.

To a valve on top of the tank you fasten a hose, at the free end of which is a mouthpiece. This you hold between your teeth. When you inhale, the demand opens the valve and lets as much air out of the tank as your lungs require each time.

As you dive—this happens in snorkeling, too—your ears hurt. To counter this, you'll be taught to pinch your nostrils together, and exhale against the closure. As soon as the outer pressure against the ears has been equalized by this rather simple means of building up the internal pressure, the pain goes away.

Down to thirty-three feet, the pressure is close enough to normal air pressure at the surface so that you needn't be concerned with decompression. If you start making deeper dives, you will have to learn to allow enough time, while coming up again, for your body to accommodate itself gradually to the change. There are many other things you'll learn in a SCUBA course (not to swim alone; to use a surface marker in your swimming area to warn off boats), but the real goal of the course is to make you so familiar with and confident in the equipment that you won't panic. Panic is said to be the greatest enemy of the inexperienced diver, and that seems likely enough.

There's a third kind of equipment which you may have seen advertised which is great fun. This is a very light hookah rig— that is, a compressor on the surface which sends air down a hose to the divers below. Johnson makes one and Evinrude another; each has a ring for the motor and compressor to float in, so that as you swim around below you can tow it along with you. There is very little anxiety in using these; since you can't go any deeper than the hose is long, there are no decompression problems. You probably should have someone knowledgeable along the first time out, but the difference between learning to use the light hookahs and learning SCUBA is the difference between instruction and training.

As far as sport uses of the underwater breathing equipment are concerned, I'm going to take the position that there aren't any. There's the aesthetic, mind-opening kind of experience I've been describing; there are other adventures which attract amateurs, like treasure hunting, archaeology and specimen collecting.

There are various other devices invented or about to be, such as underwater sleds which can be towed by a boat, which—if used for sport—are going to be about as popular with seawalkers as waterskis are with serious fishermen, or snowmobiles with cross-country skiers.

Then, of course, there is spearfishing.

This is done only with the snorkel, free-diving, and the reason for it is all too plain, once you have been out: fish feel pretty safe down there, and will, by and large, pay little attention to a diver. To spear them while using an air tank or hookah would merely be food-gathering, like shooting a duck on the water.

To spear them while diving free, limited by the capacity of one's lungs, takes a great deal of skill, on the other hand, and allows the advantage to remain, as it should, with the fish. It attracts me not at all.

I say this, illogically, as one who loves his fly rod all too well, and might well like ocean fishing, too, if I did it like a man. But to do it like a fish seems wildly intrusive; the same beautiful creature which I might haul up with hook and line with pleasure is somehow not one I enjoy seeing with a spearhole in him.

In addition, fish do, in time, grow shy and scarce in heavily spearfished areas. There has been a start at conservation; there are, as you have probably heard, underwater parks now. There will have to be closed seasons, I suppose, and more and more protected places and species, and finally underwater game wardens. That part, the organization which will have to come, all seems rather depressing to me, but, man being as he is, I shall also have to support it.

I don't mean to make this a matter of heavy moralizing. There are harvestable species of fish, and methods of habitat improvement, just are there are for game birds, and I'd guess that spearfishermen will have to bear the costs through licensing, just as bird hunters do. What I must hope is that right now there are men, conservationists and marine biologists, planning how to preserve some wild areas of the sea, and make parks of others, and hunting preserves, commercial developments—already, as I understand it, there are artificial reefs being created by setting tripods of concrete slabs (the kind you run the wheels of your car against in parking lots) in rows, in shallow sandy areas which don't otherwise attract fish life.

To each his own violations: I shan't like being told where I can and cannot try to trap specimens for aquarium study. One of the most interesting times I've ever had underwater came when my boy and I were trying to get hold of some lovely little fish called Beau Gregories, yellow and blue, an inch long or so. We experimented with various nets and bottles before we settled on a quart jar with some sardines in it, placed on the bottom. The idea was that we would watch from the surface, and dive down to cover the mouth with a net when the fish were well inside eating.

The whole thing worked, too, except that just as the fish went in we heard a motor boat start up, looked back, saw water skiers coming, and got out of the way. The boat went by; the water cleared. We nodded at one another and swam over to complete our capture, but the sea has a new surprise for you every day.

for Ophelia

Our trap was trapped; the Beau Gregories were gone, and the whole jar was held in a pair of claws like those on an Atlantic lobster, a big one, in waters where there are no Atlantic lobsters.

It took us a couple of days to get it identified. It was a soldier crab, or so we finally decided, which is a huge version of the tiny, familiar, hermit crab which having no shell of its own inhabits discarded mollusk shells. But the soldier, in the Caribbean, needed a much grander home; he was inhabiting a conch shell which must have weighed two pounds.

This matter of identification is crucial, and difficult for three reasons: you can't carry a book while swimming, you can't communicate in any detail, and generally you can't be sure, when you come up, which fish the other guy really means.

Afterwards, looking at a book, you may say at best: "I think I saw one of those."

"A French angelfish? Yeah, I guess I did too. Did it have this white around its mouth?"

You can't remember. Moreover, there isn't, so far as I know, a good complete field guide to marine life. Seawalking needs its Roger Tory Peterson; I expect he'll be along, and when he comes, I have a suggestion. I described it recently in a letter to that same Doctor Webb in whose pickle vat I first breathed underwater: " . . . the way to do a fish and marine life field guide is to do it on plastic cards, like flashcards, a card to each species. Sets for various regions, family groups, etc. Possibly attached looseleaf to a lanyard to fasten to your safety belt. Salt water proof. Okay. You're snorkeling along, or scuba-ing (or out, forgive me, with a hookah), and want to identify something. Looks like an angelfish. Card-set has tab for the family group. Turn to family. Flip through species. AHA! Fish, not being shy, is waiting around for you to compare him to card. YUP? Show it to swimming buddy. Too much white around mouth, not blue angelfish, established by pointing. Turn to next card. White

351

around mouth. French angel fish, yup? YUP. Go back to hotel. Dry off. Pour rum. Get out large, unwieldy, nonwaterproof book. No colorplates necessary, but lots of drawings and description of habitat, feed, etc. Oh yeah. Forgot. Each card has movable tab on it, so that once you've agreed on a species underwater, you can move the tab into the we-saw-this-one position. Fact then needn't be held in small, nonretentive, middle-aged human mind. So, finding fish in book, read all about him.

"If fish not included in flash cards, book lists characteristics of rare or unlikely species, so that you may be able to key him out, as they say in conservation circles. It fact, it would not be too hard to design a keying-out card, for each marine family, where you would again be involved in tab moving, on the "not as in above choice" principle. But the card wouldn't have to make the identification; it would simply remember the data for you until you got back to the book. And the rum."

Beyond this guide, or something better, nothing more is needed for seawalking to become anybody's enchantment. But there will be other things, developed for the professionals, which amateurs may adopt. I am told, for example, that it may soon be possible to take one's air supply down in liquid form, so that a much smaller container might enable you to stay down much longer.

My friend Ramon Zapata, with whom we dove in Cozumel not long ago, has an idea of what to do when that comes.

"I want to sleep down there," he said. "Free, on the bottom."

I agreed that it would be a wonderfully tranquil place to sleep.

"And imagine," said Ramon, "how beautiful, to wake up there in the morning?"

It would be a dream that didn't stop.

5   "I taught my boy to shoot..."

Beware of good guys. They're the ones who do you in in this world.

If I didn't think that observation had fairly wide application, out beyond the small pursuit of writing stuff for magazines, I wouldn't propose and try to illustrate it. I feel it has considerable relevance to other businesses, to politics, education, marriage and the outcome of the next World Series, too.

When you ally yourself to work towards the same goal with a good guy, the moral worth of his position and the excellence of his character for holding that position are so clear that he can't imagine himself being unable to improve on your contribution to the joint venture.

When you ally yourself with a bad guy, he will look at the

contribution in a professional and practical way, acknowledging that if he could do it himself or get it done as well cheaper, he would; since he knows precisely what he's paying for, he checks only to see that he's got it, and leaves the morals up to you.

As: you know damn well you can hit the next pitch for extra bases, and the good-guy manager signals you to bunt because after all, team effort is right and good. The bad-guy manager, having hired you for the mean, somewhat talented, nasty individual you are, with a blowsy girl to impress up in the stands and a grudge against the clean-cut pitcher, lets you hit away.

Obviously, *National Wildlife,* in which something based on the first of these two concluding pieces appeared, is a good-guy publication. It stands for conservation, preservation and celebration of wildlife. "On My Place" was undertaken after some correspondence about what I might try to write for them, as something we agreed might do some good. We wanted to point out that conservation wasn't a cause to be accomplished only on huge government projects.

My notion of how to handle the subject matter so as to make it interesting and persuasive appears here for, I would have to say, the first time. To compare it with the editors' notion, you could check the magazine in which, they and I finally agreed, the piece was described as "a condensation" of the "highlights." Their title is FIND CONTENTMENT ON YOUR OWN LAND, and under it they supplied sentences like this one: "It is here that private property owners dedicated to personal conservation can ensure that our great land heritage is preserved to be passed on to the generations yet to come." *National Wildlife* prints splendid photographs, has first-rate aims, and is well worth your support. You might enjoy subscribing to it, but don't try to write for it unless you have a better character than I have.

On the other hand, *Sports Afield,* which commissioned "Going Out Less" has been a representative publication in the commer-

for Ophelia

cial, outdoor-magazine field, a field which has always repelled
me. I didn't like the way those publications fed what seemed to
me to be the worst fantasies and instincts of would-be hunters
and fishermen; I started writing some hunting pieces of my own
a dozen years ago for *The New Yorker* (the pieces collected in
The Unnatural Enemy) because it seemed to me that the American
field deserved more truth and, if I could manage it, better prose.

I don't know that my particular example has anything much to
do with what seems to be happening. Rather, I think that the
attraction of new journalism—that personal, stylistically re-
sourceful reportage which has worked so well for other kinds of
publications—has become clear to editors in the commercial
outdoor field. New men in charge at *Sports Afield* have decided
quite frankly to go for some of this stuff, in an attempt to give
their publications a transfusion of contemporary vigor. I am only
one of a number of writers not usually contributing who have
been appoached on a "You write, we'll print it" basis, and I think
they're going to get some vivid stuff that way—not because
they're personally on the good-guy side of things (about that I
don't know, or care much either), but because professionally
they're scrambling for the limited dollars in a very competitive
field.

From my standpoint, "Going out Less," a piece I'd hinted at
in "For Ophelia" when I wrote of teaching my boy to shoot, and
was now ready to write, was bought for just the right place. One
gets tired of preaching to the converted.

*Published in a heavily
edited version as described
in the introductory note to
this section.*

On My Place

I've got a couple of deep draws on my place, in the woods
above the house.

They run parallel to one another about five hundred yards
apart, from south to north downhill for half a mile each,
draining about a quarter section of mixed, hardwood timber:
burr oak, white oak, hickory, hackberry and wild black
cherry. And many old dead elms, of course, and the young
ones growing up doomed.

Water runs in my draws in spring, trickles in the summer,
stands or sometimes dries in the fall, cutting a little deeper
every year.

In dry falls the squirrels and deer, groundhogs, coons,
foxes and rabbits, and the forest birds, must travel out of the
woods to drink, and my winter dream is to dam these two

356

draws, but not elaborately. For $2500 each, five grand, the price of a fancy car I'd just as soon not buy, I could build a strong earth dam across the lower end of each, and back the water up, maybe two hundred yards, fifteen to twenty feet deep at the dams. The water source for ponds like these is only rain and melting snow.

I'd lose hardly any timber doing this, because the white oak was harvested off the slopes of my two draws long ago, by a former owner who sold them to the barrel man. Many of the trunks still lie across the draws, because the barrel man, who sells charred cooperage to the whiskey man, used only the butts of the big oak trees. I cut the abandoned tops for firewood, and the supply would last me many lifetimes.

With two new ponds in the woods—long, narrow, deep and shaded—I could try stocking walleyes, for a change from the large-mouth bass and channel catfish in the two ponds I have already built.

Of these first ponds which I built, one in the second, one in the third year that I had my place, I will have to make you a diagram, so that you will see what I am talking about. They more or less fill yet another draw, the largest of all, into which the first two that I mentioned drain, and which runs down the middle of my place from west to east, with the timber on one side and trefoil pasture on the other.

Before I try to persuade you that there is some reason for you to care (other than your noted kindliness of spirit) whether or not I ever get to build my woods ponds, let me tell you about the ducks.

Two muddy streams run through my place on their way to the muddy Iowa River, Old Man's Creek and its north branch, but when I bought my place, before we fixed the farmhouse up to live in, one rarely saw wild ducks in the creek bottoms. Occasionally wood ducks would rest overnight where brush was high on the banks, and in a wet fall there might be potholes and slack

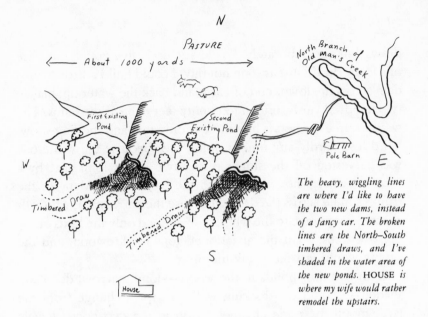

The heavy, wiggling lines are where I'd like to have the two new dams, instead of a fancy car. The broken lines are the North–South timbered draws, and I've shaded in the water area of the new ponds. HOUSE is where my wife would rather remodel the upstairs.

water where a pair of teal would be, early, or mallards late on stormy days. At that time I was more of a duck hunter than I seem to be now, but I don't recall that I ever had a shot at a duck on my own land.

I built the two ponds; I also made two sloughs with smaller dams, and blew potholes, in a sixty-acre timber piece to the northwest. I put up nesting boxes for the wood ducks, and things changed remarkably. The woodies arrive now in the spring, and stay until fall migration time, and three or four broods a year are raised on the small waters of my place. Because of a feeling of fosterhood, I guess, I do not shoot them, and therefore do not drive them off. Consequently their presence attracts other ducks, and by mid-fall there is generally a mixed flock of thirty to fifty —woodies, mallards, blue and greenwing teal, shovellers and sometimes pintails—roosting on both ponds, feeding in the shallow water at the ends, and feeding in the woods—your woodduck is a mad consumer of acorns.

Regularly a small flight of Canada geese, six or seven, comes in early October, though not for more than a day or two, so we sometimes miss seeing them, but it's in the spring that the two ponds really teem. I'm not quite certain how to explain it but diving ducks—scaup and ringnecks and even ruddies—along with remarkable numbers of widgeons—like those ponds for resting in the spring.

For a couple of weeks we can count ducks up over two hundred. Then the divers go on North, and the widgeons, too. Coming back in the fall with their new broods they go elsewhere. Perhaps it has something to do with the delicacy of pond vegetation in spring growth, because coots are more likely to hang around, diving for food in the spring, though the little pied-billed grebes stay on the same schedule as the wood ducks.

Herons, bitterns and kingfishers use my ponds. Frogs grow to enormous size in them, and bass do well (except that I lost them all last year from winterkill, and must learn to guard against this). Dragon and damsel flies thrive and, because we do not spray, there are clouds of rough-winged swallows over the ponds all summer eating mosquitos like grain.

May we go back to the diagram? When the wind is from the west, the water on my two existing ponds is rather choppy. A duck looking for comfort will pass them over. But if I should make those two new north-south ponds, then there would be protected water on my place for waterfowl whatever the wind direction. I think that instead of hatching three or four broods of wood ducks I could hope, with all that additional timbered edge, to boost production to a dozen broods, maybe a couple of hundred woodies. (Do you know about "edge factor"? Wildlife likes the edge of habitat better than the middle—and four small ponds have twice as much edge as would one large one equal to the four combined in water area.)

Next, and I haven't forgotten that you are to be caused to care whether I lay my next five grand on the local firm of Dig, Tamp and Doze or on the Ford Motor Company, I need a better feeding area. There are plans for one. They are for a shallow-water area, a man-made wetland, of about seven acres, in the creek-bottom pasture south of the house. I have a permit to pump water from Old Man's Creek to keep this wet—which would reverse a hundred-year-old practice around here of tiling and ditching the bottom fields to drain wet spots into the Creek; and that is one of the things that makes the Creek so muddy.

With the marsh and new ponds, my waterfowl attractions would be complete. Then I would have nesting, roosting and feeding situations for teal and mallards as well as wood ducks, and feeding and roosting for the other species. In addition there would be fine new winter cover in the marsh grass for pheasants, and new habitat for beaver, muskrat, mink and turtles. And for cottonwood and willow, walnut, ash, soft maple . . .

"Very nice for you, if you like that sort of thing." (I think of you saying this with your playful, patient smile.) "But what is it to the rest of us?"

Nothing by itself, of course. But multiply it by a million. That is the number of farms in this country. Spread it around all over as the farms and country real estate are spread, rather than concentrate it in a few big state and national parks. It could make more difference than parks in the lives of people who live in towns and suburbs. I think the rest of what I have to say will illustrate how.

You see, what I would essentially be doing on my place is not creating, but re-creating, restoring things that were here before the land was cleared and drained, the creeks straightened, the time (not really long ago) when Indians camped on the hill by my Second Existing Pond, where my son finds stone points now and then. Conservation is the American journey backwards from west to east, pioneers with ulcers and weak hearts, moving to preserve what's left in the West, to restore in the middle, and eventually (I guess) just plain reinvent the East. The damage has been so great, the errors so many and so detailed, that it seems to me only an army of citizen landowners, each concerned with the acres he particularly knows and cares about, can reverse what the first pioneers did to the land.

Beyond what I've described, there are three other small ponds and a huge one, almost a lake, that I'd like to make someday on my place; there's another place for an extensive marsh, and two for small ones. There are dozens of places where potholes ought to be. The timber stand should be improved. There should be many more rows of brush and evergreens and multiflora rose, for my plantings of this kind of game cover have only just begun.

Even so, all the kinds of wildlife which were native to the place, but sparse, five years ago have visibly increased. Where we saw an occasional, itinerant single deer or fox five years ago, we now find resident families around the seven hundred acres of my place, and one day last Spring we took a walk and counted fifty bluebirds—we'd looked for them the first year and never saw a one.

If I could do all the things I've mentioned (and I haven't quite got yet to the most important), the contribution of wildlife to this neighborhood and this county, already noticeable, would become significant. In addition, I am preserving here certain wildflowers, probably certain weeds; helping a little to improve water quality; and offering, I like to think, an example of what private landowners can do. And indeed, many more besides myself already have, and their work has a unique quality, for this is personal conservation. The bureaus and their engineers, who must deal with far larger tracts of land, simply do not produce the variety of conservation efforts that the private and perhaps eccentric landowners can manage.

A man who owns land and lives on it eventually creates his

own self-portrait in the fields: it may be a portrait of efficiency, treeless, tiled, tightly-fenced and level; it may be a portrait of neglect; or of single-minded adherence to a particular kind of recreation; but I think such portraits will come more and more to reflect that odd, nervous, somewhat guilty, reverse-pioneer spirit from which, I believe, a great deal of good will come.

There are costs. If, as I was saying, I could do all the things mentioned up to now, the bill would be roughly $25,000—not just a fancy car's worth, but a big tractor, a one-ton dump truck, a small front-end loader, and a medium-sized, second hand Caterpillar. Much as I would like to have any or all those things, I'd still rather move the dirt—as much rather as my wife would have a greenhouse, two new bathrooms and a warm garage.

Here is what you already know about those costs, if you're a farmer: the Government has been helping pay for conservation work on private land, as part of the agriculural program for many years. Thousands of ponds, for example, have been built already, with Government help in location, design, and a share of construction costs.

My own First Existing Pond was done that way: a Soil Conservation Service technician came to look at possibilities. The District Engineer made studies and drew plans. Both services free. Then I applied for cost-sharing for the $2700 project and was awarded, I believe, 60 per cent. I haven't kept the figures, but it seems to me I paid roughly $1300 for that pond, and the Government $1400.

My second pond I built without help; funds in that program, called the ACP, were never plentiful, and there were other applicants. I was, however, successful in getting help for smaller projects once or twice—establishing the pasture, for example, on what had been worn-out, hilly crop land. The Iowa Conservation Commission has helped, too—there are such bodies in every state—especially with plantings, and with all sorts of information and education and direct planning to turn my place, eventually, into a kind of wildlife reservoir and preserve.

There have been many other practices under ACP, a lot of them focused less on water and wildlife conservation than on soil conservation measures which often work to increase productivity; therefore, farmers have preferred the latter, which include tiling, for obvious business reasons. Because the funds are allocated by a committee of local farmers, my several applications through the years for help in making the shallow-water area, the marsh, have been denied.

This has been understandable, if a little frustrating; there really is no farming benefit at all in a duck marsh, and the policy with regard to how to distribute those funds did not discourage the commonsense view that helping a man make a bigger living might be more important than helping a duck make a better nest.

In the papers, just after New Year's, came word that this policy will change. ACP is to be renamed REAP, and the practices which contribute to farm productivity de-emphasized, those which contribute to water-quality, wildlife, beautification and the fight against pollution will be favored.

This seems to me momentous news; look out. I'm about to say something not just good but genuinely enthusiastic about President Nixon and Secretary Hardin. This new policy is just beautifully unpolitical—nothing here to fatten the farmer's wallet, a change that won't be noticed much by voters other than farmers, and one of the sweetest pieces of conservation action that anyone has thought of if it's funded big enough. It's a policy, for God's sake, that actually encourages us to be better people, dig out some of our own money and spend it on living higher-quality lives—not just higher-earning ones—and share the improvement as we see fit with our friends and neighbors. (I wouldn't, by the way, mind seeing consideration given to the idea of more than cost-sharing—full Government funding, in fact, for such projects for the poorer rural landowners; it might even make sense to pay a poor man and his sons wages to direct and labor on conservation on their land.)

Admittedly, the land to be improved will still be private, just as subsidized homes are built for private use. But the benefits, since we are multiplying my place by a million, will be shared in many, if perhaps quirky, ways. If I won't shoot ducks on my land, then neither will I give permission for you to—but if you want a place to photograph them, I'll help you build a blind. There'll be no general public picnicking here, please, but there'll be fund-raising picnics here for charities and other causes, and neighborhood pig-roasts, as there have before. No public fishing —but certain local boy scout troops will continue to camp by the ponds twice a year and learn what fishing they can from their scoutmasters. My circle of friends and neighbors and the people involved in a dozen mutual interests (how much is that times a million?) will use my place, and some of the local kids with beards and odd clothing may walk privately with their girls in the woods here, safe from harassment. The public parks may be a little freer for all this, but that is not my point. My point is that the pattern of use, like the pattern of restoration, will be personal, eccentric if you like; individual, anyway; part of the self-portrait.

If there are a million farms and private land holdings—and I think there are more—we must be talking about a couple of hundred million acres, and some of them not far from where you live. Are none owned by anyone you know?

The final thing that should be done on my place is too much to ask; more than anything else, I would like to fix the creeks, about a mile and a half of linear distance altogether. What this would take in the way of reverse-pioneer action is simple, arduous, and tremendously expensive. I'll stop saying a million, because I don't know how many muddy rechanneled American

creeks there are, but this is the procedure: first, rechannel them
again, getting rid of all the straight places where curves were
taken out, restoring the meanders. Next, slope and seed the
banks, planting willows on the insides of the curves and rip-
rapping the outsides with rock. And then reforest with wide
enough belts on each bank through the flood plains to hold back
dirt.

This would have to be done, of course, not just on my place
but upstream and down as well. But then there would be clear
water once again. It is, of course, too big a job for me to organize,
or the local funding committee to consider, and even for the
equipment available to local conservation-work contractors—
small and often expert operators who are well able to build the
ponds and marshes I've been speaking of. There are half a dozen
of these around Iowa City, by the way, and must be thousands
around the country. They're good at their jobs, and ready to go
as soon as the money shows up.

There is only one organization I can think of which might be
able to undertake the stream-bank improvement, though, watershed by watershed, and that is the Army Corps of Engineers, up
to now among the greatest and most careless spoilers of soil,
water and wildlife quality in our country. How splendid if some
Administration would now say to the Corps: time for a new
mission. Urgent. First priority. About face. You will take your
vast numbers of men and enormous machines and your brilliant
hydraulic engineers, and go fix old Vance's streambanks, and
everybody else's—and if you need 'em, we'll put a new kind of
CCC in operation for the reforestation—and that could solve
some problems too. Meanwhile, we'll let those landowners, with
their inheritance of guilt, loose on the private ponds and small
lakes and marshes and potholes, because these things and the
streambank job can mean millions of acre feet of clear water, and
tons of good dirt saved, and a tremendous new spread, not just

in the big parks but all around the country, of good wildlife habitat.

And all this not, as seems to be the depressing fact in most big conservation proposals, in a matter of thirty years, or forty, or fifty. I'd say we can damn near do it in two; give us five, publicize the opportunity, fund it properly, and I'll guarantee it.

AUTHOR'S NOTE   *January 4, 1973*

One of the recent jolts in Richard Nixon's practice of the politics of bad news has turned this rather happy chapter into a tombstone for a great Federal program.

Ever since the time of Franklin Roosevelt, farmers and country people have been offered a share of the cost of doing home-place conservation. Thousands of farm ponds, small lakes, marshes, grassed waterways, terraces, wildlife plantings, windbreaks, forest plots and other improvements on the American land have been made under this program with the love and care for detail only the people who live on and love their share of the land can give.

Millions more of these small, precious improvements, dreamed of and saved for through the years, remain to be made, but they won't be now unless Congress finds a way of insisting. The President and his Secretary of Agribusiness say they will hold back the money appropriated to help families, most of them low on the income scale, devote parts of their farms to water quality, wildlife and natural beauty, claiming "farmers can afford to do the work themselves."

Like most of the pile of lies accumulating in this Administration's barnyard, polluting the national air, this one is based on the assumption that people generally don't know any better and can't check. In truth, the only landowners who can afford personal conservation without help are Butz's corporate-farm allies and Nixon's political ones—those Southerners with the serfs and the big cotton subsidies. Those small groups, on whose behalf the farm program is now interpreted, don't undertake conservation on their land, because they never see their land.

The families who do live on farms and raise children there, who have planned cool ponds, and timber stands to break the wind and shelter birds, never could afford to pay for such plans out of income, can't now and never will be able to. They can contribute, as they have before, land and time and part of the money, but they seem to have lost the encouragement of a government which believes that only the privileged deserve encouragement, under which the decent dreams of humble men are not supported, while the rest of the Nation is supposed, for some reason, to hold its nose, look away and murmur "Thank you."

*First published under the
same title in* Sports
Afield, *February, 1973.*

Going Out Less

O ne fall, about ten years ago, there was a forty-five day
duck season during which I hunted forty-two mornings,
getting home to start work about 9 A.M., and thirty
afternoons. I have no difficulty making the figures precise; I
know I was out there for every sunrise, except for three
during a weekend I had to spend in New York.

There would have been exactly as many more sunrises than
sunsets as I had classes to teach, in that period, in the
afternoons. Two classes a week, two days when I sat trapped
indoors, the Iowa River in half-flood and the wind for
waterfowl to ride blowing past my classroom window. I sat
there more restless than my least attentive student.

First quail, then pheasant season opened, towards the end
of six weeks, and then I stopped my usual work altogether

and would spend all day in the field, and on days when I had class arrive in boots and hunting clothes with my Weimaraner, letting the day's bag cool out in the car trunk, down in the parking lot. Moon, the dog, would lie beside the desk, composed and ready to leave, looking expectantly at the brightly clothed students, wondering dimly, perhaps, why we were all sitting around on chairs when it was still daylight out there.

I don't know what my season's bag was. I doubt I averaged a bird a day on ducks, and we seldom found quail, but we had pheasants to give away, and knew a secret place where, with luck, perseverance, and an endless supply of shells, I could sometimes shoot a limit of Wilson's snipe.

Last fall, ten years later, I shot no ducks at all, though I wouldn't have had to leave my farm to do it. Ducks were coming in beautifully to the lower of my two farm ponds, almost every evening, a roosting group of wood ducks, teal and mallards. After the teal left there were more mallards, and there were various odd-specie stragglers there sometimes—gadwalls, pintails and once a pair of blacks. There were quail in my fencerows, pheasants in the ditches, rabbits and squirrels, snipe in my pasture puddles, geese overhead now and then—but the figure I can recall precisely this time is the season's bag for last year on all game species: four squirrels and a pheasant, the result of going out twice to the timber, once to the corn stubble. On another afternoon I took a couple of neighborhood boys out with the slower of my two present dogs, a good-natured Springer Spaniel named Bix. Bix found the boys a nice covey of quail and three or four cock pheasants. The kids shot up a lot of shells, and got one bird. I left my own gun home. That was the hunting season.

At home, we'd wanted two squirrels each time to stew, and the pheasant to roast on a spit. But fond as we are of eating game, plentiful as it is on the farm, and though my afternoons were pretty free, some mornings could have been, and I was feeling vigorous, I didn't seem to be going out much any more.

I'd better tell you about the fourth squirrel I shot, a young doe and a perfect shot, too. I was hunting with a scoped .22, and had had her spotted for about ten minutes. I worked my way quietly, almost casually, into easy range of the tree she was in, so sure of her I let my mind play with other matters as I moved. It was an easy stalk through moist, silent leaves to a clear lane of fire, a comfortable, partly hidden place to wait. I knelt behind a white oak stump, steadied my left hand on a hickory sapling for a rest, and was about as firm as I ever am when she came back in sight, walking along a branch, and stopped. It was pretty clear she hadn't seen or heard me. I was able to hold on her eye, as a matter of fact—that's how open the shot was and how still the squirrel. I fired, and feel quite sure she was instantly dead, though as she swung under the branch her front claws hooked it reflexively and held her there for a count of ten before she dropped.

There wasn't much reflex when she hit the ground, not much more than the end of the shudder which must have begun up in the tree and shaken loose the claw-hold. My shot—and I can't remember ever making one like it before—had gone in one eye and out the other. A quick, clean kill, I told myself; the squirrel couldn't have suffered, couldn't even have felt fear. Yet I realized as I picked her up that I minded. Why?

I sat on a log, skinning her out, and wondered at myself.

Why, after many years, should I feel sorry, self-reproachful, for the neat, traditional death of a small, expendable forest rodent which my family would enjoy eating? The explanation was not in what had changed since I was a boy, hunting squirrels in the hills of western Virginia, but rather in what had changed in a single decade of my middle years, in my country, in Iowa where I live, and in myself.

By the time I got the squirrel dressed, looking reflectively at the small internal organs as I cleared them of extra tissue—the little kidneys, heart and liver—I still hadn't made much headway analyzing my unfamiliar impulse of regret. I could only be sure that what I'd felt was not a result of trying to personify the small beast, a sentimental habit of mind I've never developed, but exactly the reverse: in thinking about hunting these days, my tendency was to beastify the small man. Me.

That is, I had gradually stopped thinking of myself as a human with certain rights in nature which culminated in an elegant and exciting exercise called hunting, and to see myself rather as a relatively inefficient member of a repulsive species of predator, worse than all the foxes, weasels and coyotes that have run since time began. Granted I couldn't destroy squirrels on the scale proposed by the jolly engineers for a pipeline company which I'd been churl enough to fight to keep out of my woods three years ago. Nor could I compete, using nothing more than a .22, with the merry geniuses of my species who poisoned air and water. Or the waggish scientists who sneaked chemicals into the tiny liver I held in my hand, via the addition of agricultural pesticides to the food chain—for squirrels use a lot of corn around here.

No. I might not count for much among them, but men were bad animals, and I was one. Though I had kept the pipeline bulldozers from clearing a five-rod strip, half a mile long, of nut-bearing oaks and hickories and good old den trees, preserving that much good habitat, was I therefore entitled to a harvest from it? Perhaps. But did I want one any more?

In the days of my hunting passion, I wrote a defense of the sport which appeared in the *Saturday Evening Post.* When I got back to the house, I jointed the two squirrels for my wife and sat down with a gin and tonic for anesthesia and a copy of the ten-year-old defense. No one had ever answered it in a way that seemed persuasive to me, so I supposed I was now going to have to write some sort of commentary for myself. It wasn't that I found the piece to be wrong, in terms of what things were like when I first worked on it in 1963 (it appeared in February, 1964), but that apparently it no longer applied to me.

I'll quote only the first line: "I think a reasoned defense of hunting, an activity I enjoy very much, would be as difficult to compose as a reasoned defense of drinking whiskey or going to the theater." I went on to point out that there had been prohibitions in America against whiskey and, in Colonial times, against the theater; that these were in the category of morals legislation. And concluded that to forbid regulated hunting, as long as it didn't deplete game species, was also in the category of morals legislation—pointing out along the way that hunting, through its contribution of license money, actually helps protect and increase game species.

All that seems to me to stand up perfectly well, the last item being not unlike pointing out that you get the best plays when the theater audience is enthusiastic, and the best whiskey when the whiskey audience pays well for its tickets. One or two details in my case seemed weak, but what really failed me now was the first clause: ". . . an activity I enjoy very much."

I couldn't, apparently, say that any more. The first-nighter was surfeited with theater; the whiskey drinker's liver had turned and the stuff sometimes tasted bad. Something similar seemed to have happened to the hunter's enjoyment, not just for me but for certain friends with whom I'd hunted during the years; they too seemed gradually to be giving it up, not as converts to a late-blooming tenderness for birds and animals. And not suddenly. Just going out less, as I was.

But it didn't seem to me that, as a group, we were slowing down much physically yet.

We'd been bird hunters. My squirrel wasn't much of a case in point—the small mammals, being good for the pot, might invite harvesting, but they did not challenge the skills and rituals we

371

valued: working dogs, knowing coverts, flight and behavior patterns, and wing-shooting which, when it works, seems more magical than skillful.

I'd suggest that environmental deterioration (will you have a rose from the garbage can?) was only the first thing that bothered us, but of course it did and still does. Hunting might not cause depletion of species, but the species were being depleted any way, by draining and clearing and polluting and paving, if not by guns. Granted, for example, that the passenger pigeon was a casualty of tillage and market hunting, would you, if there were a few thousand left and a brief season open, wish to shoot one?

As depletion occurred, the thing that caused most of it—destruction of habitat—also reduced the national acreage available for hunting, for they were the same acres, the marshes, weedy uplands, fencerows, resting ponds for migration, timbered areas, and all the rest. And along with fewer birds and less hunting ground came more hunters. More hunters in less space meant more irritation for private landowners; hence more posting. And still less space.

Admittedly the group to which I've assigned myself are among the more aloof and snobbish of hunters, with our inclination towards Eastern hunting manners and side-by-side doubles. But the men with whom I've enjoyed hunting have often been of this sort (not invariably), and as the American hunting field has diminished and become crowded, these elitists have been the first to withdraw, or to confine their hunting to private land. I make no case for them—or for myself, if I'm to be included; I only want to point out that when it becomes necessary to fill the tennis courts with ping-pong tables, the tennis players won't be stopping by much.

If I seem doubtful about including myself among the elitists, it's for two reasons: I was not exactly born to it, had never stepped into the gun room at Abercrombie's till I was well past thirty, and waited five years more before I first went on horseback after pointers through Southern quail coverts. The other is that, even more than the mannered sportsman's ritual, I have enjoyed hunting alone. Perhaps that will seem even less admirable, selfish rather than snobbish, but ten years ago it was quite possible to hunt around here in Iowa farm country day after day without seeing another hunter if you avoided the obvious hot spots. Now the only way it can be done is to own one's own land, and I will come soon enough to the difficulties of that.

Let me illustrate first, with ducks, what is happening to the possibility of solitude on public land.

Ducks were always for me the enchanted quarry, materializing where the air was thinnest, driving at the wind's speed towards some point beyond imagination, but sometimes forming cloud-like overhead, swarming, skimming—maybe, if everything were done right and luck held, spiraling in to the decoys and the call. And the shot that dropped one was a mystery, as if I were not myself in the moment of shooting but an agent of some old repository of human skill, atavistic and arcane.

It was in hunting ducks, at those strange, quiet half hours before sunrise and after sunset, that I felt the most profound excitement.

I had clear sight of the future, for the kind of nut who wants to maintain duck hunting for himself as some sort of mystical experience, the fall that Collins Radio Company of Cedar Rapids, Iowa, went on strike. I had long since given up weekend hunting, and would go out to the ten thousand acres of open river-bottom land the Government owns near here only from Monday through Friday. Now I guess the couple of thousand Collins employees on strike were nice enough guys, but I suspect that, being used to vacations in the summertime, they were mostly fishermen. Boat fishermen. Suddenly here they came, reporting for duck hunting like it was the early shift, having an unexpected fall vacation and a little strike pay to buy guns with, and needing something to do with their time; and not being sure just how to do it, they did what boat fishermen do. They moved around until they found someone who seemed to have some idea of how to proceed, and got as close to him as possible.

Several days running I'd go out and get set, and might or might not take my first shot before I'd see a couple of them, struggling in their new waders across the marsh towards me; or driving fast towards a pothole I'd walked in to, jumping out, car close by, grinning and waving and settling in opposite, in thin cover on the wrong side, where the rising sun would be in their eyes and reflecting off their gun barrels.

I am suprised now at how little I really resented it. But there wasn't much point in staying, in a situation where the dumbest duck ever hatched wouldn't even get close enough to flare away. So I'd wave back and, after a tactful ten minutes, pick up my decoys and go home, perhaps checking to see if anyone had walked Knapp Creek today to jump woodies. Generally some-one had.

For all their good nature and happy intentions, the Collins men had given me a dismal preview of what the vaunted new leisure is going to bring. Every day will be opening day, and the crowds will never thin. And among those crowds, more noticea-ble in the reduced hunting field (I don't really know whether statistically more common) one will too often meet that most unpleasant of all fellow hunters, the intentional violator. The men with whom I went out as a boy, mountaineers in Virginia, were intentional violators I confess, but with reason. During the Depression, the deer and small mammals they took all year round helped feed their families. The game was plentiful, hunt-ing pressure light, and they had my boyish sympathy. Nor am I much offended by the occasional poaching for economic reasons of the rural poor around here.

374

But there are men around—more and more, so goes my impression—in big cars with new hats, to whom hunting is not really the sport. Violating is. And a damn low-risk sport, too, with wardens assigned impossibly large territories. The chance of getting caught is one the violator invents for himself and his friends, to make things more exciting I guess. Or to feel superior to the dumb jerks who go for that shooting-time stuff; and that limit stuff; and that no-car-hunting stuff, and no-trespassing stuff. I must be wrong, but there are days when these hunters seem as numerous to me, and as unattractive, as the beer cans they throw out along the road. And I think, If that's a hunter, don't call me one.

In my old defense of hunting, I used this phrase: "Nature lovers (which includes most hunters)," but I do not feel that is accurate any longer. I'm not sure, as a matter of fact, that it wasn't my most dubious point ten years ago. Most hunters, I think I would have to say now, love not nature but their guns. And though I own six, and have had a lot of pleasure from them, I do not love guns generally nor even my own very much any longer.

The assassinations of the past decade—civil-rights workers, students, the Kennedy brothers, Dr. King. The made-up violence of movies and television which seems to be my country's favorite artificial thrill. The real violence of Vietnam, which has been the favorite real-life adventure of the corporate and political community, which leads us and confines our lives. A violent death, of another sort, in my own family. Friends beaten, knifed, robbed, killed in cars. All this has sickened my feeling towards guns, towards whatever machines and devices draw blood, tear flesh, shatter bone.

I would trade four of the six (they are not collector's guns, but were chosen with some love for their function) for a decent, second-hand binocular microscope with which to look at mushrooms. Do you want them? I do not expect to be holding the sweet little Browning autoloading .22, with its 2 1/2-power scope, on squirrels any more. My all-purpose, rough-weather, bird and deer gun, a Browning light-12 automatic with poly-choke, hasn't been out of the gun cabinet for a year. The other two are only single-shot, folding Berettas, a 12-gauge and a .410 cut to boy's size; they were for inexperienced guests, who wanted to try what the hunting field was like as safely as possible, but I do not think I will be starting people off any more. The one of the others, which I think I'll keep awhile, is a nickel-plated H & R revolver, which is a tool of farming, being needed some-times for the dispatch of injured or deformed domestic animals, a chore the performance of which haunts me. The sixth gun was a gift from my wife, a high-grade Beretta over-and-under, and I think I'd keep it, too, for every now and then, fitfully, there is a return of the impulse to shoot, and if anything I'm not dis-pleased when it comes.

With these various feelings I've described for background, I became a landowner during the decade I'm writing of. Ours is a fairly remote part of the county, and I can recall coming down here, before my landowning days, knocking on doors to ask hunting permission (generally for pheasants) and being wel-comed. Amiable men from town, red hats or no, were visitors from town to farms which rarely saw strangers. We'd be asked in, as often as not, to drink coffee and chat, before being directed out to where the birds were. If we had luck we'd always stop back and offer to leave off part of what we'd got, and would some-times find ourselves driving back to town with a bag of apples or a couple of jars of preserves in token of a pleasant occasion.

Those same farms are posted now and so, I'm afraid, is mine. It is, for my neighbors, a simple matter of numbers—too many red hats going up and down the road, scanning the ditches. Too many accidents, generally minor but irritating. Too much push, as they compete for space with one another, in silent quarrels the farmer finds forbidding. I remember driving by, on my way to town one day last fall, a man of some years who was standing at one end of a road ditch with his gun, while an older lady, his wife most likely, worked dogs towards him. He wasn't much for walking any longer, I guessed, and was hoping there'd be a rise of pheasants past his stand to shoot at. As I drove past, he waved but, being irritable because I'd just lost half an hour of time running some trespassers off my place, I didn't wave back. Immediately, I felt sympathy for him and was sorry I hadn't. As writers do, I began to give him a character and a set of circumstances, and perhaps was not far wrong: I imagined him one of those, of whom there are many around here, who had been raised on the land and forced off it years ago by Depression economics. Now, I thought, he comes out only once or twice a year, mostly with nostalgia for a country boy's excited sense of nature as a rich resource for humans. It must be dismaying to a man like that to find everything posted and the farmers grim, so that he had to hunt ditches. His question would be not so much, *Why can't I hunt?* as *Why are they so unfriendly?* I should have waved, even stopped to talk with him, but the trespasser chase had made me late and I was busy, and what I'd have had to try to explain not all that simple.

Start again with squirrels: 250 of my 700 acres are in timber, which I have chosen to preserve against the pressure to increase their value by clearing or increase their yield by pasturing. Meanwhile, neighbors, who have all their livelihood from farming, have had to clear land: a ten-acre woodlot here, a bottom for tillage; or sold off timber rights and turned livestock into the stumps. So the squirrels around here are now on Vance's place. Squirrel hunters, finding their old timbers gone, look enviously across my fences—or climb them, or are sometimes nice enough to ask. If I were to say okay (in the first years I did) and to close my eyes to the trespassers, I'd have a dozen hunters in my woods continuously, and three times as many on weekends. I would be endlessly involved with making and enforcing rules for where they could and couldn't go, what they could and couldn't do, when they could and couldn't come back. There would be no privacy, and it would not be safe for my wife to ride horseback on the trails, or my children to wander. So I say no, post, patrol the place, and feel badly about the whole thing.

But I do not have it in me, having been pushed into this attitude by American circumstances, to shake my head, grin secretly, pick up my gun and stroll off to enjoy it by myself. I do not like buying privilege. Hunting, in some irrational way, was always part of personal freedom, and I do not seem to feel that it, any more than the other parts, should be for sale to guys like me at real estate offices. So, if I begin by excluding others, I end by excluding myself. Then something further happens: if I am preserving squirrels, and, even more emotionally, the ducks that come to the ponds, from everyone now, myself included, my sense of human ownership lessens. I built those two ponds, and have since built another, for ducks to use. I meant to hunt them there, too, of course, but gradually the ponds weren't mine any longer. They belonged to the ducks, safe water in the middle of dangerous territory, and I had no right to molest them.

Am I beginning to sound silly? Let me turn to something else.

In addition to feeling my share of environmental shame, to minding the decrease in the size of the American hunting field and increase in hunters, to my dislike of feeling privileged, and apparent surrender of the sense of having, as a human, any rights in nature, something quite individual has tarnished my love for hunting: I began, indirectly, doing it for money. That is, I began to write about it, and thus to earn a couple of thousand dollars a year from being a hunter. Never, if there is something in the world you like very much to do, get around where the money is in it, for then the thing is no longer the goal—only the money is—and the thing itself becomes a hustle. Amateur (as E. M. Forster pointed out) really means lover. If you love hunting, do not cease to be a lover—do not give lessons, train dogs, guide, travel to hunt on anybody's payroll—and do not write about it. Now, you see, you have begun to use it, not enjoy it. Now it is work, grab, grub and collect. How can you love something that leads to that?

So I am going out less. There are hunts I feel I'd like to make, still. I think I'd like to go to Russia and hunt the country Turgenev wrote of in *A Sportsman's Notebook.* I'd like to go back to a special place in South America where the waterfowl are endlessly plentiful, and I could shoot selectively just the birds I wanted to look at, have cooked, and eat. I'd like to try to hunt birds of Africa, I think, the guineas and sand grouse. I think I would still find both game and solitude enough in the northeastern woods of this continent, in ruffed grouse and woodcock time. I'd like to do collecting and help with classification in the Mexican rain forest. I'd like to see—I don't know about shooting, but perhaps—the different kinds of pheasants in the Himalayas, and in China. And there are a lot of animals I'd like to see wild—just see them, not shoot, and not even take their pictures: lions and elephants, whales and caribou, kangaroos, tigers . . .

To see, not shoot. But I'd be lying if I said I didn't miss the love of shooting. It had a great deal to do with how and where I live. It was one of the things around which I organized my life, and there is nothing really that could altogether take its place. That's why I'd keep the Beretta, I guess. Because I can't help hoping that a morning might come, next fall say, when I'd wake early, before dawn, and suddenly it would all feel right to me again. Then I could get up, silent and excited, call a dog; slip out to the corn-crib where the decoys have been waiting three years now, their anchors tied on, the anchor strings coiled and ready.

And be off in the dark to the pond, to hide in willows, duck call at my lips . . . to spirit, say, two mallards out of thin air, touch off the modified barrel, the full-choked barrel. A double! Steady, boy. Steady. All right, bring it. Bring it back.

for

MYSELF

U p to here, this collection seems to me to have a certain unity to it—the pieces are mostly about living in the country, in a midwestern state; or they derive from that life, and deal with the people and preoccupations of that state. There is, in my mind, even a kind of logical, but hardly flawless, sequence to it. You begin by meeting someone, a first-person character if you want to read it that way; learn something about his origins and present life, go back from that to watch him involved in certain experiences and attitudes, and then, I think, you see the experiences begin to accumulate and the attitudes to change.

There has been, along I hope with other things, a sort of continuous self-portraiture, with digressions and excursions along the way. I hope the digressions haven't been so jarring

as to cause the reader to lose a sense of intermittent focus, if he
has been inclined to give my collection that kind of reading.

If he has, then admittedly the book was finished on the page
before this one.

And I can make no case that the two pieces which now follow
belong even in so casually organized a book as I've described.
I offer them, I guess, as Appendix A and Appendix B. The man
in whose sheep and shotguns you have been good enough to take
an interest has been away from Iowa sometimes, in that decade
of his life which the foregoing accumulaton of reports represents.
He has written other things, too, besides his novels.

Much of that other writing I am content to leave ephemeral,
along with the newspaper stories, the book and drama reviews,
the television scripts and unsuccessful plays written through the
years. But there are two pieces which meant something to me
when I wrote them, and still do apparently. I'd like to include
them, even if they don't fit.

Because I am fifty now, and hope to put as much as I can of
what remains of my writing years into fiction and into trying new
things. That is not to say that I will not write nonfiction, and
sometimes take assignments, and likely sometimes have to seek
them. That will be determined, I guess, by finances, just as it has
been generally before. But I don't expect to accumulate enough
stuff for another collection of essays, in which these final two
pieces would seem more relevant to the others.

So, if I may, I want to publish them here.

It's odd to begin to see that the hours of work left to me are
finite now, and perhaps even odder to be convinced that there
are still things within my power to achieve that I should try for
—damned if I know why I can't just relax now, and do a little
of this and a little of that, and have things pleasant. You might
think (or might not; it's hard for me to judge) that you'd just read
a bunch of sequences from the life of a man who found himself

for Myself

pretty well all set. But I hardly ever feel that way about myself, and hardly ever have; I don't know why. Something my mother and my father taught me, I suppose, and the other people of my country, along with whom, for good or bad, whether I want to or not, in comfort or in pain, I continue to evolve. I don't mean to make this final presentation of myself that of a discontented or an overburdened man, only of a sober one—until five thirty this evening, anyway. Good-bye.

First published in The
New York Times
Magazine, *January 25,
1970, in the same form,
under the title "An
Epitaph for Biafra."*

Death in Africa

It is possible to describe the fall of Biafra, a man might say,
as one of those African tales of ignorance, savagery and
contempt for human life—our ignorance, Britain's savagery,
and Russia's contempt.

Such a man would be intemperately committed, if you like,
to the most lost of causes. Take ignorance newly instructed,
add to it guilt for former blindness, and you would have his
partial sight and prejudice—more violent than the inborn
kind. His would be the kind of account you might expect—
shallow, one-sided, irrational, angry—from one who spent a
single week in the land where two million people died.

He would begin by saying that for two and a half years,
neither the American people, their press, nor their
government seemed to know or care that Prime Minister

Harold Wilson of Britain was being allowed to win his African Vietnam with no greater problem than how to come out of it ahead of the Soviet Union in Nigerian affections.

Because of this, Nigerian arms by Christmas morning, 1969, resembled what a little boy might have if he could walk through a munitions store, saying, "Gimme some of those and some of those and some of those."

From Uncle Harold there were swell, sixty-mile-an-hour Ferret reconnaissance vehicles, with revolving machine-gun turrets. There were neat Saladins, with bulletproof treads, that shot 76-mm. shells. There were Saracen troop carriers, and Uncle Harold hurried to furnish even big, self-propelled artillery when he heard of Uncle Alexei's wonderful surprise.

Because sly Uncle Alexei, in addition to the keen MIG fighters and Illyushin bombers he had been good for right along, had now slipped in twenty-four of his best new 122-mm. guns—beauties that could knock the eye out of a sand flea, or the runway off a jungle airstrip, thirteen miles away.

We heard about the new Soviet guns from a priest, waiting for our plane in Libreville, Gabon.

The priest was Father Finucan of the Holy Ghost Order, a big warm man, whose job it was to load and dispatch the relief plane for Caritas, which flew into Biafra every night as soon as it was dark enough.

I asked him how the news was, and he frowned at me to be still until there was no one else to hear besides Miriam, Kurt and me.

"It's bad, I'm afraid," he said, and told us about the guns.

We were sitting in a beach joint called the Tropicana, half a mile from the airport, waiting for the eleven:o'clock flight. Miriam Reik's father, the distinguished psychoanalyst Theodor Reik, had died four days before. She is a tall, tough, determined girl in her early thirties, who teaches literature at Temple. Her

387

involvement with the Biafran cause was deep. She had recruited
Harvey Swados and Edward Keating to go with her to Biafra, to
judge for themselves and bear independent witness to what was
going on. Six months later she had taken Herb Gold and Leslie
Fiedler there.

Kurt Vonnegut Jr. and I, neither of us the-man-intemperately-
committed yet, were the pair she had chosen for her third trip.
We had no reason to feel that there would not be others and
spent a fair amount of time in the next few days talking of other
writers we knew who might be willing to make the trip in June.

The sea smelled like night in Florida, and Father Finucan said:
"Mind you, the guns were seen unloaded about six weeks ago
in Lagos, and haven't been reported in position yet, but they've
range enough to shell the airstrip at Uli." The priests had pretty
good intelligence, and most of what is reported here we learned
from them, from the Biafrans or from what we saw.

A little after eleven we watched our plane, a DC-6, loaded
with nine and a half tons of powdered milk fortified with corn
and soybean meal in bags marked "Gift of the People of the
United States." There was one other passenger, a middle-aged
Biafran who had been registrar of a local university before the
war. He said he was glad to be going home.

The flight officer, who was Irish, said they had been shot at on
the first flight of the evening but that since the antiaircraft was
not effective above seven thousand feet and they had been going
in at ten thousand, he had chuckled over it. About midnight the
pilot—I believe he was Belgian—turned off the cabin and the
running lights, and the engineer reported that they could see
dots on the radar indicating that we were passing over Soviet
trawlers or Nigerian gunboats, which logged all flights to Uli.
Uli was the only supply point left for the Biafrans and in addition
to the relief planes, others came in all night from São Tomé with
small-arms ammunition.

We flew another hour in the dark, before we began to circle. Lights went on below, we saw a plane go in, and the lights went off again.

"The lights stay on three minutes for each plane to land," Miriam said. But when it came our turn it seemed like less than that. We were low and nearly to the runway before I saw them come on for us.

Kurt wondered that the Illyushins couldn't hit the airstrip, and we decided the antiaircraft must be good enough to keep them too high up for precision. They were flown by Egyptian crews, who may not have had much taste for low-level work. But we were told the chilling news that German conversations had been heard recently in plane-to-plane communication, and that East German aviators were reported seen chatting with the Soviet technicians who serviced the MIG's at Kano in Nigeria.

There was a curious restraint, we thought, that night and the next two days, in the use being made of all the armaments we heard about. We didn't understand until later that the Nigerian commanders had just finished opening their Christmas presents and were not quite ready to start playing with them.

At Customs and Immigration near the airport weary officials were conducting Government formalities by the light of a lantern or two, which they passed from one barely partitioned office to another. They were clinging, we sensed, to the reassuring formalities of governing and did not begrudge the long while it took.

The list of distinguished African writers would be small without Biafrans—Christopher Okigbo, Gabriel Okara, Cyprian Ekwensi, Wole Soyinka, Chinua Achebe. Chinua was at the airport to meet us with the chief of protocol. And Kurt and I, each of whom had been reading one of his novels, felt considerably privileged to be greeted by him.

He is a slight man, not quite forty, who smiles less often than

389

other Biafrans. However, there is great kindness in his manner. He was busy these days, he told us, doing Government work, and had no time or inclination to write.

The Government guest house was at Owerri, the only town the Biafrans ever managed to recapture during the war. A stucco town on flat, sandy country, where the grass grows wiry and the palm trees small, it was full of refugees and beggars, of little boys selling cigarettes one at a time for five to seven shillings each, depending on brand. That was a range of sixty to eighty-four cents for each cigarette in Biafran currency, the only kind permitted.

The kids didn't have anything else to sell, and there weren't many shoes to shine and probably no polish. As for the money, people were almost indifferent to it—a Biafran pound, which cost $2.40 at the border, would not buy a full pack of cigarettes, and it took two to buy a pineapple.

The cigarette hawkers were the lucky kids; the others we began to see that morning at a hospital run by the French Red Cross at Awo-Omana. The French doctors there were young and bearded. Kurt said they looked like moving-picture saints.

The Biafran doctor who took us around was older and had got his M.D. in London. He had a white spot in his dark gray hair the size of a half-dollar. They were treating six hundred tiny children there for kwashiorkor, a protein-deficiency condition.

The children looked just as you've seen them in photographs, except that you may not have seen them photographed from the rear. In advanced cases, the muscles that hold the lower bowel extremity in place have let go, the tissue turns inside out and protrudes several inches from the anus.

The children are apathetic, except for a few who cry. If you stand still, the littlest ones start toward you reaching their hands up to grab a finger. You could stand there quite a while with several fingers immobilized. And you might as well: You didn't feel anything like taking pictures.

They treated the kwashiorkor cases there for six weeks. A transfusion of whole blood in small quantities came first and then gradually food. Most of the patients would respond well enough to be moved to a convalescent hospital, newly established down the road, and we went there next. The sound of children yelling and laughing was one of the best I'd ever heard.

On the way back to Owerri, a MIG swept along the road. Our driver ditched the car and we piled out into the bush until he was past. He didn't fire, possibly because he didn't have a friend along. The MIG's generally work in pairs, we were told, one sweeping the road, the other strafing the bush into which people ran as we had, when they saw the first plane coming.

We did not see fighting. Neither Kurt nor I had any business wanting to, though Miriam kept asking people to take her to the front. She had an assignment to photograph it. There were a war photographer and a reporter from the *Times* of London who were having the same problem of getting up forward. They, Len Hall of the *Manchester Guardian,* and a Japanese journalist were the only newspapermen in Biafra as far as we could learn, and there were none in the country on permanent assignment, only men going in and out for a few days as we were.

The reporting of the war all came from Lagos, the Nigerian capital, and the only news stories we learned of while we were there were the ones carried by the British Broadcasting Company. The B.B.C. reported the Nigerians shelling Owerri every day we were there. The Voice of America repeated whatever the B.B.C. said. There was small-scale air activity over Owerri every day we were there, but the Nigerians didn't shell it. Not once.

It turned out they didn't need to.

Instead of the war, we saw officials and learned what we could from them: It was a great deal. I think every man we talked to

—except the M.D.s—had a Ph.D. from a British or American university in fields ranging from diplomatic history to plant biology. In the case of the younger people, the university was more likely to be American. We had dinner the next to last night with Commissioner for Information Isegwu Eke and his wife. His Ph.D. was from Harvard and hers was from Columbia.

According to my notes, we had long interviews with eight Government officials before, on Wednesday, we met and talked with General Ojukwu, the Biafran leader.

I'll try to summarize what we learned from the others, as articulate and persuasive a group of men as I shall ever have the privilege of meeting. It was the equivalent of what it might be like to be taken around Washington, introduced to the most knowledgeable and interesting man in each department of government, and being permitted to talk with him as long and candidly as you liked. The one best known outside Africa might be Chief Justice Sir Louis Mbanefo, formerly of the World Court.

The Biafrans didn't have many foreign guests in their final week—in addition to ourselves, there were a couple of Finnish pacifists. But the Biafrans could not have done more with what the relief plane brought them if we had been ranking officials or in positions to influence the course of things.

• On Mr. Wilson: His role as their true enemy was as clear as Lyndon Johnson's role in Vietnam. He had placed his government fully at the service of the lust of British Shell and British Petroleum for the great Biafran oilfields, which produced crude oil so pure it can be used directly in diesel engines.

The Ibos, who made up nine million of Biafra's prewar population of fourteen million—five times the population of Ireland then, but perhaps only three times Ireland's now—were the people whom the English could never control in Colonial days.

Mr. Wilson's goal was neocolonialism for Nigeria, a condition, I may add, that one sees in other presumably independent African countries. There, at the first sign of an administrative complication, from immigration procedures to hotel bills, a white man materializes to straighten things out. As long as their lanterns burned, this never happened in Biafra. But it was estimated that as many as twenty official missions—trade, sanitation and so on—had been sent to Nigeria from London in 1969.

• On mercenaries: Biafra had used them in the beginning. They were all gone. The only whites fighting were the volunteers in the Swedish Count Von Rossen's little group of small planes.

On the other side, in addition to the Egyptians, East Germans, Belgians, Algerians and Soviet technicians, there were British "military advisers," recruited by advertisements in London papers for men ready to retire young from the army and navy. And if you saw the war as Wilson's Vietnam, then Yakubu Gowon didn't seem to be as successful as Johnson's Thieu at recruiting his own people for the fight. Gowon was making considerable use of black mercenaries from the neighboring countries of Chad and Niger.

• On American black radical support for Nigeria: Biafrans were disappointed, but could understand that American blacks had had pride in the idea of a large, powerful federated Nigeria. Biafrans understood that as Christians defending themselves against Moslems, they could not hope for religious sympathy, and that the apparently inborn Ibo affinity for individual enterprise probably prefigured an independent Biafra as an African dynamo of capitalism. They had hoped that these religious and social traditions would be offset by the realization by American blacks that Biafra was truly independent; that unlike Katanga, whose secession was sponsored by the former colonial power, their fight was against the former colonial power.

• On American diplomacy: It strongly supported Nigeria. It might have been used, if it were truly neutral, to stop the flow of arms from Britain and the Soviet Union, or to allow some of the other sympathetic powers—Israel perhaps, and France certainly—to give more adequate military supplies.

But American diplomacy simply followed the old rule—Britain knows best in Africa, America knows best in South America. The chief lobbyist for this was Joseph Palmer—"an abominable monster," one highly placed man called him, but not without a smile—former chief of the State Department's African desk, who is now Ambassador to Libya.

Though they did not doubt his goodwill, the Biafrans shook their heads over the ineptness of C. Clyde Ferguson Jr., President Nixon's relief coordinator, who had tried to carry out the assignment of providing boats to carry food and medical relief, but who had wound up giving the boats outright to the Nigerians, who used them now to carry troops.

They named several Americans and some Africans as well—Representative Allard Lowenstein was one—who had been duped by a tactic so clever they admired it. Realizing that such a man's sympathy had been won by Biafra, the Nigerians would flatter him by persuading him that he could act as a mediator and bring peace. ("Sure," Kurt said, "fame, honor, the Nobel Peace Prize. What politician could resist it?")

• On genocide: Perhaps the Nigerians no longer intended complete extermination of the Ibos. However the thirty thousand killed in the pogroms of 1966—during which Nigerian government television stations in the north had urged Moslems into the "foreigners' quarters" to find Ibos and kill them—was a fair indication of how Nigerians felt toward them. And the two million already dead in the war was a massive follow-up. Nevertheless, with the world watching, the Nigerians might restrain themselves to cultural genocide. By killing off the leaders—the two generations of highly educated Ibos now existing—and by destroying the local system of education, which provided real educational upward mobility for every child in the country, the distinct and valuable Ibo personality could be wiped out, at least for two more generations.

The genocide question haunted the Biafrans. And now that Biafra exists no longer, it haunts me. Sealed off from observation at this writing by Nigerian decree and in a situation where piles of corpses are expected anyway, while diplomats squabble about the protocol of relief, people may die, be killed, be allowed to die, discriminately or indiscriminately, by intention, by whim, or by indifference. In one of President Nixon's most unequivocal campaign statements, he proclaimed that he would not permit genocide in Biafra; I hope it haunts him, too.

• Finally, on their qualifications for nationhood: Perhaps the most tragic of the world's misunderstandings was to regard the Ibos as a tribe. Their traditional territory is large, and the Ibos actually delayed acceptance of independence until the North was ready in order to advance the idea of federation. When it came, it was Ibos who went out, over the rest of the country, as civil servants, university teachers, military officers, financial, engineering, medical and mercantile personnel, to try to make the federation work. They were rejected.

"Why doesn't anybody ever ask the real question?" a colonel on Ojukwu's staff asked me. "Of the Nigerian man in the street: Does he want us back? Of course he doesn't. He wants our oil and our territory, but he doesn't want us as citizens of Nigeria. He pushed us out."

Perhaps it seemed to other Nigerians that the Ibos, with their talent and intelligence and thirst for education, were taking over the rest of the country in some sort of bloodless conquest, prior to 1966. If that is so, then it is unquestionably fair to regard the war just ended as a successful counterinvasion.

And as for talk of seeking unity it has been answered most eloquently by Tanzania, in the document explaining why its government recognized Biafra:

"There is no unity between the dead and those who killed them. . . . Tanzania has recognized the state of Israel and will continue to do so because of its belief that every people must have some place in the world where they are not liable to be rejected by their fellow citizens. But the Biafrans have now suffered the same kind of rejection within their state that the Jews of Germany experienced. Fortunately they already have a homeland. They have retreated to it for their own protection, and for the same reason—after all other efforts failed—they have declared it to be an independent state."

Fortunately, we did other things besides talk and listen. We saw a play one evening, produced by the Center for Biafran Artists and Writers, where about one hundred creative people had gathered to live and to try to investigate the roots and determine the direction of their culture. It was a remarkable play, its symbols taken from pagan tradition, about the search for peace. As Kurt said, with an amazement we all shared: "There isn't any anger in it."

We saw small homemade oil refineries in the jungle, which the Biafrans had built themselves with an ingenuity very much like that we pride ourselves on having. We saw homemade rockets, launchers and land mines. We saw a fisheries project, from which their scientists felt a great source of postwar protein could be developed. We talked with the dean of their agricultural school, now—or, rather, then—directing an ambitious food-growing project they called the Land Army. Among my saddest notes are the names of American varieties of rice and corn and onion seeds that Dean Okigbo calculated might work well for Biafra and which I had hoped the generous farmers of my state of Iowa might be interested in trying to provide.

One morning we saw General Ojukwu. We were, I think, the last foreigners to visit him on Biafran soil—or, rather, Miriam was, for she had a private audience after our more public one.

He is a large man, with sorrowing eyes, a deep, gentle voice and the same astonishing flow of wit and good humor in adversity—though inevitably with more authority in it—which seemed so universal in the educated Ibos.

During that interview, we were as close as we came to the front. "We are within artillery range here," he said. "I stay because the soldiers know I'm here.

"We are a kind of nuisance," he went on. His accent is quite strongly British. "The American people can only be touched by starvation, hunger, a ghastly air raid. They are not thinking about the struggle. . . . But I believe we could contribute, I believe there are certain things now lost which we can bring back. I am talking about a certain feeling for humanity, humanism in the old sense.

"If we lose, everything that makes Biafra will be lost to humanity."

I was to think a good deal in the next few days about that final line.

At the end of the interview he thanked us for risking the journey to his country. It was Wednesday now. His country had four days to live, and though he left it safely before the fall, I cannot attach to the man whose voice I still hear any motive other than the chance of continuing somehow to serve his people.

We were scheduled to leave on Wednesday, but decided to stay one more night. We wanted to meet Maj. Gen. Philip

Effiong, the chief of staff, and somewhat unexpectedly we did. We were sitting in Miriam's room after our regular guest-house supper—bully beef and rice, and glad to get it—daring one another to try some Biafran gin Miriam had bought, when the general and a couple of aides drove up outside.

In addition to the gin we had one pint of cognac left. We asked the men to share it.

General Effiong, a short muscular man with a brilliant smile, seemed pleased to accept "a little French gin," as Kurt called it. He spent a couple of hours with us. He is a brilliant monologist; but his conversation that night had a lot of tension in it. Nigerian troops had advanced that day, stopping only when they reached the Imo River, and I think he knew, perhaps better even than General Ojukwu, how close the end might be.

His troops were hungry, possibly even out of food entirely, and he knew they could not stand and fight that way for long. "The enemy drives refugees into our lines," he said. "And my men can't shoot into their own people."

He left about one in the morning, and I think the three of us felt tension for the first time. But it wasn't until late the following afternoon, and after the usual rather harmless air raid, that the first shells came close enough to be heard in Owerri.

There were four rounds and they were like a signal to evacuate the city. People started streaming out, on foot and in cars, with whatever they could carry. Although there was a five-hour delay before our starting, Kurt and I streamed out after them, driven to the airport by the chief of protocol.

Miriam, who was scheduled to stay another day, insisted on staying until the appointed time, and woke up next morning in the guest house in a deserted city, to the sound of distant shells. She is, I am happy to report, safely back in this country now.

As we flew out in the dark Friday morning, I kept thinking of General Ojukwu's phrase: "Everything that makes Biafra will be

lost to humanity," and wondering if there was something unique
—beyond a number of valuable and decent individuals—that was
Biafra.

I found two ways of answering that. Both are from books. The
first applies best, perhaps, to the first educated generation of Ibos
—the older men, who absorbed their foreign education and, in
so many cases, exceeded their foreign instructors unforgivably in
manners and articulateness and reach of mind. They were not
content merely to be amusing toy Englishmen.

To them perhaps there might apply a sort of fable from Amos
Tutuola's novel, *The Palm-wine Drinkard,* published some years
ago. To read it now is to find an awesome touch of prophecy:

"As they were traveling along in this endless forest then the
complete gentlemen in the market that the lady was following,
began to return the hired parts of his body to the owners and he
was paying them the rentage money. When he reached where he
hired the left foot, he pulled it out, he gave it to the owner and
paid him, and they kept going; when they reached the place
where he hired the right foot, he pulled it out and gave it to the
owner and paid for the rentage. Now both feet had returned to
the owners, so he began to crawl along on the ground. . . .

"When they went furthermore, then they reached where he
hired the belly, ribs, chest etc., then he pulled them out and gave
them to the owner and paid for the rentage.

"Now to this gentleman or terrible creature remained only the
head and both arms with neck, by that time he could not crawl
as before but only went jumping on as a bullfrog. . . .

"When they reached where he hired both arms, he pulled
them out and gave them to the owner, he paid for them; and they
were still going on in this endless forest, they reached the place
where he hired the neck, he pulled it out and gave it to the owner
and paid for it as well. . . .

"Now this complete gentleman was reduced to head and when

they reached where he hired the skin and flesh which covered the head, he returned them, and paid to the owner, now the complete gentleman in the market reduced to a 'SKULL.' . . .

"I could not blame the lady for following the Skull as a complete gentleman to his house at all. Because if I were a lady, no doubt I would follow him to wherever he would go, and still as I was a man I would jealous him more than that, because if this gentleman went to the battle field, surely, enemy would not kill him or capture him and if bombers saw him in a town which was to be bombed, they would not throw bombs on his presence, and if they did throw it, the bomb itself would not explode until this gentleman would leave that town, because of his beauty. . . . After I looked at him for so many hours, then I ran to a corner of the market and I cried for a few minutes because I thought within myself why was I not created with beauty as this gentleman, but when I remembered that he was only a Skull, then I thanked God that He had created me without beauty. . . ."

But the younger men were more than complete gentlemen in rented parts. The second generation of educated Biafrans seemed subtler, surer, in a way Kurt and I felt we hadn't met before, unless it was in the war play that had no anger in it.

They never entered a room without a smile, of the kind that makes one comfortable. Whatever they said, even the most serious things, was pleasant. They concealed the urgency of the extraordinary responsibilities they were trying to discharge with an easy gallantry that seemed almost lighthearted.

"They've gone past materialism somehow, haven't they?" Kurt said.

I don't want to name them here as individuals, because I hope so very deeply that as individuals some of them survive the death of the self-made culture of which they were the finest products. But I will tell you this: When I was with young men, whatever solemnities I felt and came close to expressing, their particular smiles always lightened and reassured. It was as if they found it important, as obliteration came on for them, to take care of me. I've never seen such grace.

And so there is a different passage from a very different book that will not leave my mind. It is from Loren Eiseley's *The Immense Journey,* and again it is about a skull:

"[A] skull lies in the lockers of a great metropolitan museum. It is labeled simply: Strandlooper. South Africa. I have never looked longer into any human face than I have upon the features of that skull. I come there often, drawn in spite of myself. It is a face that would lend reality to the fantastic tales of our childhood. There is a hint of Wells's *Time Machine* folk in it—those pathetic, childlike people whom Wells pictures as haunting earth's autumnal cities in the far future of the dying planet.

"Yet this skull has not been spirited back to us through future eras by a time machine. It is a thing, instead, of the millennial past. It is a caricature of modern man, not by reason of its primitiveness but, startlingly, because of a modernity outreaching his own. . . . It's all happened already. Back there in the past, 10,000 years ago. The man of the future, with the big brain, the small teeth. . . .

"Many of you who read this belong to the white race. We like to think about this man of the future as being white. It flatters our ego. But the man of the future in the past I'm talking about was not white. He lived in Africa. His brain was bigger than your brain. His face was straight and small, almost a child's face. He was the end evolutionary product in a direction quite similar to the one anthropologists tell us is the road down which we are traveling. . . .

"Nothing about their environment in the least explains them. They were tomorrow's children surely, born by error into a lion country of spears and sand."

I sit in the dark plane, flying out of Africa, overwrought,

wondering whether it might be that the paleontologist's tale about a race of men born before the rest of us were ready to accommodate them happened again in Biafra, yesterday.

NOTE, 1972: Most of the men I met in Biafra did survive. Many of them left reunited Nigeria, but there was no genocide. Colonel Gowon, they say, is the honorable, humane and forgiving leader we hoped he might be. It was the only hope. The exiled Ibos with whom I've talked report its fulfillment justly.

First published in The
New York Times
Magazine *under the title
"Middle Age Meets the
Kid Ghetto," in pretty
much the same form.*

Heavy, Heavy
Hangs Over Mifflin Street

In Madison, Wisconsin, September 1970 was a tense month.
October and November, said the students and the street
people, looked heavy.

"Heavy," as I understand it, means difficult, dull, ominous,
without promise of laughter, ease, or grace.

"Anyone new around with bell-bottoms and a beard can be
FBI," they said. "If he's not a narc or a rookie on the
Madison force."

It was here, of course, that an August bomb killed a man,
injured others and wrecked the Army Mathematics Research
Center. It wrecked the Physics Department, in the same
building, apparently not an intended target, and shattered
glass in a radius of about a dozen blocks.

Not far outside that radius is Mifflin Street, collective name for an area three or four blocks square where many of the students and street people live. There are other, smaller enclaves spread out around the city, some established to escape harassment, some simply because there are better deals on rent, but Mifflin Street denotes the youth community no less than Haight-Ashbury served as title for its counterpart in San Francisco.

Youth community? If you like. There are places like it by now near most large universities, in many big cities, and you could call them the urban analogues of rural communes. You could call them school-season or winter encampments. But it seems to me most accurate to call them what they are: kid ghettos.

Earlier this year I was in Europe, and saw the young in France and Italy, even in Spain of all places, moving freely around the towns. They did not seem to be confined, as our kids are, partly as a matter of their own choice, partly in an unnegotiated accommodation with local police: stay in the ghetto and you may follow your own peculiar and illegal customs without day-to-day interference; your aberrations will be out of sight, and if anything happens, we'll know exactly where to find you.

Clean-shaven, crew-cut, wearing a gabardine suit, a tennis tan and even a necktie, I went walking on Mifflin Street in September, whoring for intuitions. The arc of my country's descent, it seemed to me, for I was not feeling optimistic, might be seen in the distance between myself at fourteen, wondering if I had the personal qualities to measure up as a G-man, and the same American male thirty-four years later, careful to take all necessary measures with his appearance to avoid being taken for one of the federal secret police.

It was a pretty day and I walked slowly. I went by a small, two-story frame house; it needed paint and a new roof, and the porch was coming off. There was a flimsy barricade at the top of the porch steps, crib rails and wooden boxes. Five people were on the steps, taking the sun. I went by, not exactly embarrassed

404

but hesitant, as if my eyes were camera lenses and these people might not want their pictures taken. Three were men, two girls. The girls looked infinitely younger, but it was because beards took away the look of youth in the boys, if that's what they were. There was a toddler playing on the porch, and I might have thought the barricade was to keep the child from tumbling down the steps except that I knew this building and the three adjoining were under siege.

Rent strike; a new landlord, who had just bought in, wanted to raise rent, already ridiculously high, without making repairs. That happened in other kinds of ghettos, too.

This new landlord had a cute idea. He wanted to save himself the slow process of court action and individual eviction, so he'd turned the buildings over to a motorcycle gang. They were to carry out the evictions or enforce the new rents.

The Mifflin Street people were uneasy but not very awed. No motorcycle gang could come at them with the tear gas, riot guns and legal heft of the policemen and national guards they had faced so often, nor did the Mifflin Street people see much difference between motorcycle and police mentality.

The building looked ratty. The group on the steps, from their appearance and its frame, might more easily have been civillian survivors of a great city battle than middle-class American students at a major university. I came to the corner of Basset Street and got something, but what was coming in astonished me: it was the wedding, many years ago, of a lovely girl called Dusty Rhodes.

She was a Red Cross girl, getting married to a fine-looking Air Force captain, in Naples, in the late fall of 1943. So I was just twenty-one, the age of the kids on the steps perhaps. I knew Dusty only by sight, and the groom not at all.

I went as escort to a friend of the bride's, and never met the groom; had to leave the reception early and sober, to get back to my post, and no shortage of brothers-in-arms there, to take over my escort duties.

What was striking in recollection was the effort everyone had gone to to make that wedding look like Scarsdale. They'd found a white wedding gown, complementary dresses for the brides-maids, and there was a tall, fancy cake baked with gray, unrefined wartime flour and some bad, sweet, white sparkling wine we agreed to call champagne. There'd been a bachelor dinner, I understood, and I saw, as I was leaving, the jeep hung with cans and ribbons in which the couple would get away, to go down to the dock and take a boat, past the wreck of a Liberty Ship still smoking from last night's air raid, to Capri.

That was us. Struggling then and later towards conventional-ity, whatever the situation, never stopping to question very seri-ously whether the conventions were worthwhile. A writer like John O'Hara, in his prewar books, could lay out the hollowness and potential tragedy of American upper-middle class lives; and we read O'Hara, but all we saw were the lives we wanted to live.

Dusty Rhodes's daughter, okay? Sitting back there on the steps, on Mifflin Street, living with one of those bearded boys, waiting for the motorcycles. Dusty herself, a large, fair, sparkling girl, might not find it possible to understand. Her own triumph, in white Italian silk, was too absurdly hard-won ever to be under-valued.

I turned and walked back past in my conspicuous suit. One of the girls had left the steps, taking the baby to a vacant lot next door to play. A sign designated the lot a "People's Park," and some effort had been made to mow and plant it once, but it was worn and weedy now. I smiled at the baby. The girl, who was quite pretty, but dressed like a poor fortune-teller's little sister, met the smile but did not return it. To be quite honest, she looked annoyed, and I thought: hey, wait. If that's a daughter, it makes the baby Dusty's grandchild, doesn't it? And it could, except that my life didn't happen to go that way, be mine. And wasn't that part of the trouble?

We were, whatever our other characteristics, the most desperately reluctant grandparents imaginable. Grandparents? But we still wanted to be counted with the young. We wanted to dance their dances, learn their songs, revel in their movies, share their drug experience, be their lovers—we were a couple of million Mrs. Robinsons—and it seemed to me that a great deal of the national anger at our children was a product of the utter gracelessness with which their parents were accepting middle age.

Suppose in our own youths of Depression, War, and their aftermath, circumstances did not permit us satisfactorily to be young—if we refused to get over it, that was our problem, not Mifflin Street's.

I went back, then, to my motel. It was named to go with the gabardine suit: The Ivy Inn.

I'd been walking for a couple of days, talked a little, listened a good deal, and I seemed to have accumulated a lot of emotion. The outline of what was going on was clear enough, if too familiar to write about in much detail:

There had been, from the ranks of American youth, building through the peace movement, becoming massive in response to Nixon's Cambodian invasion, followed now by scattered acts of violence like the bombing of AMRC, a kind of pararevolution. Or how about, since it was essentially an uprising of troops stockpiled for eventual use in the Cold War, an American Cold Revolution?

Now the cold counterrevolution was here to no one's surprise, least of all the kids'.

There was something I felt urgently needed to be said to the counterrevolutionaries, if I could get my mind around it, a kind of view from no-man's-land.

First they should recognize, if they didn't already, that the alliance fused in the Cambodian demonstrations was an unstable one which would resolve back into separate parts quite naturally, unless repression or another Cambodia kept it together. This was because the four chief groups of the alliance had different continuing goals, and were attracted to quite different methods.

Two of them, the black militants and the New Left, had really drawn away from the peace movement (which included the other two) even before Cambodia. I made Moratorium Day speeches in November last year to audiences which included members from both radical groups, and there was no sense of common cause. They were there to jeer at and debate whatever sounded pacifist, liberal or nonviolent. They wanted hot revolution, and I was not the man to explain or defend them; my mind has grown quite rigid around the notion that Gandhi was the only leader produced in our century worth following, and his the only political methods which wouldn't, as things were now, do more eventual harm to the gun than they would to the target.

The other two elements in the alliance were Mifflin Street, and the kids in the middle.

The kids in the middle, who had come pouring out of the dormitories and even the fraternities to protest Cambodia, were back in again, their cause won really since Nixon was out of Cambodia, and while they regard him with considerable suspicion, they believe they helped force him to work for peace and an end to the draft in the same way that they helped defeat Johnson. Therefore they are willing, if they haven't simply lost interest, to work in establishment politics as they did in the McCarthy movement.

That left Mifflin Street, and as I sat on my bed at The Ivy Inn, reading through my notes, I realized that they had told me what they wanted: they just wanted to be left alone to create a new culture, that's all.

They'd told me how they felt about the Army Mathematics

Research Center bombing, too, and I thought I'd better try to understand that, and what the relationship was between Mifflin Street and the hot revolutionists who took credit for or justified the violence. Here was one boy I talked to:

"I'd go by Army Math on my way to class every day, and see that damn building there. It was such an affront. It was like a man I wanted to kill, a man I hated enough to kill, only I wouldn't. Killing isn't in me. But if bombing was in you, there it was, and I used to wonder how those who had bombing in them could stand seeing it, day after day."

Another said: "You see, it was a symbol—not just to the left but to the peaceniks and the freaks and anyone who didn't like the hypocrisy of the university taking money from the Army and doing work for it, pretending it was pure research. We'd been demonstrating against that building for years. I heard the explosion. It just about tossed me out of bed, and I went out on the street. Pretty soon word came that Army Math got hit, and we all cheered. Then I heard a guy was killed and I thought, oh God. Oh no."

They cheered the destruction of the symbolic building, then, with a kind of mindless, Fourth of July elation, like some kind of sporting victory, but regrets started quickly. Beyond that moment, it is my clear feeling that Mifflin Street is not radical—or liberal or conservative—but it is a ghetto, and I expect it has the traditional ghetto impulse to provide sanctuary and alibi for political criminals who have some claim on it.

Mifflin Street will defend itself, but essentially I believe it is nonviolent. Its days of street-fighting and trashing (as they say) the stores that exploit students are over. Perhaps the bombing ended that.

If so, there are two reasons: one is that they make a perfectly realistic acknowledgment of superior force. The truncheons of John Mitchell, who seems to them to embody counterrevolutionary leadership, will crunch the bones of the violent and the nonviolent unselectively.

The second is that something is growing in Mifflin Street. Something fragile is growing, or so I now believe. Its spokesmen call it "the alternate culture," and the very least we owe them —because damn it they are our children—is to examine those terms. Are they proposing an alternative, or is it just a collection of kid fads? I think it is more than that.

Is it then, a complete culture or only a revision which can be placed in accurate perspective not by citing the failure of my generation to modify American values but by citing the success of my parents'—the kids' grandparents'—generation, the people who brought us out of Victorianism, Edwardianism, in the 1920s. Opposed as they were by those who hungered to return to normalcy with Harding and Coolidge, those forebears, their jazziness now venerable and remote, led the country out of stagnation without having to break completely with the political and cultural past.

That description has profound appeal for me, because I know that, if the kids in the dormitories and fraternities will not take political leadership from the New Left or the Old Right, there is a good deal of evidence that they are accepting cultural leadership from the creative spirit of the kid ghettos. Whatever part of the cultural past and present I occupied as a writer, I sure didn't want broken away from completely, but sitting there in The Ivy Inn I found myself prepared to argue that it might be happening.

I think it was that suit. It came from Brooks Brothers, it cost two hundred bucks, and I'd always wanted one like it. I'd bought it quite recently in the way Dusty Rhodes's wedding guests make such purchases—not because it was fun and I could finally afford it, but because I was anxious and not at all sure when I'd be able to pay the bill.

Okay.

I do not pretend to know how many elements it takes to make a culture, but it seems to me quite clear that many such elements do exist already in the kid ghettos. I can do no more than list and comment briefly, inadequate by training and particular capacity to analyze in detail. But perhaps the list will show something like a whole. It will be an eclectic culture, if it does show one; but what new culture could be anything but eclectic with the world the age it is?

A culture, to begin with, has an origin, some condition that presses it to develop. This one begins, it seems to me, with the incompatibility of being young, well fed and high spirited in a stalemated world. The dreariness of the Cold War and of nuclear power politics produced an extraordinarily boring twenty-five-year period. The response of growing up in it and trying to turn to an alternate culture seems to me far less a manifestation of atomic fear, the cause so often given, than it is one of simply needing an outlet for zest, and warmth, and creativity—a relief from grinding dullness.

A culture must have a history. The history of this one might begin in the middle 1950s, with what was called the Beat Generation. The marking off of American age groups into generations is too often an advertising copywriter's exercise, but I think one can recognize times when an age group, engaged with or finishing its education, began to see and feel in a new way. The Beats seem to me to have made the first such break since I was old enough to notice. They were engaged by their own present rather than (as we were) crippled by nostalgia for their fathers' pasts.

A culture must have a nationality, and, tentatively, this one does. I saw it when traveling, I thought: the American, Canadian, British, French, German, Scandinavian members of the alternate culture seemed to have trust in and recognition of one another in a way that went beyond merely being the same age. I thought

411

them more confident of one another than of the older citizens in their respective countries of origin. And though it was probably less true of other (former?) nationalities, the Americans had the ethnic similarity of being nothing in particular—they were the melt from what had been a melting pot.

A culture should have its own language, perhaps, but it may not need to. I thought it probable that here in America the alternate culture had not yet developed much beyond having its own slang.

A culture has its own art forms. The development of its own music by American youth is too obvious to do more than note, but there is one point to be made about it, in comparison to the swing music I danced to, which is rather overlooked. Swing was played and arranged by men ten or fifteen years older than we were, men who had been the young jazz musicians of an earlier decade. Today's musicians are the kids themselves.

To go on with art forms: the poetry of rock lyrics has been cited often, and there is a great flow of poetry not tied to music, and a great interest in writing it, reading it and hearing it read. I am not aware of much fiction yet from the alternate culture, except in the work, perhaps, of Richard Brautigan; I am aware, of course, of a strong taste for fantasy, somewhat confounding to a writer like myself (though, let me acknowledge, somewhat liberating, too). Brought up on television, which was their baby-sitter but which failed to grow up with them, their preference for film seems logical enough; beyond that I don't think I can comment on what is happening in the visual arts. Perhaps they are satisfied by what half a century of continuous innovation has already established.

The alternate culture produces great quantities of its own handicrafts, work in leather for example. If a lot of it looks like stuff we did as boys in camp, still, young craftsmen are developing self-taught on Mifflin Street as they haven't in the world for a long time. It is not dilettante or hobbyist's work: they produce garments their community needs, bypassing mass production.

In fact, since a culture needs it own approach to production and economics, Mifflin Street has one, and I was surprised to learn how well developed it is. Easy enough to see in the cooperative food growing on rural communes, its metropolitan application depends on understanding how to work the established system. Let me quote the proprietor of a record store:

"First, music is a necessity for us. When I started selling records, I discounted as much as I could, not to get volume but to share the difference between wholesale and retail with people who had a need for the product. That made some of the straight record stores in town start discounting to meet my prices, so I became a wholesaler. Now the straight stores can get records from my wholesale operation cheaper, too, so a lot of them have started buying from me. There are still profits, and we're using them to develop our own musical groups, and the musician's union is delighted. We'll soon be able to make our own records, with our own groups, which will bring the price down even more. Eventually," he said, "we'll have our own studio."

I asked how that would be different from consumer cooperatives of the past. "They all got too big," he said, and the implication was that in the alternate culture each community, like each individual, should do its own thing—making and distributing locally and not for profit in its own, idiosyncratic way.

The nonprofit spirit is very strong in what they themselves call freak-owned businesses. I know of a youngster who has a health-food store who is setting up his own competitor eight or ten blocks away because, says the first, he's making more money than he needs. This approach to doing business earns a certain amount of harassment, too; they are often searched, not always with warrants, and, as a matter of fact, sometimes get trashed.

The windows of the Mifflin Street Cooperative, a grocery,

were plywood at the time I went in, but I wasn't thinking about economics at the time. I was thinking that a culture has its own cuisine, and if that is too elegant a word to be appropriate, nevertheless the alternate culture has a very distinct approach to food. It favors organic foods, various health foods, abhors processing, and is faddish about eating in a way I grew up associating with rather elderly people. It cuts considerably across the image of healthy, young, all-consuming appetites requiring mountains of hamburger and pizza; it has, in fact, considerably more self-denial in it, whatever its nutritional merits, than we generally want to credit our young with.

The alternate culture, in fact, is not self-indulgent. It has its own ethic: a reverence for life, for example, in all its forms—they have seen so many of those forms destroyed, not on the frontier scale of shooting a hawk because it's a hawk but on the scale of technological society: the wiping out of whole species through careless use of pesticides and other pollutants. Self-realization would seem to be another part of the ethic, and while I can't offer specifications, there is a great deal of religious curiosity. To seek personal fame seems to them a curious aberration and to want more money than one needs another. Their only nonnegotiable demand is for personal freedom, their own and every man's, which makes them poor material, I should think, for disciplined political action.

A culture, once it exists, must develop a system of education —education, that is, in the culture itself. There is, near Mifflin Street, a free school. If it follows the pattern of the free universities I have seen in other communities, then it offers courses created to fit the particular demands of students, taught by whoever is willing and feels able to teach the particular subject matter. What is perhaps more characteristic are the attacks on the present educational system—the direct one which criticizes its relevance, and the indirect attack of nonparticipation. Drop-out is an honorable term in the alternate culture, and that leads me to another explanation: many of the street people came originally as students at Wisconsin, dropped out, and were now criticized locally as outsiders. The point was that they weren't outsiders to Mifflin Street, only to the university they'd decided was no longer relevant. Mifflin Street was no less an institution than the other place, and they had created it themselves.

The alternate culture has not begun, as far as I could learn, to develop its own system of law, but I would guess it may have to. It expects the courts of the country in which it is growing to treat it with routine unfairness. In the case, for example, of an underground newspaper editor who refused to testify about the AMRC bombing before a Wisconsin grand jury, as a newsman protecting his sources, they were far less surprised than I at the judge's remark in convicting the editor of contempt: ". . . something has to give. What has to give is the First Amendment. . . ."

Some of the other attributes of the alternate culture need only be itemized: they have their own ritual celebrations, rock festivals. Their own game: Frisbie. Older heroes: Vonnegut, Ginsberg, the Beatles, Buckminster Fuller. Stimulant: marijuana.

There is, of course, a neat parallel between the way marijuana functions for them and the way alcohol functioned in unifying their grandparents as they fought for and won the cultural revisions of the 1920s. It is not hard to imagine the move for legalization growing and becoming politically respectable, as Mifflin Street grows older and votes more consistently—just as the repeal movement became respectable when I was twelve or fourteen.

And of course the alternate culture has, as any culture must, its enemies: most adults, their government, their police. It is some of them I would hope to persuade by writing this; I have tried before, in talks at midwest service clubs and women's clubs going back four years now. There are always some who will listen, sometimes one or two who will agree, and it is to them I feel I owe an explanation. I owe it because I understand and even sometimes share their irritation, anger and despair—despair because, of course, kids always win. Unless we kill them. They outlive us.

I have never been able to make this explanation as fully before. It has taken a long time for me to learn and acknowledge my own conclusion. Here is how I learned it:

It was ten days since I'd left Madison, a serious occasion, and I found myself speaking to a group who were fifteen, sixteen and seventeen, and saying to them:

"You're good people. You're a special part of the best American generation I've ever seen or ever hope to see. I am impressed with the quality of your thought, the courage of your actions, and astonished at how young you have learned to value kindness . . ."

Where did they learn it? Not from you and me, Dusty; Mifflin Street.

That night I sat up late, in the dark, with a drink in my hand, looking out the bedroom window through the warm, moist October air, a trouble light staring back at me through the mist from the next farm, half a mile down the road, and thought of Mifflin Street again, and thought: couldn't we just try loving them?

It didn't matter much if they loved us back or not.

They were so beautiful, with their funny hair and curly beards, the boys elegantly scruffy, the hostile girls lovely and young for all their grimness, and they were trying to make something.

I didn't want what they were trying to make destroyed.

I had been, earlier this year, in two of the places where the world hurt worst: Biafra and Greece. I had not been to the others, the Middle East and Southeast Asia, but my imagination told me the same grief was there, the irreparable grief of people who have made a culture and seen it destroyed. They may live on physically, as American Indians do, but there is nothing left to belong to, nothing to be in the world that matters to you, unless you agree to join or rejoin the destroying culture on its own terms.

In a way, those who gave their vision and energy, the strength of their youth, to building the alternate culture might be doing something more radical, perhaps equally courageous, certainly more joyful, than the New Left extremists. The latter, when they answered social injustice with violence, knew the consequences of being caught, understood their risk and were presumably willing to take it. But there were no known consequences of trying to create a new culture, unless you wanted to think in terms as broad as the early history of Christianity.